STAR WARS

THE COMPLETE GALACTIC TIMELINE

COLLECTORS EDITION

DAMIEN M. BUCKLAND

ISBN-13: 978-1518890345

ISBN-10: 1518890342

THIS COLLECTORS EDITION BOOK HAS BEEN CREATED THROUGH THE WRITINGS AND CONTRIBUTIONS OF HUNDREDS OF STAR WARS FANS AND HISTORIANS. EACH CONTRIBUTOR, AND THERE ARE TO MANY TO NAME, HAS PIECED TOGETHER POINTS OF INTEREST TO CREATE THIS SPECIAL EDITION. IT IS TOO THESE HISTORIANS THAT THIS BOOK IS DEDICATED.

SOME OF THE PROFITS FROM THE SALE OF THIS EDITION CONTRIBUTE TOWARDS THE SAVE THE CHILDREN CHARITY

Save the Children®

Also by the bestselling author:

TROJAN LAW FOR SECURITY OFFICERS (2013) (Retired)
LAW & PRACTICE FOR SECURITY PROFESSIONALS (2013)

COLLECTION EDITIONS: TOP GEAR (2014)
COLLECTION EDITIONS: NCIS (2014)
COLLECTION EDITIONS: MERCEDES IN FORMULA ONE (2014)
COLLECTION EDITIONS: GAME OF THRONES; An Inside Guide to the Hit Show (2014)
COLLECTION EDITIONS: SPACE SHUTTLE (2015)
COLLECTION EDITIONS: THE WALKING DEAD: Behind the Show (2015)
COLLECTION EDITIONS: FERRARI IN FORMULA ONE (2015)
TOP GEAR: 1977 – 2015 (2015)
JAMES BOND: THE EVOLUTION OF BOND (2015)
TRUTH JUSTICE AND THE SUPERHERO COMIC (2015)

COLLECTION EDITIONS PUBLISHING 2015

Contents

THE TIMELINE OF GALACTIC HISTORY

So where does the Galactic History come from? The Star Wars Expanded Universe originally encompassed all of the officially licensed fictional material of the Star Wars Saga including the books, comics, video games, toys, and other official merchandise but did not include the six feature films nor The Clone Wars series or The Rebels series. Where stories would interlink and explain an area, the Expanded Universe would be updated to record these events much the same as any other history.

Early development of the Expanded Universe had always been sporadic and unrefined as there had previously been very little official material for creators to build upon. In February of 1978, Alan Dean Foster's Star Wars spin-off novel, Splinter of the Mind's Eye, was released. This novel had drawn inspiration primarily from an early draft of the Star Wars script and had originally been conceptualized as a possible sequel for the big screen. Whilst George Lucas was given the sole writing credit for the original Star Wars novelization, Alan Dean Foster actually ghost-wrote it, contributing heavily to the Universe in the process. While he worked on the novelization, he was given a copy of the working script and a tour of the production.

Much of the early Expanded Universe material from the early 1980's contained analogies to the real world, rather than embracing the holistic fiction of the Star Wars films. A turning point was reached when West End Games began publishing the Star Wars Roleplaying Game in 1987. In order for players of the game to create new adventures, West End Games needed to provide supplemental material describing the Star Wars universe in previously unknown detail. For example, the Aurebesh alphabet was originally a random piece of set dressing in Return of the Jedi. Stephen Crane copied those symbols and turned them into a complete and coherent alphabet (which would be used later in the feature films). Developing details like this in a consistent fashion turned West End Games' Star Wars products into a de facto reference library for the Star Wars universe, to the point where LucasFilm actually sent copies of the game supplements to other Expanded Universe developers to use as source material.

Shortly thereafter, in the early 1990's, Bantam published Timothy Zahn's Thrawn trilogy. Widely publicized as the "sequels which were never made", Zahn's novels reignited Star Wars fandom and sparked a revolution in Star Wars literature. Around this same time, Dark Horse Comics acquired the Star Wars license and used it to launch a number of ambitious sequels to the original trilogy, including the popular Dark Empire stories.

All this development began to feedback on itself. West End Games were producing roleplaying supplements detailing the material from Dark Horse's comics and Zahn's novels. Novelists and comic creators were using West End Games' supplements as reference material. Sequels to the novels were being published as comics and vice versa. The scope of the Expanded Universe was growing at a prodigious rate.

To date, the bulk of the Expanded Universe has detailed the Star Wars universe after the end of Return of the Jedi, as numerous topics, including the rise of the Galactic Empire, the personal histories of Anakin Skywalker and Emperor Palpatine, and the Clone Wars had been declared off limits by George Lucas before the development of the prequel trilogy.

It was also decided in the late 1990's that using the Empire as the villains had become repetitive and monotonous. Hence a new threat, the Yuuzhan Vong, was introduced in The New Jedi Order, more specifically, in the first book of the series, Vector Prime. Vector Prime proved controversial; as it marked the first and only time a major character from the films (Chewbacca) was killed off in an Expanded Universe work.

In November of 2012, The Walt Disney Company acquired LucasFilm and announced that all the previous released Expanded Universe would from now on be non-contradictory to one another and any previous storyline would be valid to the story told throughout the films. In doing so, the Star Wars Expanded Universe has become a universal "diary" of events which is recognised across the planet as an official source and guide.

Throughout the Expanded Universe a standard measurement of time is used. This is known as The Galactic Standard Calendar and is centred on the Coruscant Tropical Year. The Coruscant solar cycle lasts 368 days with a day consisting of 360 Net Degrees (or 24 standard UTC (universel coordonné or Coordinated Universal Time)). The most recent of these calendar eras used the Battle of Yavin (i.e. the destruction of the first Death Star) as its epoch, or "year zero": BBY (Before the Battle of Yavin), and ABY (After the Battle of Yavin).

THE EXPANDED UNIVERSE AND THE PREQUEL TRILOGY

Prior to the release of The Phantom Menace, LucasFilm specifically prohibited development of the time period before A New Hope in the Expanded Universe (with the exception of the Tales of the Jedi series which took place thousands of years before the movies). The release of Episode I, however, created an entirely new storyline for writers to work from.

Since The Phantom Menace was set in a time of peace, it was hard to invent any kind of threat for the heroes to fight against. Thus most material that built on The Phantom Menace was either set before or during the film, rather than after.

Attack of the Clones, on the other hand, introduced another fresh conflict. One which fans had wanted to see for over twenty years. Aside from being explored in comics and novels, the Clone Wars would be given their own animated series Star Wars: Clone Wars, which would serve to lead up to the release of Revenge of the Sith. In this series, many battles throughout the galaxy are shown, with the Force shown to seemingly its full extent in fantastic fights, such as Mace Windu single-handedly destroying a whole droid army, without even using a lightsaber. The first season of the series, in 2004, concludes by introducing the newest villain, General Grievous, an important character in Episode III. Grievous was also a main player on episodes 21-25, released in 2005 and leading directly to Episode III. Following the release of Episode III, events between the two trilogies are now being elaborated, like the Great Jedi Purge.

In addition to adding new possibilities, the prequel trilogy contradicted a number of statements involving the Clone Wars in existing novels. In Timothy Zahn's Thrawn trilogy, for example, the dates given for the war were inaccurate. This was since retconned by explaining that the dates were given using the Noghri calendar. Also, the character Admiral Pellaeon makes a specific statement about fighting clones in the Fleet (presumably under the Republic) and that the early clones were "unstable, sometimes spectacularly so." This completely contradicts the prequels, but was later addressed in Karen Travis's Republic Commando books by the addition of the Nulls. And again, in book three, True Colours, Pellaeon makes his first chronologically appropriate appearance as a fresh Republic officer. As well, with all six films officially released, more and more ties between the prequel and original trilogy eras are being made. Rogue Planet's introduction of Zonama Sekot, for example, was both an important tie-in to Episode II and part of the resolution for the New Jedi Order series. And Outbound Flight linked The Phantom Menace with several Zahn novels (the Thrawn trilogy, Spectre of the Past, Vision of the Future, and Survivor's Quest).

DISNEY'S ACQUISITION OF LUCASFILM

After LucasFilm was purchased by The Walt Disney Company on October 30th, 2012, it was decided that a sequel trilogy would be made. These movies will not tell stories of the Expanded Universe, and instead be completely original stories. On April the 25th, 2014, it was revealed that existing Expanded Universe material would be republished under a new banner, "Star Wars Legends". Also, a new line of Expanded Universe material would be published by Disney Publishing Worldwide, starting with Star Wars: A New Dawn by John Jackson Miller, a prequel to the TV show Star Wars Rebels. This would be followed by Star Wars: Tarkin by James Luceno, Star Wars: Heir to the Jedi by Kevin Hearne, and Star Wars: Lords of the Sith by Paul S. Kemp and more. To ensure continuity within Star Wars canon going forth, a close story group has been formed by LucasFilm to watch over all Star Wars development.

Unlike the films, which are set over a span of more than 66 years, the "Legends" branded Expanded Universe takes place over 37,139 years in the Star Wars "Legends" universe. The earliest work involving the expanded universe chronologically is the Dawn of the Jedi comic series, whose earliest events take place 37,000 years before the films. The most recent is the Legacy comic series, which is set at most 135 years after Return of the Jedi.

THE PRE-REPUBLIC ERA

Pre-trilogies story eras. Set before the rise of the Republic and first mentioned in the Knights of the Old Republic, this era saw the Rakata, a bipedal species from the world of Lehon in the Unknown Regions, establish an empire using the Dark Side of the Force. This era ended with the collapse of their Empire and the establishment of the Galactic Republic in 25,053 BBY.

13,000,000,000 BBY

By the year 13,000,000,000 BBY, long before the Galactic Republic was founded, the Big Bang had already taken place, creating the universe. Many believed that it was approximately the year in which a cloud of dust and gas within the universe that was one-hundred-thousand light years across experienced a gravitic collapse; the cloud collapsed to form a disk of the same dimension that revolved around an extremely massive black hole... the galaxy.

The galactic disk came to have three vertical layers: one in the middle that was 2,000 light years thick called the "thin slice" sandwiched between two 3,500 light year sections on either side of that called the "thick slice." The majority of the galaxy's approximately four-hundred-billion stars fell within the thin slice, though the thick slice had some and there was also a great sphere around the galactic disk called the "stellar halo" that consisted of billions of stars with highly elliptical orbits. Many of the stars ended up developing planets that orbited them over the succeeding eons. Half of these star systems, primarily within the thin slice, maintained conditions favourable to life, ten percent of this half actually developed life, and only one in a thousand of the life-bearing worlds went on to bear true sentience. Life would still be emerging on planets in the galaxy by 5,000,000,000 BBY. Many of these forms of sentience would try to explain their conditions, forming religions. A number developed creation myths, detailing how their existence came to be, whether that meant the creation of the galaxy, the formation of their world, or the origin of life. The Mandalorian religion had a creation tale called the Akaanati'kar'oya, "The War of Life and Death" in Basic, and it posited that the stars in the sky were ancient Mandalorian leaders that had died. Life that grew on worlds separated by great distances, primarily twenty million sentient species, would go on to interact and integrate, experiencing and eventually recording galactic history.

By the reign of the Galactic Empire, which began in 19 BBY, much would be known about the physical properties of the galaxy, from its stars to its planets, but only about a quarter of all stars in the galaxy were surveyed. Contemporary estimates stated that of all the stars, 7.1 billion were not dangerous to life while 3.2 billion of those supported actual star systems. It was proposed that at least one billion of them were inhabited to some degree and Imperial census data showed 69 million that were populated significantly. There were 1.75 million planets considered by the Empire to be advanced and populous enough for full member status. Imperial records further showed five million catalogued examples of sentient species, but it was accepted plainly that there were many more undiscovered species in the galaxy.

5,000,000,000 BBY

Following the creation of the galaxy, stars began to form within it, developing planets and becoming star systems. One of these systems, which would go on to be called the Goroth system, developed around a star named Goroth Alpha, with a second, Goroth Beta, orbiting. After several millennia in existence, the system had four planets revolving around Alpha between the suns. The system's second planet would become known as Goroth Prime.

Xenobiologists native to Goroth Prime who lived during the reign of the Galactic Empire, formed in 19 BBY to begin the Imperial Period, studied their planet's biological history. Their estimates placed the world's first forms of life as emerging by the year 5,000,000,000 BBY. Those forms of life evolved over billions of subsequent years until achieving semi-sentience one million years before the Battle of Yavin, the epoch of the Galactic Standard Calendar. This was relatively late when compared to the rest of the galaxy. The fully sentient Gorothites then emerged 990,000 years after that.

10,000,000 BBY

High volcanic activity on Esseles, a planet located along the Perlemian Trade Route in Darpa sector of the Ringali Shell measuring 9,186 miles (14,783 km). It was the third in position in the Essesia system and had one moon.

3,000,000 BBY

An asteroid collides with the planet Vinsoth in the Quelii sector of the Outer Rim Territories, killing most life on its surface. The remaining survivors evolve into the Chevin.

2,000,000 BBY

Kashyyyk (a Mid-Rim planet also known as Wookiee Planet C, Edean, G5-623, and Wookiee World, reaches an evolutionary crux where species must learn to adapt or die. It is during this violent period that Wookiees begin to evolve.

1,000,000 BBY

An ancient aquatic civilization thrives on the planet Jerrilek, but eventually goes extinct in the following millennia and the semi-intelligent ancestors to the Gorothites emerge on Goroth Prime.

600,000 BBY

Scientists trace the origins of the Ibliton, a swamp creature of Randorn 2, back to 600,000 BBY. The Randorn 2 was a mollusk by nature, and its shell was about two meters long with three meter long tentacles. Like many molluscs, its shell was chambered and coiled with its fleshy body protruding out. Unlike most molluscs, its segmented body and knife-like legs were covered by an insectoid exoskeleton. It was believed by the native Mizx to be an avatar of Hershoon the Destroyer, created by its demented soul so that its legacy would be perpetuated.

200,000 BBY

Around this time, the Zhell, the early ancestors of the Human species, battled the Taung species for control of their mutual home world Notron. Despite a loss at the city of Great Zhell that inspires the epic poem Dha Werda Verda, the Battalions of Zhell succeeded in driving the Taung off world.

100,000 BBY

Roughly around this time, the Celestials accomplish a number of feats including the construction of CenterPoint Station using the Killiks, the subsequent construction of the Corellian system using CenterPoint, the Vultar system and its Cosmic Turbine, the Hapes Cluster, and the Kathol Rift. The Maw black hole cluster was also constructed with CenterPoint during the Celestials' era of power to contain the Force entity known as Abeloth.

The Columi species achieves interstellar spaceflight and surveys the "primitive" people of Duro and Notron, known by that point as Coruscant. However, they are disappointed by the developing Human and Duro's civilizations and return to their home world of Columus in isolation. Around this time, the Sharu expand out from the Rafa system and the Centrality, planting their indestructible pyramids on planets such as Aargau. However, the Sharu bury their cities and revert to a primitive state in an attempt to avoid the attention of the Celestials.

The winged Thrantcills are first recorded flying south for winter on Coruscant.

The Muurshantre Extinction occurs, destroying the Taurannik Codex and scattering its remains.

90,000 BBY

Also known as 56,547 Before the Tho Yor Arrival or 86,347 Before the Treaty of Coruscant, 90,000 BBY was a year during the Pre-Republic era. Approximately this year, on the planet of Coruscant, Galactic City stood as a many tiered settlement. This was the groundwork for the 5,127 levels, which stretched kilometres from the surface that would exist by the time of the Clone Wars.

57,000 BBY

Utapau (an arid sinkhole world in the Utapau system of the Tarabba sector in the Outer Rim Territories) is colonized by humanoid species that would later evolve into the Pau'an and Utai species.

53,600 BBY

Around that year, the Quake, a series of intense ground quakes that last for centuries, began on the planet Quesh. Quesh was a world riddled with toxic waste within Hutt Space.

36,453 BBY

That year marked the Tho Yor Arrival. The eight Tho Yor pyramid ships became active and traversed the galaxy, picking up Force-sensitive passengers of over a dozen species from many different worlds. The Tho Yor then travelled to the Deep Core world of Tython, where they gathered around the ninth and largest Tho Yor. The Tho Yor arrival sparked an immense Force Storm, the strength of which would go unrivalled for almost ten thousand years, as Tython reacted to the presence of so many Force-sensitives. The Tho Yor then scattered themselves across Tython, and the pilgrims soon formed the Je'daii Order, a Force-using organization that strove to maintain balance between the light and dark sides of the Force in both themselves and the world around them

35,000 BBY

The Rakatan Infinite Empire, based on the planet of Lehon, is formed. The Rakata (also known as the Builders), were a humanoid species with distinctive amphibian features. They were a technologically advanced race that developed early in galactic history, even developing some early hyper drive technology. Long term use of the dark side of the Force corrupted their society and turned them into a race of merciless warriors. The Rakata used their potent Force-powered technologies to conquer and enslave every other species they came across throughout their known galaxy. During the reign of their Infinite Empire, they were characterized by their cruelty, savagery, and arrogance. They were known to strip entire planets of their resources, terraform worlds to fit their own shifting needs, kill entire slave workforces, and to eat and defile the bodies of slain enemies.

33,598 BBY

The Rakata interact with the terraforming computer on Kashyyyk for the last time

The Terraforming computer could change a previously uninhabitable planet or moon into a habitable one for a certain number of species. During the rule of the Infinite Empire, the Rakata became the first known culture to develop terraforming machinery and technology, and used it upon planets such as Kashyyyk. The following year (33,597 BBY) the terraforming computer on Kashyyyk malfunctions, causing a hyper-acceleration in the growth of the planet's forests.

During the Yuuzhan Vong War of the galaxy from 25–30 ABY, the extragalactic Yuuzhan Vong terraformed many subject worlds to better suit them. The Yuuzhan Vong phrase was known as world shaping, but others referred to it as Vongforming or Vongformation which was performed by Yuuzhan Vong called shapers. Coruscant, Duro, and Ossus were examples of terraformed planets. Even a century later, reconstruction of many Vongformed planets still wasn't completed, partially due to sabotage.

30,000 BBY

The Infinite Empire of the Rakata reaches its peak, spanning dozens of worlds across the galaxy. They annex the holdings of other spacefaring species such as the Gree and the Kwa.

The Killiks of Alderaan attempt to invade the planet Korriban, but are repelled by the Sith species. The Killiks later vanish from Alderaan, Alsakan and the galaxy at large, having been relocated to the Unknown Regions.

28,000 BBY

28,000 BBY King Adas begins his reign over the Sith on Korriban. King Adas. King Adas was a large creature whose skin was unusually, for his species, charcoal-coloured. He was raised as a chosen being from his youth and would later encase himself in ebon armour, wielding a massive battle-ax. His reign on Korriban would last nearly 300 years during which time Adas would unite the disparate nations in a series of bloody conflicts and eventually solidifying himself as the sole leader of his people. The Sith hailed him as "Sith'ari" or "Overlord".

27,700 BBY

The Sith species on Korriaban are visited by the Rakata of the Infinite Empire, but King Adas leads his people in driving the Rakata off world when it was found that they were intending to conquer the planet.

The Rakatan attack, turning Korriaban into a wasteland and causing most Sith to relocate to the forested world of Ziost, an ancient world made up of ice with small areas of barren tundra and dark forest. Other Sith find and use a Rakatan Force-driven hyper drive to spread out among the planets of the Stygian Caldera and the planet Tund would become a place of exile for heretics among the Sith. The Stygian Caldera was a large nebulosity that surrounded the former Sith worlds which was difficult to navigate and this protected the Sith from future attack.

27,500 BBY

The human natives of Coruscant begin to launch sub light sleeper ships over the coming fifteen hundred years, seeding a number of worlds with humans, including Kuat, Metellos, Csilla, Alderaan, Rendili, Koros Major, and the Tion Cluster. Humans also launched the Kuat Explorer which colonizes the planet Alsakan, an ecumenoplois in the Alsakan system of the Core Worlds and a key area of the Perlemian Trade Route.

27,000 BBY

The Goassam Courivers begin to colonize as a group of Gossam explorers, using the Tumble Hyperdrive, visit the planet Felucia. The Tumble Hyperdrive was an unstable device which allowed for jumps of variable distance and duration and the Devaronian species also experimented with the device around this time.

26,053 BBY

The Morodins, a large sentient herbivore species able to secrete a nutrient slime trail that promoted growth and mutation in plant life, established a colony on the planet Varonat to feed a growing population on its own struggling home world. The Morodins turned part of Varonat into a vast jungle and transported their bounty to their own home world aboard organic space vessels. Soon an ecological disaster on their home world prevented the Morodins from returning and contact with the home world was lost. The Morodins on Varonat continue to thrive and eventually human colonists reached Varonat and saw the Morodins as wild beasts intent on destroying their plantings when, in reality, the Morodins were trying to help the humans to grow their food.

26,000 BBY

The Kuat launched their own colonization ships and seeded Axum, Tepasi, and Humbarine with humans.

In the aftermath of the fourth in a series of devastating planetary conflicts, the early Nikto discover the M'dweshuu nova and form the religious Cult of M'dweshuu. This cult quickly takes control of the entire planet of Kintan and continues to rule for three decades. The Nikto were a reptilian humanoid with leathery skin, sometimes covered in spikes and horns. Most had cold black obsidian eyes which contained a protective membrane which protected their eyes underwater and during windstorms. This resulted in their "staring" eyes and seemingly blank intelligence and combined with a lack of necessary anatomical infrastructure, which limited their range of facial expressions, the Nikto were often mistankingly underestimated in intelligence.

The Roche system, located in the Mid Rim, is colonized by the insectoid sentient species called Verpine.

25,805 BBY

Queen Hadiya of Shikaakwa tries to conquer the whole Tython system by uniting the crime barons of her home world. She fails and ignites the Despot War. The Je'daii Order on the planet, seeing that Hadiya's plans were a threat to the system's stability, decided to intervene on the side of the aristocracy. War broke out between the Je'daii and Hadiya's Despot Army. When Hadiya invaded Tython and attacked the Je'daii temple Kaleth, she was killed by the Je'daii Ranger Daegen Lok, who had been undercover in Hadiya's army. Her death ended the war, but not before a hundred thousand Tythan casualties, over million casualties among the Despot Army, and thousands of injured. Tensions throughout the Tython system remained high for another decade.

25,793 BBY

The Force Wars on Tython begin between the followers of Ashla and the followers of Bogan.

Tatooine, a desert world and the first planet in the binary Tatoo star system, had once been a lush world that had huge oceans and a world-spanning jungle inhabited by the native and technologically advanced Kumumgah. Against the elder's wishes they colonized nearby star systems but this drew the attention of the Rakata. The Rakatan Infinite Empire invaded the planet, conquered and enslaved its native inhabitants and then abducted many to their other conquered worlds. After a terrible plague weakened the Rakata, the Kumumgah eventually rebelled and managed to drive the Rakata off the planet. In response they subjected the planet to an orbital bombardment that boiled the oceans dry and fused the silica in the soil into glass, which then broke up over time creating the desert sands.

The Infinite Empire, the first known major galactic government founded and ruled by the Rakata, launches a campaign of conquest against the Je'daii Order and the Settled Worlds.

25,200 BBY

The Infinite Empire is struck by a mysterious plague that strips the Rakata of their ability to use the Force. This prompts slave revolts across the galaxy and the Empire collapses.

The Toinese nobleman Xer VIII is born. He would become a pirate chieftain and later a King of Cron, forging an empire from the desperate elements of the Tion Cluster.

25,150 BBY

Xer VIII begins the Cronese Sweeps. Xer began the campaign by sending warlords and nobles he considered worthy into battle against rebellious Cronese worlds and independent planets on the kingdom's borders, taking their heirs hostage as guarantees of loyalty. The incompetents were eliminated with their families and followers. The most feared warlord of the Cronese Sweeps was however Xer's teenage son, Xim. Xim and his legions became famous after his brutality during the conquests of Pasmin, Eibon and Nuswatta and the slaughter of Cronese nobility.

25,130 BBY

Xer's son Xim takes the throne of the Kingdom of Cron and he begins a campaign to conquer the Livien League, a state located within the Tion Cluster.

25,127 BBY

Xim conquers the Livien League.

25,126 BBY

Xim begins to absorb the Thanium Worlds.

25,125 BBY

Xim's empire now begins to flourish in the Thanium Worlds

25,120 BBY

Xim begins to conquer the Kiirium Reaches to the Southwest of his empire.

25,116 BBY

Xim's conquest of the Thanium Worlds comes to a close.

25,102 BBY

Xim attacks the planet of Ko Vari, instigating a conflict between himself and the Hutt's.

25,100 BBY

The conflict between Xim and the Hutt's reaches its peak. Kossak Inijic Ar'durv lures Xim into fighting the first and second Battles of Vontor.

Kossak convinces the Klatooinians, Nikto and Vodran species, to sign the Treaty of Vontor. This secured their allegiance and their aid in the Third Battle of Vontor. With the Hutt forces now bolstered they were able to gather their fleet at Vontor as Xim sent his troops to the surface in massive landing barges. Xim did not expect to find the millions of Klatooinians, Nikto, Vodrans, and Weequay Mercenaries, who were also fighting for the Hutt's, waiting for them. Despite a huge technological advantage, Xim's forces were no match for the massive numbers they faced. Whilst Xim was sending his warships against Kossak's forces, the Vodrans and their new companions destroyed most of Xim's war robots and then wrecked Xim's orbital platforms by bombing them. Xim's fleet was destroyed in orbit except for a few ships that escaped with the last war robots. Xim is captured and imprisoned in Kossak's dungeons on Varl were he would later die as a slave. His treasure ship, the Queen of Ranroon, escaped to the planet of Dellait where it would remain hidden for millennia. The Tionese never knew that their leader had been captured and believed he had been killed in the battle.

Borte Belgoth is commissioned to construct a set of hyperspace beacons, one of which becomes known as Belgoth's Beacon. Belgoth's Beacon bears the faces of a Columi, a Cacodemon, and a Molator, and sits along the Perlemian Trade Route. The great historian, Vicendi, would later name the Belgoth Beacon one of the Twenty Wonders of the Galaxy.

25,096 BBY

Despite the loss of their ruler, the Xim Empire completes the conquest of the Kiirium Reaches.

ORIGINAL/PREQUEL/SEQUEL TRILOGY STORY ERAS

The Old Republic (25,053 BBY - 1,000 BBY)

In this era (set thousands of years before the films), the Jedi are numerous and rule the galaxy, serving as guardians of peace and justice. The Tales of the Jedi comic's series takes place in this era, chronicling the immense wars fought by the Jedi of old, and the ancient Sith. The Knights of the Old Republic series and the MMORPG Star Wars: The Old Republic takes place during this time, as well as the Darth Bane series and the Sith Era.

This time is also known as "The Expansionist Era" and was the term given to the years after the Galactic Republic formed, when transit between the Core Worlds was opened up by the newly developed hyper drive, and during the early expansion of the Republic.

25,053 BBY

The Galactic Republic was born with the signing of the Galactic Constitution in the aftermath of the Unification Wars. Its founders were a number of key Core Worlds known collectively as the Core Founders and included Couscant, Alderaan, Humbarine, and Kuat. As an early founder of the Republic, Duro entered a golden age under the leadership of Queen Rana Mas Trehalt. Later, when the Monarchy was abolished in favour of a collection of ruling corporations administered by the Duro's High House, human and Duro's scientists reverse-engineered the Rakatan hyper drive, inventing the modern hyper drive. This led to vigorous colonization in a small patch of the Core known as the Tetrahedron at first and then further outwards into the known galaxy. With the founding of the Galactic Republic, Coruscant became the new Government's capital.

25,000 BBY

To link the new Republic capital at Coruscant with Ossus in the Tion Cluster, the Perlemian Trade Route is founded. The route took its name from the Perlemia system, located in the Core Worlds, which in its early history produced the thousands of scout vessels that charted the route. To also contribute to making Corellia an economic superpower, the Corellian Run was established running through the galaxy. It became one of the largest hyperspace routes running through the galaxy and formed the southern border of the Slice.

Duro's scouts, from the newly formed Galactic Republic, make contact with the Jedi Order on Ossus and Jedi Master Haune Tiar returns with the scouts to the Core Worlds. During his tour of the Republic, the Jedi foresaw that the Order would need to be the Republic's protectors. Returning to Ossus, Tiar discussed the matter with the rest of the enclave for several weeks before declaring that they would become guardians of the Republic.

Queen Rana, with the development of the hyper drive, allows for a wave of colonization to embark from Duro's. One of the colony worlds is the planet Neimoidia, which is colonized by a group of Duro's led by Chla C'cHaan. He called upon the colonists to embrace the heritage of their original home world Duro. The descendants of the colony that C'cHaan founded eventually evolved into a separate species knowns as the Neimoidians.

Jedi Master Sar Agorn, an amorphous blob-like sentient whose form was constantly surrounded in green gases, takes on a Jedi apprentice called Cope Shykrill. Shykrill excelled in his studies at first but soon, however, it was discovered that Shykrill had fallen to the dark side of the Force. He had been responsible for the murder of three of his fellow Jedi trainees and Agorn could see no other recourse than to kill his young Padawan.

24,500 BBY

During the early history of the Jedi Order, the Kashi Mer exile Xendor was studying on the planet Ossus, fortress world of the Jedi and home to a culture devoted to the study of the Force and its light side aspect called the Ashla. A respected Jedi Knight, Xendor was a vocal opponent to the Order's increasingly exclusionary ways and eager to learn the techniques and teachings of representatives from other Force traditions also studying on Ossus. Among his closest allies was a Steel Hand of Palawa named Arden Lyn. The two of them shared philosophies away from the eyes and ears of the Jedi High Council and eventually became lovers.

Xendor, able to bear his frustration no longer, approached the High Council and requested their blessings in opening a new Jedi academy far from Ossus to focus on the darker aspects of the Force called The Bogan. When the Council refused, Xendor quietly broke with the Order and travelled to the planet Lettow to open an academy which focused its teachings on the Bogan. Drawing on Force traditions such as the Order of Dai Bendu, the Followers of Palawa, the Kashi Mer Guardians of Breath, the Baran Do, and the Chatos Academy, Xendor's academy drew a trickle of interest which quickly transformed into a roaring river. It was these acolytes which named their new group the Legions of Lettow, as they knew that they would one day be forced to defend their traditions from the Jedi High Council's wrath. At the academy, the Legionnaires followed similar initiation ceremonies that were practiced by the Jedi Order, for example, the forging of Force-imbued blades was carried over from ancient Tythonese practices. Initiates shaped high-carbon steel in the furnaces of the academy in an extremely challenging ritual, melding the blade's molecular lattice with that of the energy crystal, making the blade and the crystal one-in-the-same. With the furnace-forged steel, the Legionnaires adopted the ancient Jar'Kai fighting art, calling it Niman, after the triumvirate of Kashi gods.

The Jedi Order had grown weary of the dissidents' continued existence and decided to put an end to the Great Schism which had torn at the Order's fabric for too long. Forming a massive army, the High Council forced the Legionnaires into open combat. Reluctant to take up the title of General, Xendor hoped to avoid massive bloodshed by bringing the war directly to Ossus. During the battle, Xendor's forces were pushed back and forced to commit troops to several fronts as the Order pushed the Legionnaires towards the galaxy's core. In an attempt to warn the Galactic Republic of the Jedi Order's machinations in forcing the conflict into civilized space, Xendor was ignored and branded as a warlord by the Republic. Campaigns were played out on Chandrila, Metellos, Brentaal IV and Coruscant until the Jedi leader, Awdrysta Pina managed to come into direct battle with Xendor on Columus. Known as the Green Blade, Master Pina and his Jedi Knights were able to separate Xendor's vanguard from the bulk of his army through the use of a strong Force meld. Cutting through powerful warriors such as Sethul Asaiage and Tun Bohoi, Pina eventually duelled Xendor and slew him in hand-to-hand combat.

With Xendor dead, Arden Lyn took command of the remaining Legionnaires on Lettow. As Pina's forces sacked the academy, Lyn and her comrades held off the Jedi until the surviving Legionnaires could flee Republic space. Separating from the rest of the survivors so they could not be cornered together, Lyn attempted to hide beyond Kitel Phard but was hunted mercilessly by Master Pina and he finally cornered her on Irkalla. There, Lyn used a Kashi Mer talisman gifted to her by Xendor to shatter Pina's blade and send the shards through his body. As he lay dying, Pina poured his last bit of life into attacking Lyn with the Morichro technique, stopping her heart and nearly killing her. All remaining Legionnaires were hunted down or left to die in exile, their attempted schism put down with crushing exactness by the Jedi Order, leaving the Legions of Lettow to descend into myth and legend, barely remembered in the footnote of galactic history.

24,000 BBY

The Tionese War begins between the Galactic Republic and the Honourable Union of Desevro and Tion, one of the feuding states that rose in the Tion Cluster from the ashes of Xim the Despot's empire in the century after his death. The initial Tionese assault down the Perlemian Trade Route met little resistance. The Tionese seized Abhean, Roche, Lantillies, and Tirahnn before the Republic mounted a serious effort to construct its own war fleet. Tionese raiders destroyed the shipyards of Axum and Perlemia with a pressure bombs before unleashing more pressure bombs upon Alsakan and Coruscant itself.

After a last-ditch counterattack repelled the Tionese offensive, new Republican warships were launched from shipyards at Corellia, Rendili and Humbarine. Nearly a century of offensives and counteroffensives up and down the Perlemian followed. Republic agents managed to steer the Hutt's into attacking the Tionese border, and eventually the Jedi joined the war, leading Republic forces in the hope of saving galactic civilization from sinking into barbarism.

With the Republic's overwhelming industrial might fully committed to the struggle, defeat for the Tion was only a matter of time. Believing that their culture would be annihilated, the Tionese resorted to sneak and suicide attacks. These tactics served only to enrage the Republic, whose leaders embraced a doctrine of total war. Key Tionese worlds were pounded with pressure bombs, and eventually Desevro itself faced destruction under the guns of the Republic navy.

Desevro's attempt at unconditional surrender was ignored. The Republic's leaders were committed to making an example of that world in order to intimidate the rest of the Tion into surrendering, and the planet was turned into a blasted wasteland. As the Tionese War comes to an end 100 years later and the Republic devastates the worlds of the Tion Cluster, the Republic's sterilization of Desevro prompts the Jedi to break with the Republic. The Republic later negotiates with the Jedi, who eventually agree to serve as the Republic's watchmen.

23,643 BBY

The planet Uphrades experiences a period of significant volcanic activity, resulting in especially fertile soil tens of thousands of years later.

22,800 BBY

A Jedi scout follows the Force's call into the Unknown Regions, discovering the crystal world of Ilum. Ilum soon becomes an important religious world for the Jedi Order. The planet crucially was one of the main sources of the valuable Adegan crystals used in the construction of Jedi lightsabers. Unlike the crystals of other planets, the crystals of Ilum were limited to blue and green in colour and the caverns containing the crystals were turned into a Jedi temple.

22,000 BBY

The planet Nubia was colonized by hardy human settlers after the discovery of large subterranean aquifers below the planet's surface. Installing massive pumps to bring water to the surface, they created an instantly habitable world and soon other colonists came to settle. Within just a few decades, Nubia had become an agricultural powerhouse and an organised democracy soon established rule over the planet. The Government was however corrupt and would rig its own elections to maintain power. The planets true leader was the head of PharmCorp, a Hutt by the name of Prail. The Galactic Empire coveted Nubia's massive grain production to fuel their war efforts and the Empire feared that Nubia Star Drives Inc. might be utilized by the Rebel Alliance to manufacture ships. In response they placed an Imperial class Star Destroyer in orbit over the planet and instituted martial law on the surface. Within hours, Stormtroopers patrolled the streets and an Imperial Governor assumed authority.

20,100 BBY

B y this time, most of the Colonies and the Inner Rim have been settled.

THE GREAT MANIFEST PERIOD

The Great Manifest Period of the Galactic Republic was a span of time that lasted from 20,000 BBY to 17,018 BBY. It was characterized by increased movement into the Slice and the establishment of the Expansion Region in its Rimward territories. Even as the Republic expanded astrographically, the government expanded its bureaucracy. The limit of fifty systems per sector that had been set by the early Republic continued to be ignored, causing already burgeoning sectors in the newly colonized areas of galactic space to be virtually ungovernable. Additionally, the era featured the creation of the Metellos Trade Route, which connected Coruscant to Metellos and other points west of the galactic centre. The new hyperspace route increased trade among the newly connected systems. Around 2,000 years thereafter, the bureaucracy expanded with the establishment of the Bureau of Ships and Services to regulate and manage transportation across the galactic community.

Culturally, the Republic was undergoing change, as well. Vianism, a religion that had developed among the Core Worlds, became non-extant on its generative planets; however, it spread into the expanding regions of the galaxy and took hold within the Kanz sector. Additionally, the famed Shawken Spire saw its destruction during the Great Manifest Period, an event that was remembered over 8,000 years later. All the while, outside of Republic space, the two planets Neona and Kamino underwent dramatic climate changes. These events, which began during the Great Manifest Period, caused extinction for the native species of Neona and forced adaption of the Kaminoan species. Nevertheless, the era and its corresponding boom were brought to an abrupt end by internal strife in the form of the First Alsakan Conflict.

20,000 BBY

This marked the end of the Expansionist Era and the beginning of the Great Manifest Period in the Galactic Republic. Now approximately five thousand years old, the Republic began a period of rapid expansion out from the Core Worlds and into the areas of Wild Space "east" of the galactic centre. Other cultures, such as the Etti, had already begun Rimward migration. Further development and exploration took place in the Core as well. The planet Metellos, suffering from a lack of trade and overpopulation, began its attempt to blaze a new hyperlane connecting it to both Coruscant and points westward to alleviate these issues. Once completed, the route stretched from Coruscant to Orooturoo.

19,997 BBY

Neona, was a temperate world in the Tapani sector's Freeworlds Territory populated by an indigenous sentient species, experienced a period of intense geological warming that melted the ice caps and plunged the landmass below massive oceans, sparing only two ice-continents, one located at each pole. The native species was consumed by the tides and succumbed to extinction, leaving behind only extravagant ruins interred beneath the waves as proof of their existence.

19,000 BBY

The planet of Kamino began a dramatic climate shift. The surface ice, which was confined to the planetary glaciers, began to melt. As it melted, the low-lying marshes that gave rise to the Kaminoans and the narrow oceans began to flood, covering the then-extant land area. Within two centuries, all the surface land on Kamino was buried under water, which was hundreds of meters deep at places. The former cities, such as Derem, and architectural wonders, such as the Clock Spires of Harai Nova, were submerged. For survival, the Kaminoans adapted the technology they possessed to build their cities on stilts above the water level. Furthermore, the Kaminoans turned to genetic engineering to preserve many of the species that drowned in the rising waters.

Elsewhere, in the Galactic Republic, the Great Manifest Period was continuing. The Republic continued its expansion and settlement of the areas east of the Core Worlds, into the area that eventually came to be known as "the Slice.

18,780 BBY

The Republic continued its expansion eastward into the uncharted Wild Space areas of what later became "the Slice." In the Core, the Shawken Spire had become a super-tall structure that reached low-orbit altitude. Made of ancient building materials, the building was famous across the known galaxy. The iconic construct, however, met its destruction at this time.

18,000 BBY

The Bureau of Ships and Services is established. BoSS was an extra-governmental galactic agency responsible for assigning unique transponder codes to starships and tracking their movements through space.

A fixture in intergalactic travel, the Bureau of Ships and Services fielded offices in most major spaceports. Its unique structure and neutrality, complete with its own customs, traditions, unique personality and even language, allowed it to operate across political borders and through the transition of major galactic powers. Offices and field positions were often filled through hereditary means, so much so that after a millennia of operation the Bureau was both a closely knit family and a civil agency. According to Platt Okeefe, the Bureau was full of secrets and even the Galactic Empire dared not trifle with it.

Acting as the galaxy's record keeper when it came to starship and spacer information, it kept extensive record of starship registrations and transponder codes, captains' flight certifications, and listings of all weapon load outs on all registered ships in the galaxy. It also kept track of astrographical and navigational information as well as data on hyperlane's used in navigation computers. The Bureau's databanks were continuously updated and transmitted to spaceports, systems, and enforcement agencies throughout the galaxy. Files bearing information on the millions of registered starships were held in secure, encoded computer cores. These information details were frequently kept in cold boxes, which also made public access to transponder codes contraband. However, at least one BoSS owned cold box ended up stolen, where it eventually ended up as part of a droid sale by Nebit's clan in 0 BBY/0 ABY.

All registered spacers were issued with a BoSS datapads, which was to be shown to all port officials and Imperial boarding parties upon request, to ensure the legality of a ship's position, cargo and crew. BoSS was not attached to any one government, remaining omnipresent through the reign of the Galactic Republic, Galactic Empire, New Republic, and well into the age of the Galactic Alliance.

THE INDECTA ERA

The Indecta Era was the period of time from 17,018 BBY to 15,000 BBY. The period was noted for the introduction of assassin droids used by the Judicial Department.

17,018 BBY

During the Great Manifest Period, the planets Alsakan and Coruscant openly competed for worlds in the Expansion Region of the Slice for colonization and natural resources. This rivalry grew throughout the era and was fuelled, as well, by the politicking of the Galactic Senate and other officials. The Republic backed the Duro's merchants, sparking a war between the two factions when they attacked Virujansi in 17,018 BBY. Six years later, Alsakan forces liberated the planet. Corellia would remain neutral by protecting its interests in the Rim.

17,000 BBY

While the Republic was busied with the First Alsakan Conflict, the arboreal hunter-gatherer Xexto species on the planet Troiken was discovered by rogue scientists from Arkania. The Xexto spoke the language Xextese. They had 24 fingers and 6 arms (two were used as legs). Their eyes were normally a dark purple or black. Their skin could range from chalk white to a pale yellow or purple. Their brain was split between two parts of their body; the part located in the skull controlled primitive emotions and basic body functions, while another portion in their chest controlled higher functions such as creative thinking and logic. The scientists sought to perform genetic experimentation on sentient species outside of the Republic's borders, because such actions were illegal within Republic space. Around 17,000 BBY, the Arkanian scientists secretly took a sample of the Xexto and relocated them to the nearby planet Quermia. There, the planet was terraformed, and the transplanted Xexto became helpless subjects of genetic experimentation and manipulation. The experiments were not confined to Quermia, however, as the Arkanian's also performed some experiments on those who had remained behind on Troiken.

16,921 BBY

The Battle of Kes occurs during this year, resulting in a tactical draw between the Galactic Republic and Alsakani forces.

16,820 BBY

The First Siege of Porus Vida occurs.

16,782 BBY

The Celebratus Archive is founded on the planet Obroa-skai. The Celebratus Archive was a library that held complete records from over three hundred thousand different species. The creation of the library secured the reputation of the planet as a bastion of research. The archive was included in the list of the Twenty Wonders of the Galaxy by the historian Vicendi in his 10,000 BBY publication Arturum Galactinum.

16,800 BBY

The Siege of Belasco occurs.

16,700 BBY

The First Alsakan Conflict is ended by the Bureau of Ships and Services, which uses its control of the hyperspace beacon system, used by both the Galactic Republic and Alsakan, to force a peace between the two sides by threatening to withhold access.

16,200 BBY

The Second Alsakan Conflict begins. The Conflict saw fighting in the Outer Rim Territories with the Second Siege of Porus Vida around 16,100 BBY and the Gizer Campaign about a century later, while the later years of the war saw fighting in the Core Worlds, primarily during the Core Campaigns around 15,600 BBY. The planets Skako and Commenor were both attacked during this time and Belgoth's Beacon, one of the original hyperspace beacons commissioned by Borte Belgoth around 25,100 BBY, was destroyed during fighting along the Perlemian Trade Route. The Republic planet Abhean was the site of a battle known as the Strontium Raid in 15,480 BBY, though the Conflict ended in a draw in 15,400 BBY like the rest of the wars.

THE KYMOODON ERA

The Kymoodon Era was an era of time in the galaxy that started circa 15,000 BBY and marked a second boom in expansion similar to the Great Manifest Period. Hyperspace travel became more commonplace during this time and some of the most noted starship manufacturers noted this era as the time of their founding.

In the last centuries of the era, Republic colonists spread beyond the frontier into what was then the Wild Space between the Republic and Hutt Space. The Hutt's sponsored numerous raids against these planets with the aim of enslaving the colonists. Lexrul, Drogheda, Hathrox, Imram and Parcovey Minor were among those colonies targeted. The successful defence of Parcovey Minor was one of the few bright spots for the colonists amid the raids.

The Kymoodon Era stretched from the end of the Indecta Era in 15,000 BBY to the Pius Dea Era, which began with the election of Contispex I as Supreme Chancellor in 11,987 BBY.

15,000 BBY

The Anomids of Yablari join the Republic. Anomids were tall, well-built humanoids ranging from 1.7 to 1.9 meters tall. Anomid skin was translucent with a faint colouring ranging from a light violet to a pale purple and was smooth, but wrinkled with age. They had large, slender hands with six fingers on each; two end fingers, two centre fingers and two thumbs, with a sharp claw on each. The fingers were paired in twos and slightly spaced apart from the others. The eyes of the Anomids were solid, with no visible irises or pupils and have been seen in varying shades of yellow or blue. The Anomids had pointed, fin-like ears that protruded from the sides of their heads. Anomid hair was often long and well kept, and were always found in shades of black, grey or white. Some Anomids had bald domes with wrinkled skin and sparse hairs, though this could have been an effect of aging as other, presumably younger, Anomids were seen with full heads of hair. The most notable thing about Anomids, appearance wise, were the metallic, often elaborate and aesthetic masks they wore on the bottom half of their faces. These were not breathing masks, as many 'offworlders' might have assumed, but rather vocalizer units. The Anomids were born without vocal chords so many decided to adorn their faces with these machines to better communicate with the galaxy, as learning or even understanding the six-fingered sign language of the Anomids was difficult to near impossible for most humanoids or humanoid-built droids.

The Hutt Cataclysms come to an end. This had been a civil war which had torn through the Hutt Space, leaving the Hutt homeworld of Varl and other ancient Hutt colonies lifeless wastelands. The Hutt's established a Council of Elders to prevent clan rivalries from erupting into open warfare and instituted a new philosophy called The Kajidic, which rejected war and territorial conquest in favour of enslavement of minor species. Many of the Hutt's were forced to relocate to the planet Evocar

During the early Alsakan Conflicts, a series of seventeen wars between the Republic and the allies of the planet Alsakan, the Galactic Senate resisted calls for the Navy's reinstatement. In the early conflicts, both Alsakan and the Coruscant-controlled Republic attempted to use massive battle fleets to secure victories, but neither side had the military resources to split their forces between attack and defence. During the Duinuogwuin Contention of 15,500 BBY, when the Duinuogwuin species attacked the Republic capital of Coruscant, further calls for the Navy's return were blocked by internal feuding in the Senate. Around 15,000 BBY, however, the Senate finally heeded the pleas of the outlying systems and re-established the Navy with its headquarters on Coruscant.

The Cremlevian War began in the wake of an invasion by a droid species in the Yuuzhan Vong's galaxy. Threatened by extinction, the Yuuzhan Vong developed new weapons and technology, eventually defeating their droid enemies. After this victory, the Yuuzhan Vong continued waging war on other species in the galaxy, conquering a number of worlds. However, the species also began warring amongst itself.

At some point, the two most powerful tribes, one led by Warmaster Yo'gand and another led by Warmaster Steng, clashed. The resulting conflict known as the Cremlevian War saw the destruction of many planets. It came to a close when Yo'gand utilized a technique that was later named after him, to drop a moon on the planet Ygziir, which was allied with Steng. The tactic destroyed the planet, and killed many of the leaders of Steng's faction, who were stationed on Ygziir. Steng was also killed in the battle, bringing the war to an end.

The Aquala and Quara species fight a civil war, but unite when an offworld exploratory vessel lands on Ando. The united Aqualish species kill the explorers and take their ship, learning to reproduce it. A few decades later, the Aqualish embark on a campaign of conquest, but are quickly stopped by the Republic.

Dahrtag, later known more commonly as Necropolis and a tombworld located on the Giju Run of the Core Worlds, is first settled by a religious order who are appalled by the way that Core cultures have grown more similar to each other. They set aside parts of the world for each culture, and invite any culture to inter their dead on the planet in their specific tradition.

14,743 BBY

The Caliginous Automaton of Tomo-Reth was a black droid of more than fifty meters in height that sat upon a brick throne on the planet Tomo-Reth. It amazed visitors by breathing fire but was destroyed during the Herglic Crush.

14,500 BBY

The Third Alsakan Conflict, between Coruscant and Alsakan, began in 17,000 BBY. During the conflict, the famed Alsakan Mosaics found in the city Rucapar on Alsakan were destroyed during the Cleansing of Rucapar. The centre of the mosaic had been featured at the city square and extended to five equidistant mountains. Only remnants survived the war. Another major battle was the Commenor Run Campaign.

14,300 BBY

The Duros Red Credit Brigade was a faction during the Third Alsakan Conflict presumably composed of members of the Duros species. They were defeated by the rival Machinists of Nikato who then established an independent state known as the Nikato's Bootheel on Raxus Prime in the Tion Cluster, bringing an end to the Third Alsakan Conflict with it.

14,000 BBY

A number of Sith establish a library-temple on the world of Krayiss 2 where they slumber and their spirits supposedly haunt the temple for the next 10,000 years.

The noble Korden family first appears. Throughout history, members of House Korden could be found in both the Galactic Senate as well as the Jedi Order, using their influence to promote peace. Members of House Korden also contributed to the efforts of the Alliance to Restore the Republic in its fight against the Galactic Empire.

Duros scouts discover the planet Sneeve and the Sneevel species in the Expansion Region.

13,800 BBY

The Fourth Alsakan Conflict begins.

13,649 BBY

The Defence of Drogheda was a battle that took place in 13,649 BBY, during the Fourth Alsakan Conflict.

13,649 BBY

The Defence of Drogheda was a battle that took place in 13,649 BBY, during the Fourth Alsakan Conflict.

13,220 BBY

The Conquest of Manaan was a battle that took place in 13,220 BBY, during the Fourth Alsakan Conflict.

13,200 BBY

The Fourth Alsakan Conflict comes to an end.

13,050 BBY

The Fifth Alsakan Conflict begins. the conflict lasted until around 12,700 BBY, and saw fighting across the galaxy. Alsakan began using a new class of cruiser during the conflict, and Admiral Hirken made great use of the cruisers during his defence of Alsakan colony worlds in the Northern Dependencies region in 12,980 BBY. His campaign included battles at Iridonia, Glee Anselm, Xa Fel, Dachat, Borleias, and Twith. Near the end of the conflict, a battle later known as the Resistance on Cyrillia occurred at the planet Cyrillia, though the war as a whole ended in a ceasefire that lasted almost a millennium.

13,000 BBY

The Herglic Trade Empire joins the Republic, sparking development around the Hidakai Pool route. The Herglic Trade Empire was a trading Empire in the Colonies established by the Herglics of Giju presumably not long after the Corellians achieved hyperspace travel, prior 27,500 BBY. There was some archaeological evidence that the Herglic Trade Empire achieved a superior level of technology that was not paralleled during the Rebellion era.

The heavily-fortified planet of Ailon in the Inner Rim becomes a member of the Republic.

12,980 BBY

Admiral Hirken, a human Admiral who fought on the side of Alsaka during the Fifth Alsakan Conflict, defends Alsakani colonies in the Northern Dependencies, a campaign that was a major turning point in the conflict.

12,720 BBY

The planet Pelagon in the future Tapani sector is first settled by large colony ships, and the colonists soon settle other worlds in the region.

12,700 BBY

The Resistance on Cyrilia occurs and the Fifth Alsakan Conflict comes to an end.

12,293 BBY

An expedition led by Doctor Beramsh conducts the first surveys of the planet Tandun III. The expedition was led from Ord Mantell to Tandun III. Beramsh supervised the exploration of the planet and found massive ancient population centres the doctor theorized were constructed by the Rakata. Though Dr. Beramsh's survey had proven that Tandun III was suitable for colonization, it was never colonized before its destruction in 43 ABY.

12,000 BBY

During the years of the Old Republic, the governing body gradually but steadily expanded its boundaries. Most of the settlements, however, were in a wedge-shaped region of space known as the Slice. Aside from occasional protrusions into unknown areas and isolated settlements, most of galactic society lived within the confines of known hyperspace routes and the established hyperlanes. Settlers and explorers, however, continued to search the wild and unexplored areas of the galaxy. In the years leading up to 12,000 BBY, this steady advancement continued.

The expansion of the Republic continued around 12,000 BBY as colonists from Corellia continued to explore uncharted space. A group of colonists settled on the Mid Rim world of Ord Mantell. The colonists established an advanced military outpost on the planet for the expanding Republic, even though it was isolated from Republic space by uncharted area. This planet was an Ordnance/Regional Depot (Ord) world whose purpose was to also protect Human colonists in the surrounding systems. Elsewhere, the Ithorians of Ithor had their first contact with the Republic, further expanding the reaches of known space.

Starting from the planet Gyndine, scouts start to establish the Ootmian Pabol route, bridging the gap between the Republic and Hutt Space.

Haddius Korden, a successful merchant from Corulag, turned his family business into Korden Outfitting and Surveying, which supplied a wide variety of equipment to colonists headed for the farthest frontiers of the known galaxy.

THE PLUS DEA ERA

The Pius Dea Era was an era of time in the galaxy from 11,987 BBY to 10,966 BBY. During this time, the Contispex dynasty of Supreme Chancellors initiated the Pius Dea Crusades against outlying alien cultures, reversing a previous trend of cultural integration. Those under persecution fled to Hutt Space, transforming the Rimward Slice into a staging grounds for soldiers, as well as an area for war profiteers to operate. Also during this time, Ordnance/Regional Depots proliferated and were a constant reminder to those outside the Galactic Republic.

11,987 BBY

A cult of conspiratorial religious zealots known as Pius Dea usurped power over the Republic with the help of a secretive society called the Malkite Poisoners. The zealots impeached reigning Supreme Chancellor Pers'lya and installed the Pius Dea figurehead Contispex I, assassinating the Bothan not long after he was removed from office. The new chancellor, housing Humanocentric beliefs, then unleashed a series of religious-based crusades against alien species and those who worshiped other deities. The rise of the Pius Dea cult marked the end of the Kymoodon Era and the beginning of the Pius Dea Era.

11,965 BBY

The First Pius Dea Crusade was a punitive campaign waged by the Pius Dea Supreme Chancellor Contispex against Hutt Space beginning in the year 11,965 BBY. A humanocentric sect, the Pius Dea had come to power by impeaching the incumbent Chancellor Pers'lya in 11,987 BBY. Shortly after coming into power, Contispex was able to exploit popular anti-Hutt sentiment amongst the Galactic Republic citizenry.

The first major conflict since the Hutt Cataclysms in 15,000 BBY, the First Crusade launched over a millennia of religious conflict. The Republic dispatched a military expedition to Hutt Space, a crime haven which had threatened the Republic's frontiers in preceding millennia, launching three simultaneous assaults from the edges of Republic space. One fleet moved along the ancient Ootmian Pabol trade route from Ubrikkia to Kwenn and then into Hutt Space, while a second and third fleets moved from Ord Yndar and Ord Wylan into the crime-ridden region. The Hutt's would again be targeted in the Second and Third Crusades, starting a trend of religious persecution of alien species.

11,947 BBY

Contispex I steps down as Supreme Chancellor after a forty year reign and is succeeded by his son Contispex II. He continued the Pius Dea Crusades, instigating the Second and Third Pius Dea Crusades against the Hutt's.

11,939 BBY

Contispex II sanctions the Third Pius Dea Crusade, yet another invasion of Hutt Space.

11,933 BBY

The Jedi Order retreats to Ossus and severs all ties with the Pius Dea dominated Republic, beginning their Recusal. A number of Jedi who are loyal to the Pius Dea form the Order of the Terrible Glare and settle on the planet Garn. The Order becomes a violent and dangerous cult led by shamans, the Order waged war against the Jedi before being destroyed at the end of the Crusades. The sole survivor, Rur, lived on in a computer and lured Jedi to Garn for thousands of years, taking vengeance on them one at a time. However, Rur was finally defeated by Luke Skywalker during the Galactic Civil War, which brought an end to this ancient Order.

11,920 BBY

The Fourth Pius Dea Crusade begins against the Hutt's.

11,884 BBY

The Seventh Pius Dea Crusade, also known as the Great Northern Crusade, begins against the Zabrak and other species native to the northern region of the galaxy.

11,820 BBY

The Sixth Alsakan Conflict begins as the Alsakani ally with the Duro's, Herglics, and the Hutt's against the Pius Dea controlled Republic; however, the conflict ends with a Republic victory.

11,791 BBY

The Tenth Pius Dea Crusade, also known as the Crusade of the Wilds, begins. The Galactic Republic, under the control of the Pius Dea religious group, initiated a campaign against various alien species and suspected alien sympathizers.

11,708 BBY

The Colonial Era of the Tapani sector ends, beginning the Twelve Kingdoms Era. This period was marked by the fragmentation of the original Pella Compact colonists into twelve primary Houses. Each House ruled their own colonies without interference until Shey Tapani initiated a twenty-year civil war. Two houses were wiped out, and another collapsed on itself, but Shey Tapani succeeded in uniting the Houses and ending the Twelve Kingdoms Era.

11,707 BBY

The Eleventh Pius Dea Crusade against the ancient spacefaring species The Herglics begins. It was a religious crusade orchestrated by the Pius Dea cult In 11,707 BBY, over eighty years after the previous crusade, the Pius Dea-controlled Galactic Republic launched an invasion of Herglic Space to the south of the Deep Core.

11,660 BBY

The Twelfth Pius Dea Crusade begins. When the planet Zarracina III was discovered by the Galactic Republic in 11,660 BBY, the Republic forces attempted to conquer the native Zarracines. However, the Zarracines resisted the Pius Dea controlled government's attempt, and in response the Republic bombarded the planet's surface. The attack drove the Zarracines to extinction and irradiated the planet's surface, destroying all life.

The Republic's attack provoked outrage across much of the galaxy, and the Teirasans of the planet Teirasa expressed significant anger with the Republic. The Teirasans' response caused Pius Dea to strike out at the Teirasans as well, starting another crusade. Republic forces launched against Teirasa from Ord Dorlass and Ord Zynthar, battling the Teirasans to an unknown outcome

11,600s BBY

Republic citizens fleeing the Pius Dea settle on the planet Prefsbelt IV. Prefsbelt IV, also referred to as simply Prefsbelt, was a green planet in the Prefsbelt system, a star system in the Prefsbelt sector of the Outer Rim Territories.

11,591 BBY

The Fifteenth Pius Dea Crusade against the Baragwin begins. The Baragwin were a species of sentient reptilians native to the lost world Old Barag. One of the earliest spacefaring races, the Baragwin could be found across the galaxy.

11,198 BBY

The Twenty-Third Pius Dea Crusade against the Bothans and the Lanniks begins. The Republic launched forces from Ord Segra against Bothawui, the homeworld of the secretive Bothans, and Ord Dycoll against the warmongering Lanniks of Lannik.

11,100 BBY

The Inquisitions begin in the Core Worlds and the Colonies, and the Jedi Order end their Recusal.

11,057 BBY

The Thirty-Fourth Pius Dea Crusade against the Hutt's begins. The Thirty-Fourth Pius Crusade was the last of the religious crusades orchestrated by the Pius Dea cult and their leaders, the Contispex dynasty. The Pius Dea controlled Republic launched an assault against Hutt Space, using the nearby Ord Dycoll, Ord Wylan, Ord Klina, Ord Ortag, and Ord Lonesome as staging points for their attacks on the southern end of the region.

10,970s BBY

Pers Pradeux joined the Republic Navy when it was a bastion of the Pius Dea religion, and rose to the rank of Admiral: for nearly a thousand years beforehand, the Republic Navy had been the tool of the theocrats controlling the Galactic Republic to launch Crusades against the alien species of the Rim. By the 10,900s BBY, however, a heresy stoked by Jedi and Caamasi agents was circulating throughout the Pius Dea Republic, and Pradeux became influenced by Renunciate thought. Admiral Pradeux became part of a conspiracy to overthrow Pius Dea and restore the Republic.

Pradeux discovered the secret colony of Prefsbelt IV, founded by Republic citizens fleeing the Pius Dea, and used the world as a secret base and a retreat for his fellow Renunciate naval officers while plotting the overthrow of the Pius Dea Faithful.

Following the Battle of Uquine in 10,966 BBY and the collapse of Pius Dea rule, Pradeux and his colleagues held meetings on Prefsbelt to plan the reorganization and rebuilding of the Republic Navy. Consequently, Pradeux became remembered as the "Father of the Navy", with Castle Pradeux on Prefsbelt named for him.

After his death, Pradeux's body was entombed in the Naval Crypt, a few kilometres from Castle Pradeux. As a tradition, the night before graduation from the Prefsbelt IV Naval Academy, navy midshipmen would walk from Castle Pradeux to the Crypt and pledge their dedication to the service.

The Imperial Navy named the Imperial I-class Star Destroyer Pradeux in his honour.

10,967 BBY

The Renunciate movement, a splinter faction of the Pius Dea that has renounced their faith, reveals itself and allies with the Alsakani, Caamasi, and the Jedi Order. This splits the Pius Dea faith from within, pitting the Faithful against those who have abandoned the faith, and signals the start of the Seventh Alsakan Conflict. Renunciate forces later clash with Faithfuls at Fondor, Ixtlar, and Cyrillia, supported by the Jedi, Alsakani, Duros, Herglics, and Hutts.

10,966 BBY

After a year of conflict, the Bureau of Ships and Services abandoned its traditional neutrality and secretly agrees to aid the Jedi Order. Coordinating with the Renunciates and the alliance, the BoSS secretly seeded Pius Dea's fleet of cathedral ships with rogue navicomputer code. The Order and its allies gathered their forces at Uquine, baiting the Faithful into attacking the Renunciate fleet there. Just before the Pius Dea's fleet jumped to hyperspace, the BoSS sent a signal to every ship in the fleet that activated the implanted code and caused the Puis Dea's ships to jump randomly to hyperspace and become lost forever.

More than half of the fleet disappeared, lost in hyperspace. Many of those missing cathedral ships found themselves stranded in deep space, with their navicomputers wiped clean and their hyperdrives and communications systems rendered useless. Those aboard would be unable to return, and would eventually die from lack of supplies. The remaining ships arrived at Uquine to find themselves under attack by the combined forces of the Renunciates and the Jedi-led alliance.

A strike team of Jedi Knights boarded the flagship Flame of Sinthara and captured Supreme Chancellor Contispex XIX, ending the Pius Dea's rule of the Republic. Contispex was taken to Caamas, where he was found guilty of crimes against the galaxy and imprisoned for the rest of his life. Without their leader, the Pius Dea faith crumbled after their defeat at Uquine. Every single member of the faith was removed from office, and Jedi Grand Master Biel Ductavis assumed the office of Supreme Chancellor. The Jedi capture Contispex XIX aboard the Flame of Sinthara, taking him to Caamas where he stands trial and is imprisoned.

THE DUCTAVIS ERA

The Ductavis Era was an era of time in the galaxy from 10,966 BBY to 9000 BBY. It was considered a time of rebuilding after the crusades of Supreme Chancellor Contispex I during the Pius Dea Era.

10,966 BBY

Grand Master Biel Ductavis assumes the position of Supreme Chancellor; his ascension heralds the end of the Pius Dea era and the start of the Ductavis Era. Biel Ductavis was a male Jedi Master who led the Jedi Order as its Grand Master at the end of the Pius Dea Crusades, a series of conflicts that began in 11,965 BBY and lasted for nearly one millennium. When the Order suspended the Galactic Senate following the arrest of Supreme Chancellor Contispex XIX, aboard the Flame of Sinthara, in 10,966 BBY, Ductavis was installed as the leader of the Galactic Republic in an attempt to rebuild the galactic government.

10,000 BBY

The historian Vicendi compiles a list of the Twenty Wonders of the Galaxy for his Arturum Galactinum, a work commissioned for the Republic's anniversary.

Ryloth enters the Galactic Republic. Ryloth, also known as Twi'lek, and Twi'lek Prime, was the harsh, rocky homeworld of the Twi'leks, an Outer Rim Territories world located on the Corellian Run and forming one endpoint of the Death Wind Corridor. One side of the planet perpetually faced its sun and the other remained in darkness, a phenomenon known as tidal locking. The dayside was referred to as the Bright Lands and the night-side was known as the Nightlands.

The Gran species begin to record their history. Gran could easily be identified by their three eyes and their goat-like snout. Gran were also able to sense one another's emotions and disposition by noting subtle changes in body heat and skin color and female Gran had three breasts. The Gran had excellent vision, able to resolve more colors than most species, and even able to see into the infrared. They had two stomachs, having evolved from herbivorous grazing animals who lived in herds on the mountains and highlands of Kinyen, surviving on the local goatgrass, for which Gran kept their taste. Gran chewed and digested their food quite slowly, savoring the flavor carefully. A single meal could take almost an entire day to finish, but a Gran would often not need to eat for several days afterwards.

A recessive genetic mutation sometimes caused some Gran to suffer from misshapen extremities, with hands and feet swelling to abnormal sizes. While not affecting the individual's ability to do finer work, the handicap nonetheless often resulted in social isolation. Gran scientists intently studied the trait to attempt to find a cure.

Ammuud, a cold planet with a short rotation located in the Corporate Sector, is settled as a religious retreat by colonists from Thokos. The planet had been ruled by seven major clans operating under Corporate Sector Authority subcontract.

The Kumauri Empire, a realm of more than thirty star systems, comes into conflict with the Republic They deploy planet-busting battleships including a series of massive capital ships capable of planetary bombardment, beginning with the warlord's flagship Kumauri Battleship, and culminating in the three kilometre long Cal-Class battleship, with mass drivers which flung asteroids at surface targets and could only be rendered obsolete by the development of effective planetary shields. The Kumauri are soon defeated though.

The planet New Plympto and its Nosaurian inhabitants are discovered by Corellian traders. New Plympto was a temperate terrestrial world in the Core Worlds region populated by the Nosaurians. It was discovered by Corellians around 10,000 BBY, although the Jedi Order apparently had contact with it since at least 25,000 BBY, using the native population as potential recruits. The planet was also the homeworld of Podracer pilot Clegg Holdfast.

Madilon is discovered and becomes a principle component in Hyperdrive manufacturing. Madilon was a type of naturally-occurring alloy, which had a unique molecular structure that gave it high tensile strength, while retaining a large amount of elasticity. These properties meant that the alloy could withstand the stresses of hyperspace travel, and so it was useful in the construction of hyperdrives. The amount of Madilon required for a single Hyperdrive was relatively small, but allowed the hyperdrive to be almost ten times smaller in size than one that did not contain madilon. Scientists were unable to develop a method for synthesizing madilon, so the only sources of it were the few planets in the galaxy that contained deposits of the alloy.

9757 BBY

The Republic rocket-jumpers participate in the Second Herglic Feud. The Rocket-Jumper Elite Advance Unit (R-EAU), known commonly as the Republic rocket-jumpers, was an elite soldier equipped with a rocket pack, used by the Galactic Republic millennia before the rise of the Empire. They were organized as a part of the Republic Army.

9400s BBY

Planetary shielding begins to see widespread use across the galaxy.

9349 BBY

The Korden family officially becomes the noble House Korden.

9200 BBY

Planetary Turbolasers are first commonly deployed around this time.

THE RIANITUS PERIOD

The Rianitus Period of history lasted from 9000 BBY to 8000 BBY. It was remembered for the 275-year reign of Blotus the Hutt. Around the end of this period (c. 8000 BBY), the Republic established an outpost on Malastare's eastern continent.

9000 BBY

The Rianitus Period begins. The Rianitus Period of history lasted from 9000 BBY to 8000 BBY. It was remembered for the 275-year reign of Blotus the Hutt. Around the end of this period (c. 8000 BBY), the Republic established an outpost on Malastare's eastern continent.

Jiroch-Reslia, a planet in the Mid Rim, joins the Republic. The planet was saved from Lortan invasion by the Galactic Empire, ensuring its loyalty to the Empire, but it did join the New Republic in later years.

THE SUBTERRA PERIOD

The Subterra Period was a period of time in the galaxy that lasted from 8000 BBY to 7000 BBY. During this time, there was new mapping of the galactic southern quadrant. The planet of Malastare acted as an anchor for short hyperlane snippets, also known as praediums. The supply lines that linked the galaxy with the Rishi Maze were also constructed.

The rapid expansion however led to lawlessness in the Rim and Coruscant lost its control on its new territories. This was thought to have contributed to the Second Great Schism in 7003 BBY, which led to the start of the Hundred-Year Darkness.

8000 BBY

The planet Malastare becomes a member of the Republic. Malastare was the high-gravity homeworld of the quadrupedal Dug race, on the Hydian Way. Malastare had a variety of terrains including forests, deserts, methane lakes, and rivers. This made the planet a favourite Podracing location. There, local and interstellar stars such as the Dug Sebulba competed in events such as the Malastare 100, the Dug Derby, Sebulba's Legacy, the Phoebos Memorial Run and the Vinta Harvest Classic. The Republic soon establishes an outpost on the eastern continent of Malastare, and the Gran species begin to make their own settlements and politically dominate the world.

Goroth Prime is discovered by Corellian pirates.

The star Colu expands, swallowing the planet Clak'dor I which was originally the innermost planet in the Colu system of the Mayagil sector.

7811 BBY

The Waymancy Storm occurs, a conflict between the Galactic Republic and the government of Waymancy called the Waymancy Hollow. When the Galactic Republic came into contact with the Waymancy Hollow the Waymancy ships were equipped with energy weapons that were far more powerful and faster than any the Republic had access to, as they utilized incredibly efficient power generators designed by the group known as the Sisters of the Machinesmith, and the Waymancy warships easily destroyed the Republic ships. Despite heavily outnumbering the Waymancy forces, the Republic only achieved victory after it successfully reverse-engineered the Sif-Alulan process used to create Waymancy weapons and developed its own pulse-wave weaponry.

7700 BBY

The Verpine master crafter Lyns Skutroo pioneers the Squintpipe process for power generators, having reverse-engineered the Waymancy Storm technology. As a result, shielding technology become important in combat, evolving from simply protection against environmental phenomena. As a result of Skutroo's efforts, rapid-firing turbolasers also became prevalent in defences across the galaxy.

7500 BBY

Further refinement of the Squintpipe process allows for increases in shield power and regeneration.

7348 BBY

The Twelve Kingdoms Era of the Expanse comes to an end as the warlord Prince Shey Tapani begins the Unification War to unite the worlds of the region and initiated a series of conflicts with the other kingdoms. The Twelve Kingdoms had existed in the Tapani sector for 3,000 years after power was devolved from the Pella Compact.

7328 BBY

The Unification War ends at the battle of Shindra's Veil, and Shey Tapani unites the Expanse under the banner of the Tapani Empire. He establishes his new government on Procopia, and also dedicates the Shey Tapani University on Estalle Island shortly after the Empire's founding. At the battle of Shindra's Veil Tapani commanded 150 starships against the Rogue Houses, and the battle brought the war to an end. Thousands of years later, the Unification Gala celebrated the battle with a re-enactment.

7308 BBY

The Tapani Empire establishes a university system on the planet Mrlsst, which was recently discovered by Republic and Tapani scouts. Mrlsst was a planet located in the Tapani sector's Freeworlds Territory on the Shapani Bypass. It was the home world of the Mrlssi and a voting member of the League of Tapani Freeworlds.

7003 BBY

The Second Great Schism occurs. This was a divisive split among the ranks of the Jedi Order. Jedi who practiced alchemy and the dark side of the Force as Dark Jedi broke with the Jedi Order, and the war known as the Hundred-Year Darkness followed in 7000 BBY.

THE MANDERON PERIOD

Manderon Period was an era of the Galactic Republic which lasted from 7000 BBY to 5000 BBY, and reached its height some 6,000 years before the Galactic Civil War. It was marked by a "trio" of discoveries which changed the fate of the galaxy.

The Exiles discovered the Sith Empire. The Corellian Trade Spine was completed by 5500 BBY. Simultaneously the Herglics and Givin form the Rimma Trade Route out of preexisting praediums. The Hundred-Year Darkness is also fought during the first century of this period.

7000 BBY

Sith sorcerer Dathka Graush initiates a period of civil war on Korriban upon ascending to the throne. Graush was a brutal foe. In the war's wake, he made use of both Sith magic and alchemy to perfect the Tsaiwinokka Hoyakut spell through which he resurrected an army of reanimated corpses bound to him through the dark side of the Force. He also had his heart removed and replaced with a magical crystal that was imbued with the power of the force's malevolent side.

The Hundred-Year Darkness begins in the aftermath of the Second Great Schism. It was a conflict that began in 7000 BBY and lasted until approximately 6900 BBY, when a group of Dark Jedi, also known as "Fallen Jedi", created monstrous armies to battle the Jedi Order and the Galactic Republic. The Hundred-Year Darkness began three years after the Dark Jedi split with the Order in the Second Great Schism. After decades of fighting, the Dark Jedi lost the war, in its final battle, but went on to conquer Korriban, and found the Sith.

Mandalore warrior and first leader of the Mandalorian clan, Taung Mandalore the First, or Te Sol'yc Mand'alor in Mando'a, leads his followers from the planet Roon to a new world, which his followers rename Mandalore in his honor. It was the fifth planet in the Madalore system of the Outer Rim Territories, not far from the Hydian Way trade route. Taung Mandalore and his followers were originally Taungs from Coruscant who had settled on Roon.

Republic scouts discover the Quermian system, where the Quermians had settled and inhabited numerous worlds within only a few decades. The Quermians would become active participants in the galactic community.

As the Sith Empire expanded across the galaxy from Korriban and Ziost, it was determined that a grand library need be built to rival the Great Library of Ossus maintained by the Jedi Order. Selecting the frozen world of Arkania, home to a race with a reputation for mad scientists and genetic engineers, the Empire named their storehouse Veeshas Tuwan and filled its shelves with arcane magics and tools of the dark side of the Force. Sith Lords from across Sith-controlled space visited the complex, building upon the knowledge there and practicing their dark arts in hidden chambers. The library grew so large over the centuries that nobody was able to find what they were looking for.

Veeshas Tuwan met its end at the conclusion of the Great Hyperspace War when Lord Naga Sadow was defeated by the Jedi Order and the Galactic Republic. Discovering the location of the library, the Jedi High Council dispatched a team of Jedi Masters to seek out the library and destroy any relics which could assist in the rebuilding of the Sith Empire. Arriving at Veeshas Tuwan, the Jedi looted the building and confiscated many historical texts before destroying ancient weapons and artifacts. With the library's collection in ruins, the Jedi burned the complex to the ground and left nothing but smoldering ruins. Despite the library's destruction, the Sith would remember their ancient archives for generations to come.

6950 BBY

Dathka Graush's reign comes to an end with his death at the hands of assassins.

6900 BBY

Having fought for nearly a century, the Jedi and their rival Dark Jedi made a final stand at Corbos, a mining world. Ajunta Pall was one of the Dark Jedi leading the campaign against the Jedi; Pall himself personally slew more than a dozen Jedi before the battle's end. The Dark Jedi were defeated after an orbital bombardment wave by the Jedi. Karness Muur also participated in the battle and was one of the few surviving Dark Jedi. The other surviving Dark Jedi were exiled to uncharted space, where they discovered Ziost and Korriban, home to the primitive but unusually Force-sensitive Sith people. Using their training in the Force, the fallen Jedi amazed the Sith and elevated themselves to god-like status on Korriban and Ziost, becoming the rulers of the Sith people. As years passed, and interbreeding occurred between the Fallen Jedi and the Sith, the term "Sith" came to mean not only the original inhabitants of Ziost and Korriban, but also their fallen Jedi masters. With the Battle of Corbos came an end to the Hundred-Year Darkness.

6740 BBY

The crystal world of Mygeeto is discovered by the Republic. Since Mygeeto was locked in an ice age, giant crystallized glaciation and ice covered its surface, as well as huge crystal spurs. Because of this, Mygeeto meant "gem" in the ancient trade language of the Muuns. Mygeeto's internal fires long since cooled and had left a colossal deposit of precious stones within its crust and mantle. The immense assets of nova crystals and fields of lasing crystals made Mygeeto one of the wealthiest worlds in the galaxy. It hosted artesian crystals and relacite and the planet's ice shelves were home to a species of huge and aggressive worm-like creatures. In addition, the planet itself was enveloped by an asteroid field offering it adequate protection.

6700's BBY

The Mandalorian Crusaders drive the Fenelar species to extinction after raiding the planet Fenel, a planet in the Demetras sector located within the Outer Rim Territories. Fenel was the isolationist homeworld of the Fenelar species, who became renowned for their technologists and shipwrights, producers of powerful dreadnaughts and resilient armor. The Mandalorians claimed Fenel's shipyards, and during the Mandalorian Wars, the Mandalorian Neo-Crusaders used them to construct massive Kandosii-type dreadnaughts.

6100's BBY

The planet Tlön is depopulated and its surface largely incinerated after centuries of conflict between the Mandalorians and the Tlönians.

6100 BBY

The planet Saleucami is first colonized. Saleucami was a dim and arid world with scattered oases of plant growth. Its name Saleucami meant "Oasis" in Wroonian since it was the only habitable planet within a system filled with dead, uninhabitable worlds and meteors. These meteors would frequently cross paths with the planet's orbit and would bombard its surface creating circular patters, like huge craters, calderas, circular seas, and stirring up subterranean waters and minerals, turning the calderas into life-filled pockets on the planet's surface. Large, bulbous plants were scattered around these calderas. These craters of fertile soil were heated by geothermal vents and became the location of the earliest colonies on Saleucami. As a result, the planet became a trading post in the Outer Rim Territories. Saleucami had no indigenous sentient species, but with its pleasant climate (excepting soaring temperatures during summer) brought Weequay, Gran, Wroonian and Twi'lek colonists to it. These colonists lived in tiny townships which were the only form of civilization on the planet besides a city which also served as a spaceport. Beneath the massive caldera was a system of magma streams and geothermal vents that powered the city and provided warmth during the freezing desert nights.

6000 BBY

The planet Ession is settled. Ession was a planet in the Corporate Sector, located at the nexus of the Shaltin Tunnels and Lucaya Cross hyperlanes. It later evolved into an industrial manufacturing center, and warlord Zsinj built the Pakkerd Light Transport Company on the planet, building TIE Fighters for use in his war machine, and sent the Night Caller, under the control of Wraith Squadron, to protect the Implacable while it received the first shipment of new starfighters. However, the New Republic managed to get three squadrons of X-wings to the planet aboard the Blood Nest, and was able to knock out the Pakkerd plant before the TIE's could launch. The Republic also managed to take out the Implacable.

Intelligent life appears on the planet Altiria in the form of the Altiri and Anarrians.

5975 BBY

The planet Dorin, home of the Kel Dor, joins the Republic.

5500 BBY

The Rimma Trade Route is established by Sullustan pilots and Givin theorists, ushering in widespread colonization of the southern galaxy. The Rimma Trade Route was one of the major routes that crossed the galaxy. It started at Abregado-rae in the Core Worlds, and went all the way to the Kathol sector in the far reaches of the Outer Rim Territories. It was estimated that traveling the full length of the route would take at least six weeks with a Class 2 hyperdrive.

The Corellian Trade Spine is fully established, extending the ancient hyperroute that links Corellia and Duro all the way out to the edge of the galaxy. The Corellian Trade Spine was a major trade route. It began at Corellia and headed towards the edge of the galaxy, in the direction of Duro. It passed Devaron and Bestine IV before intersecting the Rimma Trade Route at Yag'Dhul. As it continued it passed through the Greater Javin region of space (which contains the Ison Corridor) before intersecting the Hydian Way and exiting into open inter-galactic space.

5451 BBY

The Pathandr Fury occurs as the Mandalorian Crusaders raid Republic settlements.

5300 BBY

The Jedi Order establishes a training center on the planet Mustafar. Mustafar was a small, fiery, volcanic world located in the Mustafar system of the Outer Rim Territories, coreward of Rutan, between the Hydian Way and the Ninth Quadrant. The planet was mined like a precious natural resource, Mustafar often served as a place to dispose of unwanted evidence, a quality which drew Black Sun to the planet. During the Clone Wars, when Darth Sidious hired Cad Bane to kidnap Force-sensitive children so he could conduct Sith experiments, Anakin Skywalker and his Padawan, Ahsoka Tano went to recover the two children already kidnapped by Bane. When nurse droids noticed the Twilight, Anakin's personal ship incoming, Darth Sidious ordered the droids to let the building sink into the lava river. They complied and hid in the dark building with the children. When the Jedi entered the doomed facility, the droids attacked the Jedi, but to no avail. In the end, Skywalker and Tano freed the children, returned them to their homes, and the facility was no more as it sank beneath the fiery waves. It also drew the Sith and it was on Mustafar that Darth Maul began his Sith training. Mustafar also served as the last capital of the Confederacy of Independent Systems, and was the site of the Separatists' downfall, an event that shaped galactic history. In a duel that followed, Darth Vader fought his former master, Obi-Wan Kenobi, and lost, as a result of which he was forced to wear dark armor for the rest of his life.

5130's BBY

The Nakat Incursions, a border conflict instigated by the Mandalorians, occurs.

5103 BBY

The child Tenebrae kills his father, Lord Dramath, and embarks on a conquest of Nathema.

5100 BBY

Dark Lord of the Sith Marka Ragnos appoints Tenebrae ruler of Nathema, granting him the title of Lord Vitiate.

5010 BBY

Teta ascends to the throne of the planet Koros Major, and soon begins the Unification Wars in an attempt to unite the seven worlds of the Koros system under her rule. Teta was the Empress of the Koros system in 5000 BBY, the instigator of the Unification Wars of Koros, and a key military commander in the Great Hyperspace War. Born into nobility on the wealthy planet of Koros Major, Teta eventually inherited the Koros empire. She quickly became known as the "Warrior Empress," after leading her army into battle and personally foiling many assassination attempts. Over 5,000 years before the Battle of Yavin, Teta began the Unification Wars, an attempt to end the lawless poverty of the system's other worlds and bring them under her rule, with her Jedi advisor, Memit Nadill, at her side. Teta commanded her forces to victory, conquering the rebels on the other planets. She was helped by Nadill and Jedi apprentice Odan-Urr, who used battle meditation to prevent a bloodbath at the Battle of Kirrek.

THE POST-MANDERON PERIOD

This time period, following the Manderon Period, lasted until the outbreak of the Great Sith War that marked the beginning of the Old Sith Wars in 4000 BBY.

5000 BBY

The Unification Wars come to an end, with the Koros system united under Empress Teta's rule.

Marka Ragnos dies, prompting a duel between the rival Sith Lords Ludo Kressh and Naga Sadow, who both seek to succeed Ragnos. As Ragnos's spirit looks on, Sadow emerges victorious and is anointed the new Dark Lord of the Sith.

The Great Hyperspace War, a galactic conflict between the Galactic Republic and the Sith Empire, erupts when two young hyperspace scouts, Gav and Jori Daragon, accidentally make contact with the Sith. The conflict encompassed the entire Galactic Republic, though the main forces focused their attention on three Republic worlds, and later took the war to the remote star system Primus Goluud, and the Sith mausoleum world of Korriban. After it overcame the initial shock of the Sith invasion, the Republic's armadas regrouped and annihilated the Sith Empire, forcing the Sith Lord Naga Sadow to exile himself to Yavin 4.

Sadow instigates the Great Hyperspace War in hopes of conquering the Republic, invading major Republic worlds such as Coruscant and the Koros system along the Daragon Trail hyperlane. The Daragon Trail was an extension of the Goluud Corridor and a hyperspace route. The route was named after Gav and Jori Daragon and ran from Koros Major, which was later renamed Empress Teta, in the Deep Core to Korriban in the Stygian Caldera of the Outer Rim. The remarkable part of this discovery was that the Daragons made it the entire way from Empress Teta to Korriban in a single, uncharted jump. This was the longest blind jump to have ever been made successfully. Sadow's forces were ultimately driven back when his forces were revealed to be largely illusions, and Sadow fled back to the Sith Empire, where he is confronted by Ludo Kressh. Sadow later escapes after destroying Kressh's fleet just ahead of a Republic fleet pursuing him, and ultimately finds refuge on the moon of Yavin 4.

King Adas's holocron is lost on the planet Ashas Ree following the death of its owner, Lord Garu. Adas's holocron was the original Sith holocron, made by King Adas around 27,700 BBY. He learned how to create the holocron from the Rakata who had come to conquer Korriban, and whom he had driven off.

The Sith starship Omen, carrying members of Sith Lord Naga Sadow's Sith Empire, crashes on the remote planet Kesh, stranding its crew as the Lost Tribe of Sith, while its sister ship Harbinger is thrown into the future and arrives around 41 ABY. The Lost Tribe of Sith became a marginal Sith Order and the Tribe quickly dominated the native Keshiri species, who believed the newcomers to be their gods. Sith Captain

Yaru Korsin became Grand Lord of the Tribe and of the Keshiri, a title that was passed on to his daughter, Nida, after his death. Isolated from the outer galaxy for years, the Sith built a Temple in the Takara Mountains over the Omen's crash site and moved their headquarters to the capital city Tahv. Although the original Tribe consisted of several members of both the Human and Sith species, Yaru Korsin ordered a purge of all members of the latter in 4985 BBY. Over time, the Sith formed a ruling Circle of Lords, made up of Lords and High Lords, and ruled by the Grand Lord. The Sith remained isolated for millennia, but after the end of the Second Galactic Civil War in 41 ABY, the Sith Meditation Sphere Ship found the Tribe. The Ship informed the Tribe of the Jedi's newfound dominance in the galaxy and of the recent destruction of the last remnants of the Sith. They assisted the Tribe in traveling offworld and forming a new armada, and two years later, the Tribe felt the presence of Jedi Grand Master Luke Skywalker in the Force and became determined to kill him. However, the Ship was suddenly overcome by the will of Abeloth, a dark side entity living in the Maw, and deserted Kesh for Abeloth's world. The Sith quickly launched a strike team to assassinate Skywalker. The team encountered Abeloth in the Maw, and she weakened the strike team before allowing the Ship to return to them so that they could continue on their mission. Their attack on the Jedi failed, however, and Skywalker and his son Ben tracked Vestara Khai, the team's sole surviving member, to the planet Dathomir. There, a team led by Viun Gaalan captured a group of the darksider Nightsisters and dueled with the Skywalkers while attempting to retrieve Khai, although again the Sith were defeated. Shortly afterwards, a fleet led by High Lord Sarasu Taalon convinced the Jedi to form an alliance against Abeloth, who was causing a psychosis among the Jedi Knights. The allied mission resulted in the Sith betraying the Jedi in hopes of killing the Skywalker's and forcing Abeloth to serve them, but the Sith failed yet again to kill the Jedi. Abeloth was defeated, and the Jedi and Sith temporarily repaired their alliance in order to learn more about her origins. However, the alliance was soon broken, and a later confrontation between the two parties and Abeloth resulted in the death of Taalon. Meanwhile, the Sith perfected their piracy techniques and built a war fleet in preparation to conquer the galaxy.

Supreme Chancellor Pultimo orders an invasion of the Stygian Caldera to wipe out the remains of the Sith Empire.

A supernova occurs in the Moddell sector, forming the Din Pulsar. Its magnetic pulses complicated hyperspatial travel along the nearby route between Endor and Trindello, damaging hyperdrives. The shimmering nebula surrounding the pulsar was known to the Ewoks of Endor as the Gorax King's Heart, after an old legend in which the Ewoks' Golden Sun God imprisoned the Gorax king in the night sky.

Duros scouts discover the planet Adnerem. The Adnerem were a tall, thin, humanoid species of mammal native to the pleasure planet of Adner in the Yataga sector of the Expansion Region. Descended from scavenger-hunters, they had large triangular heads with wide eyes and a large lump in the center of the forehead called an echo chamber. Their thin arms each ended in four talons with no opposable thumb. Adnerem society was based on small, non-genetic social units known as steri, the singular of which was steris, who dwelt together in steri-houses. The members of a steris were known as sterisi, and individual couples who formed a close friendship within a steris were known as a sterika. An Adnerem's status was judged entirely by the status of his or her steris, and different steri sometimes battled for balance of power in a conflict known as a raid-war.

Csilla undergoes an ice age, blanketing its surface with glaciers and forcing the Chiss species to move underground.

The symbol of the Academy of Carida is carved into the moon of Carida, earning it the name of the Mascot Moon.

4999 BBY

Vitiate becomes the Sith Emperor not long after he returned to Nathema. Vitiate was informed by the head researcher that they had discovered a hyperlane connecting Korriban and the long-lost colony world of Dromund Kaas. Three days later, Vitiate announced the commencement of his ritual, and eight thousand Sith Lords answered his call, including the surviving members of the Empire's ruling Sith Council. However, as each Sith arrived at his palace, Vitiate dominated their minds and bound their wills to his own, placing their strength at his disposal. He then began the ritual itself, which took ten days to perform and enabled him to consume the life force of every living thing on the planet. The combined power conferred immortality upon Vitiate, granting him immense strength in the Force at the expense of the entire world. Later, blaming Nathema's destruction on the Jedi, Vitiate gathers the remains of the Empire and embarks on a length exodus from Sith Space.

4985 BBY

Ravilan Wroth poisons a Keshiri village with Cyanogen Silicate in an attempt to encourage the Lost Tribe to escape from Kesh, but Seelah Korsin poisons more villages and frames Wroth for the massacre. Cyanogen Silicate is a chemical compound used as a cauterizing agent in its solid form to heal the wounds of the Massassi warrior caste of the Sith species, as their tough hides proved resistant to treatment by other agents. However, the compound became incredibly deadly when exposed to moisture, killing members of the Human, Keshiri, and Sith species within minutes after exposure, regardless of whether it was ingested or simply touched. Moisture also broke down the compound as it intensified its effects, which meant that a single particle per billion could kill hundreds of people if it was inserted into a settlement's water supply. Wroth and the fifty-seven remaining pureblood Sith were executed as a result.

4980 BBY

The Sith exiles arrive on the planet Dromund Kaas, where the Sith Emperor establishes a reconstituted Sith Empire.

4975 BBY

Yaru Korsin dies following an uprising led by his wife Seelah, and his daughter Nida succeeds him as Grand Lord.

4960 BBY

Nida Korsin bears a son named Donellan. Donellan lived on the planet Kesh during the Post-Manderon period and was the heir to the throne of the Lost Tribe of Sith. However, he died as an old man, before he could become the leader of the tribe, and following his passing, Nida Korsin replaced the tribe's dynastic succession system with one that was based on merit. The Lost Tribe of Sith later established the celebration Donellan's Day, to commemorate the birth of Donellan, and to serve as a warning for Sith who chose to be too patient when trying to engineer their own ascensions.

4904 BBY

Grand Moff Odile Vaiken's final campaign against alien species ends with his death. Vaiken grew up within the borders of the original Sith Empire and was, like other citizens, a loyal servant of his Sith overlords. The Great Hyperspace War between the Empire and the Galactic Republic ended badly for the Sith, and their subjects were forced to flee their homes to escape retribution from enemy forces. The young Vaiken joined his fellow countrymen in a massive exodus from their decimated capital of Korriban, led by a reclusive Sith Lord. After wandering the stars for twenty years, the migrant fleet that carried the Sith expatriates happened upon Dromund Kaas, a forgotten Sith colony world.

After the Sith Lord leading the exodus chose Dromund Kaas to be their new homeworld and proclaimed himself the new Emperor of his people, Vaiken dedicated himself to helping build the new Imperial society. Vaiken was instrumental in establishing order among the Empire's non-Force-sensitive subjects through the creation of the new Imperial Military, which comprised an expertly-trained army and a technologically advanced navy. Vaiken's contributions to the ascendant government earned him the recognition of the Emperor and the governing Dark Council, who named him the first Grand Moff of the Empire.

4896 BBY

Nida Korsin's seventy-nine-year reign as Grand Lord ends with her death.

4800 BBY

The Gank Massacres begin with the discovery of the spice Ryll. After the discovery of Ryll, the Neimoidians acquired the distribution rights to the drug. The Porporites, a newly discovered species, quickly became addicted to Ryll, whipping them into a homicidal frenzy. The Galactic Republic attempted to stop the Porporites by sending the Jedi Knights and conventional military, but they withstood everything the Republic used. Terrified for their safety (and their product), the Neimoidians hired several Gank mercenaries to protect them. Sadly, the Ganks decided that the best course of action was to exterminate the Porporites. After that, the Ganks embarked on a full scale war against the Republic. Supreme Chancellor Vocatara was forced to commission the building of Juggernaut war droids to end the fighting. The massacres also saw the first use of the modern lightsabers, independent of the power packs used during the Great Hyperspace War some two centuries earlier. Also, the Republic rocket-jumpers were part of the Republic forces that participated in the conflict.

4775 BBY

The Gank Massacres are brought to an end by Jedi Knights and the Juggernaut war droids.

4645 BBY

The Sith Lord Darth Drear establishes a Sith academy on Odacer-Faustin, under which he builds a secret temple to store his holocron.

Darth Drear was a male Sith Lord who served the Sith Empire around 4645 BBY. He founded a Sith academy on the planet Odacer-Faustin and worked his students to death as they labored in the construction of the academy. Beneath the academy library, Drear built a temple, where he practiced Sith alchemy and searched for a pathway to immortality. He developed an elixir to fulfill his goal, effectively creating a disease that turned all those infected into zombies, knowledge he recorded into a holocron. Before Drear could successfully implement the final stage of his project, however, he succumbed to the effects of the disease and died.

4606 BBY

The Sith Lord Kel'eth Ur is killed for his heretical light side teachings by the Sith Emperor, and his body is entombed in the Dark Temple on Dromund Kaas.

4600 BBY

A group of Jedi, including the Duinuogwuin Willm Lywin, establish the Teyan Praxeum on the planet Teya IV. Willm Lywin was a male Duinuogwuin Jedi Master. During the first four hundred years of his life, Lywin was part of a group of "living snubfighters" which escorted a praxeum ship. He was one of the founders of the Teyan Praxeum, where he guarded the pathway to the Cave of Truth for six hundred years.

4500 BBY

Parties from the Republic begin to contact the planet Kamino, seeking to make use of the Kaminoans' exceptional cloning technology.

Republic scouts had discovered the star systems of the future Corporate Sector. The Corporate Sector or "CorpSec" was an independent sector created in order to resolve differences between Galactic Republic lawmakers and the heads of many of the galaxy's largest corporations. It was located in the Outer Rim Territories, at the front end of the Tingel Arm region.

The Altiri and Anarrians come into contact with each other, sparking a global conflict that lasts for almost six hundred years.

An independent scout vessel drops out of hyperspace too close to the gravity well of the planet Iol, causing the pilot to crash on the planet and inadvertently uncovering a large vein of ore used in the creation of durasteel. The pilot names the planet Iol and submits a claim to the world, but Tangan Industries intercepts and modifies his claim to give the company rights to the world. Durasteel was an incredibly strong and versatile metal alloy, created from carvanium, lommite, carbon, meleenium, neutronium, and zersium. It was capable of withstanding blistering heat, frigid cold, and monumental physical stress, even when very thin. Because of these properties, durasteel was used for almost everything, from smelting pots for other less hearty metals, to spacecraft hulls. Despite that, however, it could still corrode in the same manner as lesser steel alloys, and likewise required maintenance. Jango Fett's armor was partly made of durasteel, and General Grievous also had some parts of his body made of this material. Darth Vader's armor was mostly made of durasteel, as was Boba Fett's before he upgraded during the Second Galactic Civil War to armor made of beskar.

The Barabel War, a millennia-long conflict among the Barabel species, erupts due to disputes over hunting grounds on their homeworld of Barab I. Centuries before the rise of the Galactic Empire, the largely unknown world of Barab I became rife with dispute amongst the native sentient species, the Barabels. Two large factions had become embroiled in an argument over hunting territory, and their angry words were bordering on open combat, threatening to engulf their neighboring tribes and possibly the entire planet.

4500 BBY

Parties from the Republic begin to contact the planet Kamino, seeking to make use of the Kaminoans' exceptional cloning technology.

Republic scouts had discovered the star systems of the future Corporate Sector. The Corporate Sector or "CorpSec" was an independent sector created in order to resolve differences between Galactic Republic lawmakers and the heads of many of the galaxy's largest corporations. It was located in the Outer Rim Territories, at the front end of the Tingel Arm region.

The Altiri and Anarrians come into contact with each other, sparking a global conflict that lasts for almost six hundred years.

 An independent scout vessel drops out of hyperspace too close to the gravity well of the planet Iol, causing the pilot to crash on the planet and inadvertently uncovering a large vein of ore used in the creation of Durasteel. The pilot names the planet Iol and submits a claim to the world, but Tangan Industries intercepts and modifies his claim to give the company rights to the world. Durasteel was an incredibly strong and versatile metal alloy, created from carvanium, lommite, carbon, meleenium, neutronium, and zersium. It was capable of withstanding blistering heat, frigid cold, and monumental physical stress, even when very thin. Because of these properties, durasteel was used for almost everything, from smelting pots for other less hearty metals, to spacecraft hulls. Despite that, however, it could still corrode in the same manner as lesser steel alloys, and likewise required maintenance. Jango Fett's armor was partly made of durasteel, and General Grievous also had some parts of his body made of this material. Darth Vader's armor was mostly made of durasteel, as was Boba Fett's before he upgraded during the Second Galactic Civil War to armor made of beskar.

The Barabel War, a millennia-long conflict among the Barabel species, erupts due to disputes over hunting grounds on their homeworld of Barab I. Centuries before the rise of the Galactic Empire, the largely unknown world of Barab I became rife with dispute amongst the native sentient species, the Barabels. Two large factions had become embroiled in an argument over hunting territory, and their angry words were bordering on open combat, threatening to engulf their neighboring tribes and possibly the entire planet. Into this fray stepped the Jedi Knight Noga-ta, in some versions of the legend, Noga-ta was accompanied by a team of Jedi as well, who sought to end the conflict before fighting began. Noga-ta managed to give a fair judgment on the matter by listening to both sides and finding a way for both sides to come out as equals. As a result of the Jedi's efforts, the Barabel never fought over hunting grounds again, and indeed shared all territories between their numerous tribes. A tribe's largest kill of any given night had to be given to a neighboring tribe, thereby building a tighter community as well as gaining prestige for the victorious tribe while also rewarding the lesser of hunters.

Jedi were forever revered by the Barabel, and any judgement passed by a Jedi was thought, in their minds, to be the final word on any matter. Though open combat thankfully never began, the dispute was referred to by later generations as the "Barabel War".

4498 BBY

Tangan Industries has completed a full mining colony on Iol, which would expand into three cities scattered across the planet over the next few centuries.

4400 BBY

After being denied a Knighthood, a Padawan named Freedon Nadd explores the Yavin system and encounters Naga Sadow's spirit, who sways Nadd to the dark side of the Force. Nadd kills Sadow's spirit and establishes himself as a king on the planet Onderon, where he institutes a policy to banish criminals into the wilds beyond the walls of the city of Iziz. The exiled criminals manage to tame Onderon's wild beasts to become the Beast Riders, and the Beast Riders wage war on Iziz, sparking the Beast Wars.

The Mon Calamari of Dac begin to launch starliners to colonize planets around their homeworld over the next two centuries.

Around this time, a team of Jedi Knights including the Devaronian Chamma are sent to investigate a distress call on the planet Athiss. There, the group is attacked by Sith devotees, and Chamma succumbs to the dark side during the encounter. Disappointed in his failure, Chamma goes into self-imposed exile on H'ratth.

4300 BBY

The Miraluka Jedi Master Noab Hulis arrives on H'ratth. Noab Hulis was a male Miraluka Jedi Master who served the Jedi Order in the years leading up to the Great Sith War. He sired three daughters, each of whom would go on to serve the Jedi Order themselves. Hearing of the Jedi Chamma, Hulis set about attempting to bring Chamma back to both the light side of the Force and the Jedi Order. Seeking out the former Jedi on H'ratth, the Miraluka at first found it exceedingly difficult to get through to Chamma. Eventually Hulis was able to relay Chamma's own story to him, evoking century-old memories. Hulis remonstrated that Chamma had not been betrayed by the Force, but rather that he had betrayed it, and so the former Jedi returned to the Order, going on to become a significant Jedi Master himself.

4250 BBY

The Third Great Schism erupts as Dark Jedi wage war against their fellows on Coruscant. The Dark Jedi are eventually driven off-world and retreat to the Vultar system, where their attempt to harness the power of the Cosmic Turbine ends in the Vultar Cataclysm and with it the annihilation of the entire Vultar system.

The Wingmaw and its primary predator, the Balmorran Maweater, are accidentally carried from their home island chain to the mainland of the planet Balmorra.

4225 BBY

Jedi Master Vandar Tokare and his two Padawans lead Republic troops in conquering the corrupt world of Kaikielius. Vandar Tokare was a male Jedi Master of Yoda's species who was the head of the Dantooine Jedi Enclave Council during the Mandalorian Wars and Jedi Civil War, holding a seat on both the Jedi High Council and the Council of the Jedi academy during this time span. He was friends with fellow Council member Vrook Lamar, usually having the last word in their frequent disagreements, most notably on the choice to train Revan once again in the ways of the Jedi after his fall to the dark side of the Force. One of the attendees of the Conclave on Katarr, Tokare was killed during an attack from the Sith Lord Darth Nihilus in which the entire Miraluka colony and many of the survivors of the First Jedi Purge were lost.

4200 BBY

The Mecrosa Order is founded as a group of assassins that serve the Tapani sector's noble houses on Nyssa by Viscountess Mireya. The organization is corrupted, allegedly by Mireya herself, by Sith teachings over the next two centuries.

The planet Tatooine is first settled by offworlders. Tatooine (pronounced /tætu'in/; Jawaese: Tah doo Een e) was a desert world and the first planet in the binary Tatoo star system. It was part of the Arkanis sector in the Outer Rim Territories. It was inhabited by poor locals who mostly farmed moisture for a living. Other activities included used equipment retailing and scrap dealing. The planet was on the 5709-DC Shipping Lane, a spur of the Triellus Trade Route, which itself connected to the Sisar Run. It had its own navigation system. However, it would still play a role in galactic events, serving as the home of Anakin Skywalker. It was here that Jedi Master Qui-Gon Jinn recognized Anakin's potential to become a Jedi and where he introduced him to Obi-Wan Kenobi, his future master and mentor. Tatooine was also the home of Anakin's son, Luke, where he lived until his early adulthood. The planet acquired a bad reputation, often being viewed as the cesspool of the galaxy due to the large number of criminals who could be found there.

The planet Argazda seeks to be admitted to the Republic.

The Hapes Cluster becomes a haven for the Lorell Raiders, a group of pirates who had prowled the Perlemian for generations, also known as Hapan Pirates. They learned of safe routes through the hazardous Transitory Mists barrier that surrounded the Cluster and took refuge there along with a number of abductees. Many of the raiders were killed around 4030 BBY when they ventured out and were defeated by Republic forces led by the Jedi under Arca Jeth. Although the era of the Raiders was at an end, they did have survivors who became known as Hapans, who developed a strong hatred of the Jedi for the death they brought to the Raiders.

The planet Arkanis is colonized by pilgrims from Ator.

4100s BBY

New navicomputer technology begins to render jump-beacons obsolete.

4166 BBY

The Mon Calamari species makes first contact with the Republic when Republic scouts encounter Mon Calamari starships near Ruisto.

The planet Darvannis is discovered by spice smugglers in the Calaron sector. Darvannis was a desert planet in the galaxy where the Hutt Cartel was building up military forces during the Galactic War.

4129 BBY

The Luire system is discovered and surveyed by the Republic.[36] The Luire system, also known as the Nyriaan system, was a star system that was located in the Mid Rim, near to the border with the Expansion Region. It had seven planets: Nyriaan, Caillte and five gas giants.

4100 BBY

Bacta is introduced to the galaxy, becoming a competitor to Kolto Bacta was a synthetic chemical substance that consisted of gelatinous, translucent red alazhi and kavam bacterial particles that were mixed within a colorless, viscous fluid known as ambori. When a patient was exposed to bacta, the bacterial particles within sought out wounds and promoted rapid tissue regeneration while preventing the emergence of scar tissue. Bacta was often thought of as a "miracle fluid", and seemed to be effective against almost every type of injury and ailment across an incredible cross-section of species throughout the galaxy. It was considered to be the best medicine available anywhere, replacing the previously-used Kolto.

4086 BBY

Trampeta's Star Guide is first published. Trampeta's Star Guide was a traveler's guide, and was best known for reviewing Taris and giving it the lowest possible recommendation, because the authors' baggage was stolen by T3 droids working at the starport upon their arrival.

4085 BBY

A vintage of wine that will become known as the particularly rare Ord Mantell 432 BTC is produced on Ord Mantell.

4070 BBY

Amanoa, future queen of Onderon and wife of Ommin, is born. Amanoa was a Human female from the world of Ondero and the daughter of a prominent nobleman, Amanoa enjoyed the wealth and privileges afforded to the Onderonian aristocracy, and eventually married into the planet's royal family as the wife of Onderon's King Ommin. The couple birthed a daughter named Galia, and together they lived in the royal palace of Onderon's capital city of Iziz. Amanoa's reign saw drastic changes in Onderon's role in the galaxy. Along with her husband, she was beguiled by the specter of the long-dead Dark Lord Freedon Nadd, to whom she became the Sith apprentice in her final years. As she and Ommin steeped themselves further in the dark side, both became masters of Sith sorcery, and used their magics to maintain rule over the Onderonian populace as dictated by four hundred years of tradition. When Ommin's health began to fail him as a result, Amanoa became the sovereign leader of Onderon, and imposed her will through the power of the dark side of the Force.

4067 BBY

The Republic exploration vessel Starveil is lost while performing a study of the Luire system. The ship's last communication indicates that the crew planned to land on the fifth planet Nyriaan, but the ship is never found.

4056 BBY

The Dynamet Corporation donates a large sum of credits to the hospital Mercy General on Taris for the construction of a wing devoted to curing the rakghoul plague. The hospital is renamed Dynamet General in thanks.

Civil war breaks out between Taris's nobility and the planet's largely alien lower class. The conflict is sparked when rising levels of toxic pollution poison the planet's oceans and famine sweeps the city-world, as the nobility begin to hoard food for themselves. The lower classes rise up against the nobility and the rebellion is ultimately crushed after millions died in the fighting.

4050 BBY

Scouts from the planet Shor discover the planet Giaca. Giaca was a lush, wild, world in the Unknown Regions, which was largely unspoiled by civilization. Although it was not a homeworld or colony for any particular species, it was not without intelligent inhabitants. Besides the numerous types of wild creatures in its dense forests and massive volcanic causeways, Giaca would later host a few scattered outposts of survey teams and criminal hideouts.

Drokko Kira is banished from the city of Iziz for challenging the dark side legacy of Freedon Nadd.

4043 BBY

The Imperial Citadel on Dromund Kaas contained the headquarters of the Ministries of War, Intelligence, and Logistics and actually had two separate incarnations. The first one built on the planet resembled both the Sith Academy on Korriban and the Sith Citadel on Ziost. This was destroyed in 4043 BBY during the Kaggath fought between Darth Qalar and Darth Victun. The two Sith Lords were executed by the Dark Council and Darth Nostrem was chosen to oversee the citadel's reconstruction. The second citadel was designed by the Emperor himself and differed greatly from the first. It was no longer modeled after the earlier citadel designs. After the completion of its construction, Darth Nostrem was locked in its depths in order to test the citadel's new labyrinthine defenses. The Sith Lord never escaped and eventually died.

4030 BBY

Arca Jeth and a number of Jedi Knights devastate the Lorell Raiders at the Battle of Lorell, forcing the survivors to retreat to the Hapes Cluster. The Raiders and their female prisoners eventually evolve into the matriarchal and isolationist Hapes Consortium.

4024 BBY

The Nevoota Extinction begins as the Mandalorians attack the planet Nevoota. The Nevoota Extinction was a war fought between the Mandalorians, a religious warrior culture, and the Nevoota species. It resulted in the extinction of the Nevoota and the extermination of the insectoid Nevoota as well as the deification of war by the Mandalorians three years later.

4020 BBY

The Czerka Corporation discovers Kashyyyk, the homeworld of the Wookiee species, and claims the planet while renaming it "Edean." Czerka Arms, also known as Czerka Weapons, formerly known as the Czerka Corporation, and founded as Czerka Mining and Industrial, was a galaxy-spanning business during the reigns of the Galactic Republic, Sith Empire, Galactic Empire, New Republic, and Galactic Federation of Free Alliances. It controlled interests on Korriban, Kashyyyk, Tatooine, Telos IV and to a smaller extent Trandosha, Taris and Dantooine along with countless other planets. The corporation exported many of their weapons to Justa Starport on Mutanda.

4017 BBY

The Mandalorian Crusaders attack the planet Basilisk in the Battle of Basilisk. The Basiliskans are supported by Republic reinforcements under Jedi Master Sidrona Diath, but ultimately are overrun and seed their own homeworld with toxins to deny it to the Mandalorians. The Mandalorians retreat from Basilisk, but take numerous Basiliskans, Basiliskian warships, and Basilisk war droids with them.

4015 BBY

The Great Droid Revolution, also known as the Great Droid Revolt, was an uprising of droids on Coruscant. The Czerka assassin droid HK-01 seized power by subverting the programming of thousands of droids and tunring them against their masters. It was during the Revolution where Jedi Master Arca Jeth learned the technique of short-circuiting a droid by using the Force. One of the memorable instances of the Revolution was when Juggernaut war droids battled Republic rocket-jumpers over Monument Plaza. Jedi intervention finally brought the conflict to an end three months later. After the rogue assassin droid HK-01 was finally captured, the Republic spent many years recovering from the attacks. Droid designers and manufacturers then turned to weapons developers to work on ion weapons that would short-circuit a droid's electronic systems. The result of this conflict would be an end to the budding "droids' rights" movement for a time.

4009 BBY

The Systino crime syndicate discovers the planet Sraato, a world rich in valuable natural resources. The Systino syndicate dominates most of the criminal activity in the sector for the next two hundred years.

4008 BBY

The Jedi Jev Sunrider dies on Krayiss Two. Jev Sunrider was a Human male who served as a Jedi Master and Watchman of the Darada system in the decades leading up to the Great Sith War. Sunrider had left his family's home on Darada and, along with three other Jedi Masters, set out for the nearby system of Krayiss Two. This mission would ultimately end in the deaths of all four Jedi at the hands of a dark side force. His Force ghost, a year later, appeared to his grandson, Andur, in which Jev told him that he would play an important role in the coming war.

4007 BBY

The Quesaya Border Conflict erupts, and the Republic rocket-jumpers play a role in ending the conflict.

Andur Sunrider's, after seeing the Force ghost of his Grandfather, dedication to his studies catches the attention of Jedi Master Chamma, who invited Sunrider to train as his apprentice on the planet of H'ratth. He studied under Master Chamma for two years and excelled at his training, learning everything that Chamma could teach him. During his time on H'ratth, he and Nomi gave birth to a daughter whom they named Vima. Once Chamma realized that Sunrider required further training from a more experienced master, Chamma advised him that he would finish his training under the guidance of Master Thon on Ambria. During Sunrider's trip to Ambria, he was murdered by criminals who were after the Adegan crystals he was carrying. Many years after his death, Andur Sunrider's memory lived on through his daughter Vima, who constructed an enormous ice sculpture of her father during her Jedi training on Rhen Var.

4004 BBY

The Jedi Master Thon takes on Oss Wilum as his apprentice on Ambria.

4003 BBY

The Giju Passage is blazed by Herglic scouts, and within twenty-five years the route becomes an established trade route into Herglic space.

4002 BBY

The Mandalorians attack the Deep Core planet Kuar and conquer the world. Kuar was the fifth planet in the Kuar system, orbiting a single star and lay on the Koros Trunk Line between Empress Teta and

Foerost. The Mandalorians, who wiped out most of the indigenous Kuarans and used the ruined, underground cities as staging grounds for their attack upon the Empress Teta system. To resolve the conflict, Ulic Qel-Droma challenged Mandalore the Indomitable to a duel. On the Plains of Harkul, Qel-Droma defeated the Mandalorian leader, winning his loyalty. The Mandalorians only used the planet briefly after conquering it, and the structures were abandoned for hundreds, if not thousands, of years.

During the Diversity Alliance Crisis, Bornan Thul met with the scavenger Fonterrat on Kuar, on behalf of the Alliance leader, Nolaa Tarkona. Jacen Solo, Jaina Solo and Tenel Ka later arrived on the planet while trying to find Raynar Thul's father

Onderon makes contact with the Galactic Republic and encounters galactic civilization.

THE OLD SITH WARS

The Old Sith Wars was the name given to the series of conflicts that started with the Great Sith War and lasted until the end of the Sith Civil War in 3950 BBY. The conflicts centered around a number of fallen Jedi. Exar Kun and Ulic Qel-Droma instigated the Great Sith War when they fell to the dark side of the Force and the Jedi Knights Revan and Malak led a new Sith Empire against the Galactic Republic in the Jedi Civil War after they were corrupted by the hidden Sith Emperor at the end of the Mandalorian Wars The exiled Jedi Master Kreia routed the remnants of Revan's empire and led them in a genocidal campaign against the Jedi Order.

4000 BBY

The Kyyr system is enveloped in a supernova, forming the Thornhedge Nebula and Pulsar and also devastating the Ootmian Pabol.

The planet Ession is colonized. Ession was a planet in the Corporate Sector, located at the nexus of the Shaltin Tunnels and Lucaya Cross hyperlanes. After it was settled the planet became an industrial manufacturing center containing the headquarters of Pakkerd Light Transport, formerly a division of Sienar Fleet Systems.

Flashpoint Stellar Research Station is established on the planet Flashpoint. Flashpoint was an airless planet that orbited very close to its star, with a day lasting just one standard hour. Being so close to its star meant that the planet was bathed in stellar radiation and thus devoid of life. Before the Great Sith War, a protective magnetic field was set up and a research station established by scientists to study stars. In 3965 BBY, this station was seized by Mandalorian warriors as part of their invasion of Galactic Republic space. The Mandalorian scientist Demagol used the research station to experiment on Jedi in an attempt to discover the source of their powers, but the Mandalorian presence was, a year later, expunged from Flashpoint by fugitive Jedi Padawan Zayne Carrick and his companions in 3964 BBY.

Jedi Master Arca Jeth sends his three apprentices, Ulic Qel-Droma, Cay Qel-Droma, and Tott Doneeta, to Onderon in order to bring an end to the ongoing Beast Wars. Their mission soon goes awry when Princess Galia is kidnapped during a Beast Rider raid on Iziz. The Jedi pursue Galia, only to discover that she intends to marry the Beast Rider Oron Kira, and Onderon's royal family are practitioners of the dark side. Their attempts to negotiate a peace with Queen Amanoa fail when she unleashes the dark side against them, and the Beast Riders lay siege to Iziz. Arca Jeth arrives and lends his battle meditation to the Beast Riders, bringing about their victory, and his powerful presence in the light side causes Freedon Nadd's spirit to abandon Queen Amanoa and leave her to die. Galia and Kira are married and assume the throne of Onderon.

3999 BBY

Nomi Sunrider becomes Thon's apprentice after the death of her husband Andur.

3998 BBY

The Freedon Nadd Uprising erupts on Onderon as King Ommin leads an army of dark side-empowered Naddists against the Jedi Order and Beast Riders. The Naddists interrupt Amanoa's funeral and capture Arca Jeth, and also succeed in recovering the sarcophagi of both Amanoa and Freedon Nadd.

The Galactic Republic and additional Jedi Knights arrive on Onderon and engage Ommin's army, and the Jedi ultimately defeat Ommin and liberate Arca Jeth. At the same time, the Tetan nobles Aleema Keto and Satal Keto, who were visiting Ommin and learning Sith lore from the king, escape back to their home system of Empress Teta and become Freedon Nadd's new apprentices.

3997 BBY

The Keto cousins stage a military and political coup in the Empress Teta system, seizing control of the system from their parents as they establish the Sith cult known as the Krath. The coup begins the Krath Holy Crusade (3997-3996 BBY), a series of battles fought before and during the Great Sith War, and comprised the bulk of that conflict. The crusade was a culmination of events that began with a violent regime change in the Empress Teta system staged by Aleema and Satal Keto, heirs to the Tetan monarchy and also leaders of the Sith-inspired Krath cult. After the war, the Krath order constructed a series of temples on several of the worlds they had seized during the Crusade. This Crusade started as the Mandalorians began their holy crusade against the Basiliskans on Basilisk, and ended after the defeat of Dark Lord of the Sith Exar Kun on Yavin 4.

A Republic and Jedi task force comes to the aid of the planet Empress Teta, which has managed to hold off the Krath, but the Sith cult drives the Republic out of the system at the Battle of Koros Major. Ulic Qel-Droma is infected by Aleema Keto's Sith magic during an attack on the Republic's command ship Reliance I, and he unknowingly begins to slip towards the dark side.

The Jedi Conclave of Deneba is disrupted by Krath war droids, and the servant droids at the conclave attack the Jedi at the event. The Jedi destroy their attackers, but Arca Jeth is killed by Krath dorids in the battle.

Ulic Qel-Droma attempts to infiltrate the Krath from within, but is seduced to the dark side by Aleema Keto. Qel-Droma kills Satal and becomes the Krath's leader alongside Aleema, and a Jedi rescue mission fails when Qel-Droma refuses to depart.

The power-hungry Jedi Exar Kun searches for Sith teachings and discovers the spirit of Freedon Nadd on Onderon's moon Dxun, where he is trained in the ways of the dark side before heading to Yavin 4 to acquire more power. Kun ultimately kills Nadd's spirit and seeks out Ulic Qel-Droma to eliminate a potential rival.

Nomi Sunrider organizes a second rescue mission at the same time that Kun arrives on Empress Teta, and Kun and Qel-Droma clash in a duel. However, the duel is ended by the spirit of Marka Ragnos, who anoints Kun and Qel-Droma as Dark Lords of the Sith as well as Master and apprentice. Joining forces with Kun, Qel-Droma refuses Sunrider's attempt at a rescue, and the two Sith form the Brotherhood of the Sith.

3996 BBY

Engaging in several small raids to test the strength of the Krath, Mandalore eventually caught the attention of Qel-Droma by destroying an important carbonite smelting station in the Empress Teta system. Wanting to crush the threat that the Mandalorians presented as soon as possible, Qel-Droma agreed to a challenge of single combat on the planet Kuar, extended by Mandalore. The duel, as explained by Mandalore, would be fought between Qel-Droma and himself, and the victor would receive full command over their foes' forces, as well as the seven worlds of Empress Teta. Qel-Droma managed to best Mandalore during the course of the fight, but refused to kill his defeated enemy. Having experienced the fighting ability of Mandalore firsthand, Qel-Droma believed that Mandalore was of more use to him alive. Seeing that his reputation had been preserved, Mandalore pledged his life, honor, and troops to Qel-Droma's cause.

After months of conquering planets from the Deep Core to the Outer Rim, the Sith launch their attack on Coruscant. During the battle, Ulic Qel-Droma is captured and subsequently put on trial for treason.

Sith Lord Ulic Qel-Droma turns away from the dark side.

Both the Great Sith War and the Krath Holy Crusade end with the Recapture of the Empress Teta system.

After the ultimate defeat of Sith Lord Exar Kun in the Yavin system, a number of Krath forces were still at large in a galaxy reeling from years of unceasing, destructive warfare. The elimination or neutralization of their primary leadership (Kun, Aleema Keto, Satal Keto, Ulic Qel-Droma) dealt a severe blow to the Krath's initiative, but the entrenched holdings deep within the Koros system remained for the Republic to contend with.

Mandalore the Ultimate begins secretly summoning clans from across the galaxy, building up arms and ships on Dxun, working toward the day when a new crusade can be launched. Mandalore the Ultimate, or Te Ani'la Mand'alor in Mando'a, led the Mandalorians during the Mandalorian Wars. One of the last Taung to claim the Mandalore title, and known to some as the Great Shadow Father, he regrouped the Mandalorian forces into the Mandalorian Neo-Crusaders and slowly began to conquer fringe worlds that had been left defenseless in the wake of the Great Sith War. Mandalore took full advantage of the Galactic

Republic's halfhearted efforts to oppose his aggression and personally led his forces as they invaded Republic territory. Under his command, the Neo-Crusaders nearly defeated the Republic during the Mandalorian Wars, and it was only through the leadership of the Jedi Knights Revan and Malak that the tide of the war was ultimately turned against Mandalore. Revan killed Mandalore in hand-to-hand combat near the end of the war.

The Jedi Order create the Lost City of the Jedi to aide the recovery of the planet Yavin 4's ecology as well as to ensure that Exar Kun never returned again.

An attack by the Sith devastates Mustafar, the gas giant Lefrani is tugged out of its orbit by a dark side weapon, causing Mustafar to be caught between the gravitational fields of Lefrani and the gas giant Jestefad. All life on the planet's surface dies as the surface is ripped apart by immense tidal stresses.

The Jedi Order relocates to Coruscant following Ossus's devastation.

THE RESTORATION PERIOD

During this relatively peaceful time period, the galaxy struggled to rebuild following the devastation caused by the Great Sith War. With the Republic on the verge of collapse for over a decade following the war, a group of politicians decided to put into motion a series of events that was meant to restore the Republic to its prior strength. By guaranteeing the various corporations throughout the galaxy safe passage and trade along the space lanes in exchange for commercial investment in the Republic's infrastructure, the Republic was able to rebuild its military and provide much needed goods to the people of the devastated galaxy. Hyperspace explorers once again began to scout the galaxy seeking to discover newer and safer routes. Across the galaxy, planets began to rebuild, commerce resumed, and the Republic's military might was restored. However, at the same time, the defeated Mandalorians who had been on the losing side during the Great Sith War began to slowly prepare for their revenge against the Republic. Small bases, such as the Unity base on the planet Caillte were built in secret during the last months of the Restoration. The Mandalorian Wars eventually put an end to this short period of relative peace.

3995 BBY

The Restoration Period begins for the Republic. The Restoration Period was a historical era ranging from 3995 to 3966 BBY. During this relatively peaceful time period, the galaxy struggled to rebuild following the devastation caused by the Great Sith War. With the Republic on the verge of collapse for over a decade following the war, a group of politicians decided to put into motion a series of events that was meant to restore the Republic to its prior strength. By guaranteeing the various corporations throughout the galaxy safe passage and trade along the space lanes in exchange for commercial investment in the Republic's infrastructure, the Republic was able to rebuild its military and provide much-needed goods to the people of the devastated galaxy. Hyperspace explorers once again began to scout the galaxy seeking to discover newer and safer routes. Across the galaxy, planets began to rebuild, commerce resumed, and the Republic's military might was restored. However, at the same time, the defeated Mandalorians who had been on the losing side during the Great Sith War began to slowly prepare for their revenge against the Republic. Small bases, such as the Unity base on the planet Caillte were built in secret during the last months of the Restoration. The Mandalorian Wars eventually put an end to this short period of relative peace.

The Great Hunt, a Jedi campaign to eradicate the Sith devotees along with their creations, left following the Great Sith War, such as Silan, giant Sith Wyrms, and Terentateks, creatures native to Korriban which fed off the blood of Force-sensitives. None of the hunts were ever completely successful, and the terentateks would always slowly rebuilt their numbers, rising again whenever the Sith did.

3994 BBY

Ulic Qel-Droma revisits Yavin 4 to learn what had happened to Exar Kun, but is unable to learn anything as to his former comrade's fate.

3993 BBY

During the Great Hunt, Jedi Knights successfully cleanse the planet Tatooine of Terentateks. The Great Hunt is officially ended, but the Jedi Council secretly dispatches three Knights, Duron Qel-Droma, Shaela Nuur, and Guun Han Saresh, to seek out and eradicate the last of the terentateks on Korriban. The trio's mission falls apart when Saresh, furious that Nuur and Qel-Droma are in a relationship, strikes out on his own and hunts down a terentatek on Kashyyyk. Saresh is killed by the terentatek, and Nuur and Qel-Droma are killed by their target in the caves of Korriban.

Krynda Draay, daughter of Noab Hulis and widow of Barrison Draay, is roused from the depression that the Sith War put her in when she meets the Miraluka child Q'Anilia. Q'Anilia's powers of precognition impress the half-Miraluka seer, and inspires Draay to found a Jedi Covenant dedicated to preventing the rise of the Sith.

3988 BBY

The Arkanian Offshoot Edessa is born on Osadia. Wyrick believes her to be his greatest success in the New Generation Project, and her name Edessa, or "triumph", reflects that.

Krynda Draay receives a Force vision that becomes known as the Prophecy of the Five. The prophecy foretells five individuals. One for the light, one for the dark, one for the dark in the light, one for the light in the dark, and one who stands alone. In it, she predicted that the next conflict with the dark side of the Force would have five key figures, ambiguously described by their allegiance, that were going to lose whatever thing was built between them. Young Raana Tey, a Togruta seer training under Krynda, eavesdropped while she was having the vision. Years later she would tell Zayne Carrick of the prophecy during their duel on Taris in the Jedi Tower, seemingly associating the Five to the Sith threat she and the other Masters of the First Watch Circle foretold in the Rogue Moon Prophecy, their own Padawans, five who would see the Galactic Republic and the Jedi Order collapse between them. Carrick retorted that it may have referred to "five traitorous evil Jedi Masters." Both the Masters of the First Watch Circle and their Padawans were actually five, but Raana Tey, Q'Anilia, Xamar, Feln and Lucien Draay murdered their students. Zayne was Lucien's Padawan, and he escaped. Since he set out to expose the Jedi Covenant, the cabal to which they belonged, the Masters were removed from Taris and reassigned to different postings, Feln and Raana Tey died, and Xamar confessed to the Jedi Council before being killed himself by the

Republic fleet. Krynda's aide Haazen then declared the prophecy to be fulfilled.

3986 BBY

Nomi Sunrider, by now the head of the Jedi Order, calls a conclave of the Order on Exis Station. However, the conclave is interrupted when Nomi's daughter Vima steals an ion mining vessel and is nearly killed before Tott Doneeta rescues her. Vima seeks out Ulic Qel-Droma on Rhen Var and becomes his student, studying the ways of the Force.

The Cathar Jedi Sylvar tracks down Ulic on Rhen Var and attacks him for his crimes and the death of her mater Crado during the Great Sith War. Their duel ends when Qel-Droma refuses to fight, freeing Sylvar from the grips of her rage; however, the spacer Hoggon shoots Qel-Droma moments later in hopes of gaining fame.

3985 BBY

The Coruscant Financial Exchange Establishment act speeds the restoration of the devastated Galactic Republic by allowing corporations to invest in the government's infrastructure in return for guaranteeing safe passage through increasingly treacherous hyperspace routes.

3984 BBY

Darth Xedrix begins to serve on the Dark Council. Darth Xedrix was an elderly male Human who was one of five Dark Lords of the Sith who served in the Dark Council of the Sith Empire. He was also the Council's longest serving member. As of 3954 BBY he and several other members of the Dark Council, including Darth Nyriss, were working to bring the Emperor down, as they considered him arrogant, powerful, and mad, and viewed his plan to attack the Republic as suicidal. In an attempt to keep the alliance unknown to the Emperor, Darth Nyriss faked assassination attempts on her life. Although it was planned to have Nyriss' own followers investigate, the Emperor sent Lord Scourge, and the plan changed. Sechel, another of Nyriss' men, and Scourge were able to discover that a group of Human separatists from Bosthirda were behind the assassination attempts, and during a raid on their compound found evidence that Xedrix was allied with them. Using a replication of the separatists' coded communications, Scourge sent a message to Xedrix impersonating the separatists and asking the Sith Lord to meet with them at a cave on Bosthirda. Xedrix traveled to the location, bringing one male Human and one female Human apprentice with him. When they arrived they were attacked by Scourge, who defeated and killed the two apprentices. Xedrix, who weak from age and use of the dark side, after watching the whole scene unfold before him without making a single move, gathered his strength for one attack and unleashed a violent and devastating attack of Force lightning at Scourge. Scourge, though taken by surprise and hurt by the elderly Human's attack, recovered and prepared to kill the Sith Lord. Xedrix attempted to turn Scourge to

STAR WARS THE COMPLETE GALACTIC TIMELINE

his side, by lying to him that Nyriss had sent him to die and, though truthfully, telling him that she was using him as a pawn in a greater game. Scourge was not convinced and, realizing that the Sith was as weak as Nyriss had said, he killed Xedrix and brought his severed head back to Nyriss as proof that the Sith was dead

---

3980 BBY

Vima Sunrider makes an entry in the Great Holocron regarding Ulic Qel-Droma's redemption and death.

3978 BBY

Mandalore the Ultimate is influenced by an agent of the Sith Empire into waging war on the Republic.

3977 BBY

The planet Vortex is inducted into the Republic.

Zayne Carrick is discovered by the Jedi Order and brought to the Jedi Enclave on Dantooine.

3976 BBY

The Mandalorian Wars begin with the Battle of Althir. The Mandalorian Wars was the term given to the sixteen years of conflict between the Mandalorian warrior culture and the Galactic Republic that with the Battle of Althir. Occurring two decades after the end of the Great Sith War, the Mandalorian Wars spanned almost two decades themselves, though historians often disagreed on the endpoints of the conflict; the Mandalorians raided star systems in the Outer Rim Territories for over a decade before they actually came into conflict with the Republic Military in 3965 BBY. Led by Mandalore the Ultimate, who pioneered the Neo-Crusader movement with the help of his lieutenant, Cassus Fett, the Mandalorians conquered systems along the eastern edge of the galaxy. Though their conquests included the near-extinction of the Cathar species, it was not until their assaults on worlds near the planet Taris that they drew the Republic's attention. After a year of small conflicts known as the False War, the Mandalorians broke through the Republic's lines and besieged Taris in 3963 BBY, and then invaded the Republic through three separate corridors in what became known as the Onslaught. The tide ultimately turned when a group of interventionist Jedi known as the Revanchists, led by the charismatic Revan and his friend Malak, joined the Republic Military in combating the Mandalorians. A tactical genius, Revan won several victories against the Mandalorians and began to reclaim lost territory, prompting Supreme Chancellor Tol Cressa to appoint him Supreme Commander in 3962 BBY. Driving back the Mandalorians, Revan forced a final showdown with Mandalore the Ultimate at the Battle of Malachor V in 3960 BBY. Revan personally defeated Mandalore in single combat as the Republic and Mandalorian fleets battled above Malachor V, and the activation of the superweapon known as the Mass Shadow Generator devastated both the planet and the participating fleets.

The Mandalorian Wars had long-reaching consequences. Revan forced the defeated Mandalorians to disarm and hid Mandalore's Mask, the symbol of their leadership, and both he and Malak were turned to the dark side of the Force while investigating the Sith influence that had caused Mandalore to go to war. Many of the soldiers and Jedi who followed Revan in the Mandalorian Wars joined the two new Dark Lords of the Sith as they formed their own Sith Empire and invaded the Republic in a subsequent conflict known as the Jedi Civil War.

A gang war erupts between the Hidden Beks and Black Vulkars, two swoop gangs on Taris.

3973 BBY

Cassus Fett leads the Mandalorian Neo-Crusaders in the Battle of Cathar. Fett's forces wipe out over 90% of the Cathar population on their homeworld.

The Mandalorians' attack caught the Cathar people completely off guard. Their military forces converged from space, bombarding the surface, first destroying all interstellar communications relays and orbital spacedock facilities, and then descending to the surface and slaughtering most of the planetary population while they slept or as they fled. Cassus Fett's Basilisk war-mounts decimated the more primitive Cathar settlements.

However, because they had stood against the Mandalorians in the past, the Cathar realized why they'd truly been targeted, and that there would be no mercy for their species or their world in the end. And because the Cathar were not members of the Galactic Republic, they were left to fend completely for themselves. Near the end of the battle, Cassus herded the surviving Cathar into the ocean and ordered that they be killed. One Mandalorian objected, saying the Cathar had already been defeated. But Cassus said the battle was about revenge, and he intended to kill all Cathar on the planet. He then gave the order to have the remaining Cathar killed, and the Mandalorian who objected died with them.

The final act of the Cathar race was to pack the last able-bodied survivors who were able to withstand spaceflight into what few ships remained, sending them off into the void as quickly as possible. Juhani's family escaped aboard one of these refugee flights, and landed on Taris. The Cathar species itself, though, was nearly rendered extinct as a consequence of the genocide of Cathar.

3970 BBY

In 3970 BBY, with the Republic preoccupied with the Mandalorian Wars, Myrial seceeded the Kanz sector from the Republic and renamed it the Argazdan Redoubt. In the ensuing revolution, Loyalist Argazdans were massacred while an Argazdan military fleet devastated the Ereesi homeworld of Ereesus; exterminating all life on the world. The Myrialites then proceeded to annex the other worlds of their sector including Amaltanna and Lorrd. In retaliation for the Lorrdians' support for the Amaltannan resistance, Myrial had the Lorrdian species enslaved. The enslaved Lorrdians were forbidden by their masters from speaking with each other. As a result, they were forced to develop a system of subtle gestures, facial expressions, and body postures. This nonverbal form of communication would still be in use millennia later, during the Galactic Civil War.

3969 BBY

The First Watch Circle of the Jedi Covenant, Feln, Lucien Draay, Q'Anilia, Raana Tey, and Xamar, are assigned five Padawans: Oojoh, Zayne Carrick, Shad Jelavan, Kamlin, Gharn. The five Padawans are transferred to the Jedi Tower on Taris, where their new Jedi Masters are stationed.

3968 BBY

The Adasca BioMechanical Corporation of Arkania begins offering "genetic solutions" to Arkanian Offshoot employees. The Adasca BioMechanical Corporation of Arkania, known simply as Adascorp, was a vast medical corporation from Arkania. Famous for its bioengineering and medical research advances, Adascorp was allied with the Draay Trust and Czerka Corporation. It was owned by the House of Adasca and brought huge amounts of profit to the planet, forming Adascopolis. For years, Adascorp headquarters was located on the massive starship Arkanian Legacy. However, the ship was lost along with Lord Arkoh Adasca in his ill-fated attempt to secure galactic power through Operation Dark Harvest. The loss of the ship and its extensive archives and research facilities set Adascorp research back by decades. Worse, with no explicit heir to Arkoh's controlling interest in the corporation, ownership of the company remained contested. Adasca's niece Aurora was the sole heir of the company, but in her absence the Draay Trust filed to take over Adascorp.

3967 BBY

The Jedi Knight Jelph Marrian is expelled from the Order after alienating the Jedi Council, and he joins the Jedi Covenant as a Shadow. Jelph Marrian became an agent whose records of existence had been erased and was notably familiar with the planet Taris. He developed a strong aversion towards the Sith due to his childhood experiences during the Great Sith War, which devastated his homeworld of Toprawa.

Following the dissolution of the Covenant in 3963 BBY, Jelph fled into Wild Space and became stranded on the planet Kesh, a remote world that was ruled by a Sith tribe. To avoid detection, Marrian adopted a new persona of a slave and became a horticulturalist on an isolate farm on the banks of the Marisota River. In secret, he worked on repairing his damaged Aurek-class tactical strikefighter so that he could return to the wider galaxy and alert the Jedi and the Galactic Republic to the presence of the Tribe. Through his work, Jelph developed a good reputation for producing high-quality fertilizers and eventually befriended Orielle Kitai, a Sith Saber and the aristocratic daughter of High Lord Candra Kitai. In 3960 BBY, Orielle and her mother were wrongly accused and punished for a failed assassination attempt against the ruling Grand Lord Lillia Venn. As punishment, the Kitais were reduced to the status of slaves. Orielle sought refuge and solace with Jelph, who provided her with shelter and lodging. During this time, Orielle accidentally discovered his "secret starfighter" while he was out hunting for wildlife. Seeing Jelph's starfighter as an opportunity to restore her family's fortunes and status, she traveled to the Tribe's capital of Tahv where she informed her mother and the architect Gadin Badolfa, who had close ties to a few rival High Lords who were opposed to Grand Lord Venn. Upon learning that Orielle had uncovered his secret, Jelph followed her to Tahv and confronted her at the city's waterworks. Following a brief scuffle in which Jelph gained the upper hand, he admitted his Jedi background to Orielle and managed to convince her to abandon her Sith ambitions for power and domination. Marrian also expressed his feelings for Orielle which she reciprocated. After Orielle acknowledged that she had informed the Tribe of Marrian's secret, the two returned to Marrian's farm on an uvak, a winged reptilian beast native to Kesh. However, they were pursued by the Grand Lord Lillia Venn and her followers. They managed to reach the farm where Jelph managed to slip away while Orielle confronted the newcomers in an attempt to make them leave by claiming her secret had been four blasters, a technology unknown to the Tribe. Despite her efforts, Venn and her followers were able to locate Jelph's starfighter. However, Jelph had prepared for the event that his secret starfighter was discovered and attacked Venn's entourage with the blasters. After killing several Sith, he and Orielle managed to escape into the Marisota river. Meanwhile, Venn was killed when the starfighter exploded since Jelph had rigged it with explosives in the event it was stolen. Following the "Night of the Upside-Down Meteor", Jelph and Orielle hid in the jungle highlands of Keshtah Minor, the continent that was the Tribe's domain. The couple also severed their ties with the Jedi and Sith respectively. Jelph came to that decision after intercepting transmissions which showed that the Jedi Order had descended into a civil war. As a symbolic gesture of severing his former ties, Marrian destroyed his transmitter, the last remaining relic of his offworld origins, with the help of Orielle. They then built a home deep in the jungles of Keshtah and had three children.

3966 BBY

The planet Taris is admitted to the Republic after a number of corporations, including Lhosan Industries, successfully bribe Senators into admitting their world. Taris was an urban planet in the fifth orbit of its star, located in the Taris system, within the Ojoster sector, of the Outer Rim Territories, in turn Taris was orbited by four moons, including Rogue. The term Tarisian was used to describe people and products from the planet. The planet's ecumenopolis quickly developed over a century of prosperity, and as a result the planet suffered from massive overpopulation. Once a galactic nexus that earned great wealth from its strategic position on hyperspace routes, Taris' importance declined with the discovery of improved trade routes, and the planet rapidly fell into decay. The remainder of the planet's history was wrought with civil disorder and social unrest. As it turned to industry as a means of compensation for its economic troubles, its oceans became polluted, eliminating the planet's main food source. Famine spread among the lower classes while the rich hoarded what few supplies remained. The resulting strife led to the Tarisian Civil War, the start of lasting prejudices between the Humanocentric Tarisian nobles and the largely alien underclass. The city became segmented, and the lower classes were banned from living in the upper levels of Taris.

The parents of Shad, Shay, and Shel Jelavan are killed in an accident in the Middle City of Taris. Shel Jelavan was a Human female who lived in the Middle City of Taris prior to the Mandalorian Wars. She, along with her brothers Shad and Shay, was orphaned when her parents died in an accident. The family suffered a further loss when Shad, who had been training as a Jedi, was killed in the Padawan Massacre of Taris. The murders were blamed on Jelavan's friend, the former Padawan Zayne Carrick, and she became determined to see him pay for his crimes. After the Mandalorian invasion of Taris, Jelavan joined the Taris Resistance and finally got her chance for vengeance when Jedi Master Raana Tey informed her that the fugitive Carrick was returning to Taris. Jelavan and Tey saw their opportunity to kill Carrick when he joined them on a mission to infiltrate the Jedi Tower in an attempt to assassinate the Mandalorian Neo-Crusader Cassus Fett. Jelavan intended to kill Carrick with her brother's lightsaber, but upon learning that it was Tey and the other members of the Jedi Covenant who killed her brother, stabbed the Jedi Master with the weapon, saving Carrick's life. Jelavan left Taris soon after, to take Constable Noana Sowrs's children safely to Alderaan. When she heard that Carrick was in trouble on the Mandalorian world of Jebble, she joined several of his friends in a mission to rescue him, and agreed to help him clear his name. Carrick's quest for vindication led him and his friends to Coruscant and a final showdown with the Covenant. With his name cleared, Carrick departed but Jelavan decided to remain on Coruscant, working with Senator Haydel Goravvus to help refugees throughout the Republic. In this role she assisted Carrick during his fight with The Crucible slaver organization.

3965 BBY

The Mandalorian Neo-Crusaders first begin to combat the Republic Military as they move closer and closer to the Republic's edge, thus beginning the "False War."

3964 BBY

The Mandalorians clash with the Republic at the Jebble-Vanquo-Tarnith line for several weeks. The Jebble-Vanquo-Tarnith line was a boundary between Galactic Republic and Neo-Crusader forces in the Outer Rim.

The First Watch Circle of the Jedi Covenant commits the Padawan Massacre, the murder of their five Padawans on Taris, after the Rogue Moon Prophecy foretells a dark figure who will bring destruction to the galaxy, a figure they believe is one of their Padawans. The Padawan Zayne Carrick arrives late and escapes with the con man Marn Hierogryph, but is framed for the Massacre.

Selected from a group of students trained at the Draay Estate on Coruscant; Feln, Q'Anilia, Raana Tey, Xamar, were decidedly the most potent seers of all of the students Krynda Draay had trained. Her own son, Lucien, was the Hand, a position that was suggested by Haazen, Krynda's retainer. He was responsible for handling arrangements, protection, etc. After being knighted, these five Jedi were often grouped together at the same postings. This was done in no small part due to the Covenant's machinations so the four Seers of the group could work closely together.

Although the was a secret society that acted separately from the Jedi High Council; the First Watch Circle's members were in the Order, and did have to answer to the newly formed Council if they wished to maintain their secrecy. All the while, they would teach their students that it is the Jedi's duty to prevent the return of the Sith.

3963 BBY

The Mandalorians break through the Republic lines and begin the Taris Siege, and proceed to invade the Republic through three separate corridors in what becomes known as the Onslaught. One of those corridors sees the nuclear devastation of Serroco, though the Mandalorians' offensives are all halted by the end of the year.

With a growing level of Mandalorian encroachment into the Outer Rim Territories during the period, Republic military forces grew increasingly stretched across that region, and were likewise hard-pressed to counter any major planetary assault.

The Mandalorian invaders outnumbered the Republic forces and they were unable to successfully defend the planet. A Jedi enclave had been established in the Taris Upper City prior to the invasion, but turmoil gripped the facility in 3964 BBY after several Jedi students were found murdered. The actual conquest of the world was a siege which lasted at least several weeks.

Ultimately, the Mandalorians were successful in their conquest of the planet; upon which, it must be noted, were a number of the last Cathar refugee-survivors from the Mandalorian genocide of their species, having fled there years previously. A resistance force, including the world's swoop gangs, was established in the Lower City. The precise length of the Mandalorian occupation of Taris is as yet unknown, but it would eventually end with the retaking of the planet by the Jedi Knights under the command of Revan, during the Second Battle of Taris.

The Revanchists, a group of young interventionist Jedi led by a charismatic Knight known as "the Revanchist," uncover evidence of the Battle of Cathar. In light of the Mandalorians' actions, the Jedi Council begrudgingly sanctions the Revanchists' entrance into the Mandalorian Wars, and the Revanchist adopts the name Revan.

3962 BBY

The Mandalorian launch a Coreward campaign known as the Mandalorian Triumph that sees them breach the Core Worlds as far as Duro. However, Revan and his friend Malak arrive at the Battle of Duro with a fleet of Interdictor-class cruisers, preventing the Mandalorians from escaping with war material. As a result, Supreme Chancellor Tol Cressa appoints Revan the Supreme Commander of the Republic Military.

3961 BBY

Over the course of this and the next year, Revan leads the Republic in rolling back the Mandalorians' advances, though often at the cost of civilians thanks to "moral shortcuts."

Lillia Venn was a female Human member of the Lost Tribe of Sith on Kesh. She was an elderly woman and was the oldest member of the Circle of Lords, the Tribe's government. In 3961 BBY, Lillia ascended to the rank of Grand Lord, the highest rank in the Tribe. She had been elected as a "compromise" candidate from among the Circle of Lords after the other six High Lords had been unable to agree on a new leader. Due to her old age, her political rivals, the Red and Gold Factions, regarded her as a weak leader who would not last that long in power. Still, Lillia sought to outmaneuver and defeat her opponents in order to maintain her grip on power.

3960 BBY

The Mandalorian Wars come to an end at the Battle of Malachor V. Revan forced a final confrontation with the Mandalorians above Malachor V. He deployed a massive Republic fleet to the planet consisting mostly of those whose loyalties to himself remained in doubt. In utter secrecy, he had prepared a superweapon, known as the "Mass Shadow Generator," which had been designed by the Zabrak engineer Bao-Dur. The weapon was the centerpiece of a trap with which he hoped to bring about a conclusive end to the destructive conflict. Commanding the fleet and overseeing the device's use was a capable and jaded Jedi General, Meetra Surik (later known as the Jedi Exile) who had taken part in the recent bloody campaign on Dxun. Revan lured the Mandalorians to Malachor V and a massive fleet battle ensued in orbit

3959 BBY

The Jedi Civil War begins. The Jedi Civil War, also known as the Second Sith War, the Old Republic Insurrection, and by the Mandalorians as the War of the Star Forge, was a devastating conflict that began when the Jedi Knight Revan, who had led the forces of the Galactic Republic to victory in the Mandalorian Wars, founded his own Sith Empire and declared himself the Dark Lord of the Sith. The war began when he, along with his friend and apprentice Darth Malak, led an invasion of the Galactic Republic in the year 3958 BBY. With the aid of veterans from the Mandalorian Wars and a host of Dark Jedi converts that had served with them, the former Jedi hoped to take over the Republic in anticipation of a greater threat posed by a Sith Empire that lurked within the Unknown Regions of the galaxy. During the war, Darth Revan brought the Republic to its knees and nearly succeeded in conquering it, however, a trap set by the Jedi and unwittingly abetted by Malak left him comatose, with his mind nearly destroyed. Barely alive, he was taken from the wreckage by the Jedi Knight Bastila Shan, whose skills in battle meditation and the Force had allowed the mission to happen. Taken to the Jedi Enclave on Dantooine, Revan was healed by the Jedi Council and reprogrammed to believe that he was an agent loyal to the Republic. Revan was assigned under the command of Shan, who was then placed aboard the Endar Spire. In 3956 BBY, with the intention of drawing out Revan's fragmented memories of the Star Forge, the vast space station that was the source of the seemingly endless resources of the Sith, he was taken to the ecumenopolis of Taris where a Sith fleet under the direct command of Malak was waiting in ambush. Eventually escaping from Taris, Revan, along with Shan, the Republic commander Carth Onasi, and several others, fled to the Dantooine Academy, where the Jedi Masters there retrained him. After several weeks, the Dantooine Council sent him and the crew of the Ebon Hawk back out into the wider galaxy to track down the Star Forge's location, at the heart of the ancient Infinite Empire of the Rakata. Later, after a number of ancient Star Maps had been uncovered, Malak led an attack against the Enclave, devastating it and further crippling the Jedi Order. After finding the last Star Map and, from it, deducing the location of the Rakatan homeworld, Revan, the Jedi, and the Republic launched the war's final battle. Revan vanquished Malak aboard the Star Forge, and the Republic successfully routed the Sith forces. With Malak dead, the Star Forge destroyed, and the Sith fleet scattered and defeated, the long and costly war came to an end.

To prove his loyalty to the Sith, Republic defector Saul Karath, captain of the Leviathan, ex-hero of the Mandalorian Wars, and later commander of the entire Sith fleet, bombed Telos IV using his codes to bypass their scanners. Eluding Republic defense systems, Sith bombers were able to infiltrate into the Republic docks before any warning could be raised. In moments, half the Republic fleet docked at Telos was destroyed. This was only the vanguard of Karath's attack, and he soon arrived with the bulk of his fleet, the Leviathan at its head. The resulting attack was devastating. While some were able to escape on in-system shuttles, millions were killed, and more died soon after due to medical supply shortages. A nearby Republic task force in which Carth Onasi was stationed arrived in the system shortly after, but by then it was too late. They were left to pick up the witnesses aboard the drifting vessels Karath and Malak let survive so that their testimony would intimidate those who would stand against the Sith Empire.

3957 BBY

Revan is captured onboard his flagship, after Malak turns against him. Bastila Shan brings Revan back to the Jedi, who use the Force to strip his memories and create a new identity for him.

3956 BBY

Destruction of Taris which results with most of the planet destroyed. Following the destruction of the Endar Spire by the Sith battle fleet in hopes of capturing Jedi Padawan Bastila Shan, the destruction of Taris was an event that took place during the height of the Jedi Civil War. Intending to capture the Jedi Padawan Bastila Shan, whose talents with battle meditation had been crucial to the Galactic Republic's effort against the Sith Empire led by Darth Malak, the Dark Lord of the Sith set his fleet around the Outer Rim world of Taris. After successfully ambushing the vessel under Shan's command, the Hammerhead-class cruiser Endar Spire, Sith troopers led by Darth Bandon boarded the ship, intent on seizing her alive. However, Shan, Carth Onasi and the amnesic ex-Sith Lord Revan were able to escape before the vessel's destruction. Afterwards, Malak ordered the conquest and blockading of Taris in order to search for the Jedi. The escape pod bearing Shan crashed in the Undercity, however, and she was taken prisoner by the Black Vulkars swoop gang. With support from the Hidden Beks swoop gang, Revan found and freed Shan. Impressed, the Mandalorian mercenary Canderous Ordo offered Revan an opportunity to leave the planet by stealing Exchange boss Davik Kang's flagship, the Ebon Hawk. Accepting the offer, Revan raided the main Sith base to acquire codes to bypass the blockade; Ordo then brought him to Kang's estate to steal the ship. Malak, meanwhile, grew weary of the protracted search. Seeking to eliminate Shan, he ordered Admiral Saul Karath to thoroughly bombard the surface. As the Sith fleet in orbit repositioned itself, Ordo and Revan succeeded in accessing the Hawk. However, they were confronted by Kang and the bounty hunter Calo Nord. After a brief firefight as the bombardment began, Kang was killed and Nord incapacitated; with the way clear, the party boarded the freighter, picking up Onasi, Shan, Mission Vao, Zaalbar, and T3-M4, and blasted off for space. The Ebon Hawk eluded a vanguard of attacking Sith fighters before fleeing into hyperspace, en route to the Jedi Enclave on Dantooine. Despite their escape, the bombardment continued until the entire world was virtually scoured of life, killing billions of beings. However, Taris's ecosystem eventually recovered over the next three centuries, leading the Republic to resettle the planet.

Revan and Bastila along with their companions begin to look for the Star Maps spread across four planets (Korriban, Kashyyyk, Tatooine, and Manaan) after finding one on Dantooine.

The Attack on Dantooine was a massive planetary bombardment conducted by the Sith fleets of Darth Malak.. The Jedi Enclave on Dantooine was believed to have been sufficiently fortified and too well-defended to invite an attack by the marauding Sith in that era. Malak and commander of Sith forces Saul Karath proved the Jedi Masters there wrong by conducting a highly effective bombardment of the planet's surface, destroying the Enclave and killing a number of high-ranking Jedi. Afterwards, a brutal large-scale subjugation of Dantooine's population was carried out, lasting for several years. The Jedi Council on Dantooine was aware of the attack thanks to the Force, but was unable to do anything about it save evacuate as they had no protection from an orbital bombardment. Their efforts proved to be unsuccessful, as only a small amount of the Jedi stationed on Dantooine were able to evacuate. However, thanks to their precognition of the attack, many high ranking members of the Jedi Council were able to escape, such as

Master Vandar Tokare and Master Vrook Lamar. Dantooine suffered greatly under the yoke of the Sith, after the location of the Jedi Enclave was exposed and the bombardment completed. Sith troops invaded and occupied the world, with many innocent settlers arrested and executed for no reason whatsoever. After the Sith were driven off some time before 3951 BBY, a sort of selective recollection gradually took hold amongst the populace, with many of them growing to despise the Jedi and holding them responsible for Dantooine's woes despite much of the good wrought by the academy for decades previous. While this event had a drastic impact on the Dantooine settlers, leaving them completely unprotected, which later led to the formation of Khoonda, the consequences for the Jedi Order itself were less significant. The Jedi that were vital for the Republic's ultimate victory in the Jedi Civil War, namely Revan, Bastila Shan, Juhani, and Jolee Bindo, were not on Dantooine during the strike, busy searching for Rakatan Star Maps, and the Council, Masters Dorak, Vrook Lamar, Zhar Lestin, and Vandar Tokare survived the attack. Moreover, most of the Jedi historical materials, including holocrons, had been evacuated to Telos IV by Atris earlier in case of an attack. Nevertheless, the deaths of much of the Jedi population of the Enclave weakened the Order and foreshadowed the Jedi purge that was to follow the Jedi Civil War.

End of the Jedi Civil War. As they flew toward the unfolding engagement, Carth contacted Admiral Forn Dodonna, who was leading the assault fleet, and informed her that Bastila had fallen to the dark side and was now using her abilities with battle meditation against the Republic from on board the Star Forge itself. With the battle turning against the Republic fleet, Jedi Master Vandar Tokare, who was aboard Dodonna's flagship as an adviser, sent a team of Jedi Knights to escort the crew of the Ebon Hawk. Together, they penetrated the outer defenses of the Forge and boarded the massive space station in an attempt to disrupt Bastila's use of her powers and, for Revan at least, to confront his old friend and apprentice. While a few Jedi stayed behind at the docks to keep the door open for the strike team, Revan, his companions, and other Knights attempted to infiltrate the station's interior. When Malak realized that the station had been boarded, he sent a number of the Forge's own battle droids to halt the impending threat. Revan and his companions were, however, equal to the challenge and pressed deeper into the station's inner workings; as a stopgap, Malak ordered all available Sith troopers, Dark Jedi and their apprentices to engage in battle. Though he knew that they would not stop his former master, the Dark Lord of the Sith knew that they would slow him down sufficiently for his new apprentice, Bastila, to be prepared to fight and even kill the one she loved in order to prove her loyalty and worth. After defeating a trio of Dark Jedi who guarded the entrance to the Star Forge's command center, Revan became separated from his companions and was forced to confront Bastila alone. Despite drawing upon the power of the Star Forge, the former Jedi was unable to overcome Revan and pleaded for him to kill her. Revan refused, however, and encouraged Bastila to see the light within herself by drawing on both the Force bond and the bond of love that they shared. Bastila accepted this, and after confessing her own love, she turned her battle meditation around to aid the Republic forces while Revan went on to confront Malak. Atop the highest levels of the station Revan confronted Malak who, after striking down two Jedi he had captured, activated a number of ancient droid-producing machines. After sealing the room, he fled further into the factory complex. Eventually working his way through the onslaught of combat droids and deactivating the factory, Revan pressed on, defeating Malak in a spectacular lightsaber duel, during which the Dark Lord attempted to siphon off the remaining Force-energy of several Jedi that had been killed when he attacked the Jedi Enclave on Dantooine. Revan, however, was able to use his own Force powers to prevent further instances of this siphoning. After defeating his former apprentice, he and Bastila, along with Carth and the others, boarded the Ebon Hawk and escaped the station's destruction. As the Jedi infiltrated the station, Admiral Dodonna attempted to hold off the Sith forces as best she could given the odds of the battle. With the effects of battle meditation working against the Republic's forces, she was unable to find an avenue of attack against the station itself. As the battle progressed, the Star Forge continued to produce Sith fighters, Sith freighters and even capital ships to be put immediately into battle. Despite the increasing odds, Dodonna succeeded in maintaining her fleet's presence at the periphery of the engagement zone. When Revan redeemed Shan, the battle began to turn, imperceptibly, at first, until while monitoring the tactical situation, Dodonna noticed a sudden break in the Sith formation. Acting quickly, she sent in two of her best starfighter units; Green Wing was ordered into the breach, followed swiftly by Red Wing, who rapidly expanded the crack into a salient through which the main fleet could attack. As the Hammerheads and blockade runners flooded through their shattered lines, several Sith capital ships were lost. As the climactic duel within the upper levels of the Star Forge came to an end, Dodonna's fleet converged on the massive station, pummeling it with their turbolasers while many fierce dogfights stained the skies with explosions. Withering from the combined firepower of many vessels, the station's orbital stabilizers were soon destroyed; Dodonna then ordered her ships to pull back as quickly as possible before the Forge's final destruction. As the Star Forge plunged into the Rakatan sun and erupted in a titanic explosion that cast glowing debris for millions of kilometers through space, the Ebon Hawk made its escape, barely keeping ahead of the wavefront of the conflagration. With the Sith fleet decimated, the vast orbital factory destroyed, and the Dark Lord defeated, the Republic forces, along with the surviving Jedi Knights, gathered on Lehon at the foot of the Temple of the Ancients to celebrate their victory. Dodonna awarded the Cross of Glory to Revan, Bastila Shan, Jolee Bindo, Zaalbar, Mission Vao, Canderous Ordo, Juhani, and Carth Onasi for their actions in the battle. With both Bastila and Revan back on the side of the Republic, and the Sith Empire's primary factory destroyed, the Sith forces were quickly scattered by the Republic. The survivors went into hiding, attaching themselves to Darth Sion, Darth Nihilus and Darth Traya in the coming years. The Sith Academy on Korriban became a focal point for the infighting that later broke out among the tattered remains of the Sith, and even under Darth Traya, they were never again strong enough to overtly challenge both the Republic and the Jedi the way they had under Revan and Malak. After the battle, wreckage of the ships and the Star Forge formed a ring around the world. The Republic declared the site a historical zone and restricted travel to it, in order to prevent Sith adepts from going to the Force-strong surface of the world. Eventually, though, during the New Sith Wars three millennia later, the travel restrictions appeared to be enforced only loosely if at all, as Darth Bane was able to travel there unimpeded to find Darth Revan's holocron. In the years following the fall of the Star Forge, the eight heroes of the battle were memorialized by a series of holostatues bearing their likenesses in Axial Park on Corellia. In the Battle of Corellia during the Galactic War three centuries later, the holostatues, disabled by Sith forces, were reactivated by heroes of the Republic, to raise the morale of Republic soldiers in the struggle to free Corellia.

The Sith Civil War begins and was a conflict that wracked the remains of the Sith Empire in the wake of the Jedi Civil War. Following the death of Darth Malak during the Battle of Rakata Prime, several of the Sith Lords who had followed Darth Revan and Malak during the war attempted to take what scraps they could from the ruins of the Sith Empire. Declaring themselves sovereign warlords, they fractured the Empire into a number of small, hotly-contested kingdoms. During the height of the Sith Civil War, many of the Sith warlords united under Darth Sion and Darth Nihilus, but upon their deaths, the Civil War escalated once more. By 3950 BBY, the remnants of the Sith Empire disintegrated entirely due to the constant infighting. As a result, the Galactic Republic was able to conquer Sith space, and reclaim worlds that had been under Sith control since the Great Sith War. Following Revan's attack on the the Korriban Sith Academy during his search for the Star Forge, and the death of Darth Malak during the conclusion of the Jedi Civil War, the remaining Sith Lords battled amongst themselves as each sought to rule the remnants of the Sith Empire. The bloody civil war began on Korriban, centered around the Sith Academy there. As a result of the chaos, the Dreshdae settlement on Korriban was abandoned by Czerka Corporation. At the height of the civil war on Korriban, Revan led a host of Jedi in an invasion of the Sith homeworld, and his forces successfully drove the Sith Lords from the planet. When Republic forces arrived on Korriban approximately a year after the Jedi Civil War's conclusion, they found the planet to be barren and lifeless. After fleeing Korriban, the Sith survivors scattered across the breadth of the Sith space and the Sith Empire began to fracture in earnest. In the year 3955 BBY, the surviving Sith Lords tore the empire apart as they battled for supremacy, and the empire was eventually divided up between the most powerful of the feuding warlords.

In the year 3954 BBY, Darth Nihilus and Darth Sion emerged as the heirs apparent of the Sith Empire. In time, they united most of the remaining Sith Lords beneath their banner. Following the deaths of the Sith Triumvirate on Malachor V, the destruction of the Trayus Academy, and the foiling of their plot to exterminate the Jedi and destabilize the Galactic Republic, the leaderless Sith descended into anarchy once again. They turned upon each other and eventually destroyed what little remained of their Empire. However, records indicate that at least one Sith Lord bearing the title of "Darth" survived, if for nothing else but to train a Sith apprentice, ensuring the continuation of the "Darth" line until Darth Desolous's time.

3954 BBY

Vaner Shan is born. Vaner Shan was the son of Revan and Bastila Shan, two famous Jedi Knights and heroes of the Jedi Civil War that was fought between the Galactic Republic and the Sith Empire. Born around 3954 BBY, Shan greatly resembled his father at the time of the Jedi Civil War, having Revan's dark brown eyes, fair skin and shoulder length dark brown hair. The Human male's name was an anagram of his father's, but unlike both his parents, Shan was not sensitive to the Force and therefore never joined the Jedi Order. Shan became a politician instead, developing into a major leader in the time of rebuilding following the Jedi Civil War, and he was a candidate to run for Supreme Chancellor in 3900 BBY. By that year, he had married a woman named Emess and had two children named Reesa and Bress Shan. In 3900 BBY, Vaner and his family visited his mother on the anniversary of her marriage to Revan, who had disappeared before Vaner had been born. Vaner's situation of not being born Force-sensitive despite being the son of a powerful Force-user was repeated generations later with his descendant, Theron Shan.

3952 BBY

The Conclave on Katarr is called to discuss the future of the Jedi Order. This was the first major event of the First Jedi Purge that took place during that time period. That year, the last known hundred members of the Jedi Order secretly assembled on the planet Katarr, a colony of the Miraluka species, a race who saw through the Force. Jedi Master Atris summoned the Jedi she had kept contact with to a secret meeting on Katarr, seemingly to discuss the future of the Jedi Order. Her real intention, however, was to use the Jedi as bait, hoping their shadowy adversaries would reveal themselves. She leaked information about the conclave, which Sith Lord Darth Nihilus received. Unfortunately for Katarr, Atris's plan backfired. The Jedi were not aware of the true extent of Nihilus`power. Nihilus arrived on Katarr before the meeting could begin and, using a unique variation of Force Drain, he stripped the Force from the Katarr's surface, killing every living being on the planet. Of all its living denizens, sentient, flora and fauna, Nihilus spared only one Miraluka woman, Visas Marr, who was subsequently recruited into the Sith as Nihilus's apprentice. 3,933 years later, the Jedi who survived Order 66 attempted to draw the Sith into a trap, with the similarly disastrous Conclave on Kessel.

3951 BBY

Canderous Ordo, known as Mandalore the Preserver, reunites the Mandalorian clans and aids in the fight against the remnants of the Sith Empire.

The Czerka Corporation, though not entirely legal means, attempts to take control over the Telosian Restoration Project, an initiative of Supreme Chancellor Tol Cressa to restore the ecosystem of Telos IV after the planet was rendered lifeless by orbital bombardment during the Jedi Civil War. The outcome of this project would determine the Republic's policy towards the Outer Rim worlds, if the project was successful, it would consider financing the restoration of other planets that had suffered from the Mandalorian Wars and the Jedi Civil War. To monitor the Restoration Project, the massive Citadel Station was built in orbit above Telos. The project itself was guided by Chodo Habat and his Ithorian herd. The surface of Telos was divided into "restoration zones," each of them having a unique code, and the Republic started importing lifeforms from other worlds, for example, cannoks, meant to keep the herbivore population in check, were taken from Onderon, its jungle moon of Dxun and Ithor itself.

By 3951 BBY, the Ithorians had been challenged by Czerka Corporation, which, through not entirely legal means, attempted to take control over the Restoration Project. Their plans were different from the ones proposed by the Ithorians. Instead of restoring the nature of Telos, they proposed urbanizing it. In reality, they saw the project only as a cover-up andwhat they actually wanted was access to abandoned Republic military bases on the planet's surface. However, the corruption within the Czerka department on Citadel Station was eventually exposed by Meetra Surik, and the Telosian Council drove the company away from

Telos. According to Darth Traya's predictions, the Restoration Project would complete successfully, and the surface of Telos would once again harbor life for years to come. The project was still underway by 3643 BBY, over three hundred years later.

Meetra Surik is discovered aboard the Ebon Hawk by Kreia. Meetra Surik, also known as the Jedi Exile after the Mandalorian Wars, was a Human female Jedi Master. As a Padawan, she chose to disobey the orders of the Jedi High Council and aid the Galactic Republic in its war against the invading Mandalorian Neo-Crusaders. Rising to the rank of Jedi Knight during the conflict, she served with distinction under the command of her fellow Crusaders Revan and Malak and was eventually commissioned as a General in the Republic Military. Surik played a vital role in defeating the Mandalorians during the latter stages of the conflict, but as a direct result of her controversial actions during the cataclysmic final battle, she effectively cut her connection to the Force. Afterwards, out of all those who went to war, she was the only Jedi to avoid the call of the dark side and return to the Jedi Council to be judged for her crimes. After being exiled from the Jedi Order, she wandered the periphery of known space for nearly a decade before returning to the Republic during the Dark Wars, at the height of the First Jedi Purge.

Lonna Vash dies. Lonna Vash was a female Human Jedi Master serving the Jedi Order and the Galactic Republic as a member of the Jedi High Council during the Mandalorian Wars and the Jedi Civil War. She was one of the Masters who banished Meetra Surik from the Order.

The Battle of Khoonda was a local conflict that followed the catastrophic Jedi Civil War in 3951 BBY and was a major event during the First Jedi Purge. The main target was Khoonda, site of the local government established after the destruction of the Jedi Enclave. It was particularly aimed at Administrator Terena Adare, the only person on Dantooine capable of uniting the surviving farmers. Territories outside the Khoonda Plains were inhabited by salvagers, who sought for Jedi relics in the ruined Enclave, and mercenaries of the Exchange led by Azkul, who participated in the Jedi Civil War under Darth Malak's command.

A blockade of the planet Onderon was the opening skirmish of the Onderon Civil War, and was also a major event of the First Jedi Purge during that time. General Vaklu, cousin of the reigning queen of Onderon, Talia and commander of the Onderon military, had been dissatisfied with his cousin's policy of what he viewed as appeasement towards the Galactic Republic. Vaklu had secretly made an alliance with the Sith, and when they informed him that the Meetra Surik (The Jedi Exile) would soon be arriving on Onderon, he saw his chance to both take his cousin's place and to spoil the Onderon citizenry's view on the Republic. Vaklu placed his right-hand man, Colonel Tobin, in charge of the orbital defenses as he himself went to Onderon's capital, Iziz. Tobin authorized a blockade over the planet of Onderon. All Republic vessels were to be seized and searched, causing delays and frustration for pilots who wished to enter the planet to deliver their quotas. The arrival of the Ebon Hawk exacerbated the issue. Under the pretense that the Exile had fired first, Tobin ordered the Onderon military to open fire not only on her ship, the Ebon Hawk, but also on the other freighters that were in orbit around Onderon waiting to dock. Vaklu declared martial law and effectively took control of Iziz. He declared that Tobin was a hero who had been attacked first, and that fifteen (as opposed to six) of their defense ships had been destroyed. He also misinformed the public that the Hawk was a capital warship. The Exile fled to Onderon's moon, Dxun, and although most of the Onderon military remained loyal to Talia, they were no match against a Sith armada that quickly appeared to support Vaklu's claim to the throne.

The Second Battle of Onderon was a battle of the Onderon Civil War, which occurred on the planet Onderon and its moon, Dxun, and was one of the last major events of the First Jedi Purge. The battle concluded the Civil War and paved the way to the end of the purge, by acting as the catalyst that goaded the Sith into revealing themselves so that they could be destroyed by the Jedi Exile.

Battle of Telos IV occurs. Kreia's plan worked as intended. Immediately after leaving Onderon, Tobin reported the misinformation to Nihilus. The Sith Lord took the bait and moved his fleet to Telos IV to feed on the supposed Academy's Jedi. Despite the surprise of the Sith's appearance out of seemingly nowhere, the Telos Security Force, led by Lieutenant Dol Grenn, managed to keep them from completely overrunning Citadel Station until reinforcements arrived. Thanks to Meetra Surik's earlier aid in stopping a weapons smuggling ring, Grenn was able to arm some of his men with the confiscated weapons. The first reinforcements were sent from Dantooine and Onderon, led by Captain Zherron of the Khoonda Militia and Major Riiken of the Onderonian military, respectively; both worlds, in the midst of political turmoil, had been stabilized by Surik during her search for the Lost Jedi. After that, Surik herself arrived on the station with the Ebon Hawk, accompanied by Mandalore the Preserver and his clans. With Surik's help, the combined Republic forces cleared Citadel Station of Sith troops and saved the fueling station.

Meetra Surik reestablishes connection to the Force, then kills Darth Nihilus, Darth Sion and , who have spent the last five years assassinating Jedi.

Destruction of Malachor V. Behind the destruction were Meetra Surik and her former lieutenant, Bao-Dur, the inventor of the Mass Shadow Generator, which had been previously used by Surik in the Battle of Malachor V to crush the Mandalorian fleet. Shortly after the Battle of Telos IV, Admiral Carth Onasi appointed an audience for Surik. Having recognized her as one of Revan's generals and her ship, the Ebon Hawk, as Revan's former ship, he asked Surik to find Revan and bring him a simple message that Carth was following his orders to keep the Galactic Republic safe. After that, Surik departed to Malachor V, the last known location of Revan, as she also had her own business on the planet, she was to reach Kreia, who threatened to sacrifice herself and kill Surik as well through their Force bond, resulting perhaps even in the death of the Force. Upon arrival at Malachor V, the Ebon Hawk crashed into part of a canyon area and was suspended far above an abyss, falling into the abyss shortly after Surik's departure into the Trayus Academy. And as Surik was descending into the depths of the Academy, one of Surik's companions, a bounty hunter named Mira fought and defeated Hanharr, whom she had previously fought, and healed by Kreia before being sent after Mira on Nar Shaddaa, and Bao-Dur sent his remote on a mission, which activated via a pre-recorded hologram. It turned out that the droid's primary objective was reactivating the Mass Shadow Generator and undoing the damage done to Malachor nine years earlier by destroying the planet itself. Once inside the academy, Surik faced off against all of Kreia's dark forces, killing them, then finally confronted Darth Sion. As they dueled, the Lord of Pain believed that Kreia would accept him back as her apprentice once Surik is destroyed. But despite his abilities to regain consciousness with the dark side, Surik defeated Sion and explained that Kreia was only using him to get to her. Knowing this to be true, Sion confessed that he "hated" her because of her beauty and became one with the Force. Following the battle with Sion, Surik confronted Kreia, having again assumed the mantle of Darth Traya, in the Trayus core. After a verbal exchange, Kreia refused Surik's offer of redemption, insisting instead that the apprentice must kill the master. After Kreia and Surik dueled, Surik severed Traya's hand, but refused to kill her, in which Kreia then used the force to make three purple lightsabers float in the air and attack Surik. Surik defeated all of them, but killed Traya in the process. Mortally wounded, Kreia declared Surik to be her greatest pupil of all, and after revealing to Surik the future of her companions, died with Malachor. On the surface, the remote succeeded in activating the Mass Shadow Generator, and the damaged Ebon Hawk was piloted out of the core and arrived to save Surik from the collapsing Trayus Core. Malachor disintegrates, freed from the mass shadows, finally silencing the echo of the Mandalorian Wars and ending the first ever Sith Triumvirate as Surik and her allies escaped the exploding planet.

First Jedi Purge ends. This purge saw nearly the entire Jedi Order disappear from the galaxy The Order publicly disbanded and most of the survivors were slain by the Sith.

During the Sith Civil War, circa 3954 BBY, Darth Traya, Darth Nihilus, and Darth Sion took command of the remnants of Revan's Sith Empire. After the exile of Traya, Sion utilized his Sith assassins to assassinate Jedi, while Nihilus would consume the life of an entire planet in search of the Jedi. Nihilus's final attack was on the Miraluka world of Katarr Nearly all of the remaining hundred Jedi died at a meeting that was being held on the planet. Despite the Sith's success against the Jedi, the purge was finally brought to an end by Meetra Surik, who not only trained a new generation of Jedi, but also personally killed all three leaders of the Sith Triumvirate in combat. After the conclusion of the purge, the Jedi who Surik trained proved essential to the Order's revival.

End of the Old Sith Wars.

THE INTER-SITH WARS PERIOD

This historical period occurred between the events of the Old Sith Wars and the New Sith Wars.

3950 BBY

The city of Bin Prime is chosen to replace Sobrik as the capital of Balmorra. It was the headquarters of planetary Governor Beltane during his administration under the Imperial occupation of the planet. Despite their income from producing Imperial war machines, Beltane wanted Balmorra free from the Empire. After the Battle of Endor, the world broke away from Imperial influence. During Operation Shadow Hand, it was attacked by Executor Sedriss QL, who sent an invasion army towards the capital. Bin Prime was saved by the numerous technological achievements Balmorra had made in the intervening years, as new battle droid models held the force at bay, before they could reach the fortified city's borders

---

3946 BBY

Go-To droids seize control of sixteen worlds in the Gordian Reach and secede from the Republic, forming the independent territory of 400100500260026. However, Supreme Chancellor Tol Cressa organizes a military campaign that liberates the territory.

3900 BBY

Queen Elsinoré den Tasia of Grizmallt sponsors one of the last colonization efforts by her world, but the colonization ships, the Beneficent Tasia, Constant, and Mother Vima, disappear from sight. It is later discovered that the ships reached the planet Naboo, where they settled and came into conflict with the native Gungans.

3809 BBY

Sraato sustains massive damage from a meteor storm, beginning a period of environmental chaos that lasts for five hundred years.

3781 BBY

The reconstituted Sith Empire begins preparations for their eventual invasion of the Republic.

3756 BBY

Jedi Master Barel Ovair, actually a servant of the Sith Emperor, undertakes a mission with his apprentice Eison Gynt to Yavin 4. Ovair's true mission is to eliminate the spirit of Naga Sadow for the Emperor, but the two are attacked by Massassi and Ovair and is forced to flee the moon, abandoning his apprentice. Gynt returns to Coruscant years later, under Sadow's possession, and is killed when he attacks Ovair.

3743 BBY

The hunter Riegenn Hetuu is hired by a Hutt to acquire and deliver a live K'lor'slug queen for the Hutt's annual gladiatorial tournament on Nal Hutta. The K'lor'slug was a dangerous vermiform native to the swamps of Noe'ha'on. On arrival at Nal Hutta the K'lor'slug had reproduced and was consumed, along with his client, by the approximately four hundred k'lor'slugs that the queen had spawned in his ship. The incident gives rise to the term a "hutt's cry," referring to the sound made by a batch of hatching k'lor'slugs.

3712 BBY

The Sith Lord Darth Ikoral is granted permission to take his flagship, the Red Reaper, on an expedition in search of pureblooded Sith outside of the Sith Empire.

3705 BBY

The Brentaalan hyperspace explorer Freia Kallea bridges the gap between the Mandalorian Road and the Sprizen End Run. Kallea was one of the first female pilots who decided to map out a part of the galaxy. She managed to blaze a trail beginning at the Corporate Sector and continuing through the Core to the other side, effectively passing through the whole galaxy. Sewing together the Dustig Trace, the Sprizen End Run and dozens other one-hop routes, she formed a larger hyperway, called the Hydian Way. Opening the galaxy beyond The Slice and joining its northern and southern quadrants, the scale of galactic civilization changed forever. In a local level, Brentaal became the only system to be at the intersection of two major hyper-routes (the other being the Perlemian Trade Route). After that, Kallea became a symbol of Brentaal's cultural strength and endurance, and her name would pass to posterity. She later retired from the life of a pilot to marry into a Brentaal family. Now a noblewoman, Kallea (who retained her maiden name) would work to turn her new family into a major trading enterprise, the Kallean League. Even years after her death, the Kallean League would still remain a large consortium of representatives of different trading houses.

3704 BBY

Freia Kallea blazes a route linking the Spurs of Celanon and the Morellian Trail, completing the northern end of the Hydian Way.

3703–3702 BBY

Freia Kallea charts a route south from Denon, linking the end of the Brentaal–Denon Route with the Dustig Trace. However, she crash-lands on the uncharted planet Nuvar thanks to interference from rivals, where she is stranded for six years.

3701–3699 BBY

Kallea's route is expanded from the Dustig Trace to Seswenna and Clak'dor VII to the south over several years.

3694 BBY

Rescued from Nuvar, Kallea extends her route all the way to Terminus near the edge of the galactic disk, and then extends it further to Imynusoph.

3693 BBY

The fully-charted Hydian Way is christened. The Hydian Way (pronounced /hʌi-diː-yæn/) was a super-hyperroute that began at the Corporate Sector on one side of the galaxy and continued through the core to the other side, past Eriadu. It was the only route that passed through the entire galaxy. The route helped open up much of the galaxy beyond the region known as The Slice, fundamentally altering the scale of galactic civilization. The route was named in honor of Duros scout, and later Kallea's colleague, Banu Hydia.

3681 BBY

The Great Galactic War, known as the Great War during the conflict and in the years afterward, begins and was a war between the Sith Empire and the Galactic Republic, lasting for a total of 28 years. Also known as the Republic–Sith War, the conflict was ultimately the culmination of a 1300-year grudge held by survivors of the old Sith Empire against the Republic for their defeat in the Great Hyperspace War. The war would cost countless lives and devastate worlds from the Core to the Rim, as well as having dramatic galactic consequences otherwise. The Republic economy was shattered and roughly half the galaxy would end up under Sith dominion, and the Jedi Order would withdraw from the galactic capital to establish a new home on their ancient homeworld. But it would not ultimately be conclusive. While a strategic defeat for the Republic, the end of the war left both powers standing, engaged in an undeclared conflict for supremacy on numerous disputed worlds

3671 BBY

The Empire is defeated at the First Battle of Bothawui. This was a naval conflict between the Sith Empire and the Galactic Republic. Following the return of the Empire and its initial victories in the Outer Rim Territories in the early stages of the war, the Sith Emperor turned his sights toward the Mid Rim in 3671 BBY, with Bothawui as his first target. Admiral Greik of the Republic Navy predicted the attack, and so took approved the daring tactics of the combat analysis droid B-3G9 and assembled the entirety of his fleet of warships over the world. The incursion, led by Darth Immern, was a disaster for the Empire, as the Republic force was ready for the attack. The entire Imperial Armada strike fleet was wiped out, but the Empire's defeat during its first attempt at taking Bothawui only served to provoke their second, more aggressive attack.

3670 BBY

The Jedi finally liberate the Kanz sector from the Myrialites, ending the Kanz Disorders.

3667 BBY

Imperial Intelligence sponsors a Mandalorian gladiator in hopes of using him to rally the Mandalorians to the Sith Empire's side. Eventually, after a string of fixed victories, the gladiator is given the ancient title of Mandalore by cheering crowds in a Geonosian arena.

3653 BBY

The Empire sacks Coruscant, destroying the Jedi Temple and inflicting mass casualties. They hold the planet hostage as the Republic, who had been tricked into attending peace negotiations on Alderaan, are forced to sign the Treaty of Coruscant, which ends the Great War, beginning the period of covert conflicts and private wars known as the Cold War . The Galactic Republic was strongarmed into the treaty following the twenty-eight year conflict with the Sith Empire that saw the galactic government crumble under the pressures of war and economic struggles. The concept of a cessation of hostilities between the Republic and Empire was first proposed by the Sith Dark Council, under the leadership of the Sith Emperor. Although wary of possible ulterior motives, the Republic's Galactic Senate accepted the offer out of desperation. While representatives of the Empire and the Republic conferred, the Sith launched an unexpected assault on the Republic capital world of Coruscant. The Sacking of Coruscant placed the Republic's capital firmly under the control of the Sith Empire, and gave the Imperial delegation on Alderaan the leverage they needed in order to demand the Republic's surrender of the war. The leader of the Imperial delegation, the Sith Lord Darth Baras, authored the Treaty of Coruscant and presented it to the representatives of the Senate and the Jedi Order for their signatures. They signed the document, ending the Great Galactic War and declaring the Sith Empire as the victor. The treaty divided the galaxy in two and demanded that all Republic forces and Jedi withdraw from open conflict with the Empire and that the Senate cede a number of outlying worlds to the Sith. The agreement was heavily opposed by certain interests within the Republic, including Jedi Master Dar'Nala, General Elin Garza of the Republic Military, and the Royal House of Alderaan. Such opposition to the treaty led to the initiation of a galactic Cold War fought between the Republic and Empire both directly and by proxy. The treaty was so significant that the Galactic Senate adopted the date of its signing as a new dating standard.

3651 BBY

Satele Shan rediscovers the planet of Tython, a deed that gains her the rank of Jedi Master and later Grand Master, and the Order relocates to Tython.[97]

3650 BBY

The Jedi Order begins construction of a new Jedi Temple on Tython

---

3647 BBY

Construction of the Jedi Temple on Tython comes to a close.

3645 BBY

Satele Shan has been made Grand Master of the Jedi Order

3643 BBY

The Cold War begins to collapse as a number of proxy conflicts erupt between the Republic and the Empire, such as Darth Angral's private war on the Republic,

3642 BBY

The Galactic War breaks out as the tense peace of the Cold War collapses. After twelve years of tenuous peace in the form of the Cold War, the actions of several powerful individuals caused open warfare to break out once more between the major galactic powers.

3640 BBY

Through Operation End Game, the Republic destroys the Ascendant Spear, a prototype warship commanded by Darth Karrid. Operation End Game was a joint mission of the Galactic Republic's Military, Strategic Information Service, and the Jedi Order that was conducted during the Galactic War. Its goal was to destroy the Sith Empire's new warship, the Ascendant Spear under the command of Darth Karrid, a Falleen Sith Lord. SIS Agent Theron Shan and Jedi Master Gnost-Dural were sent out as the forefront of the operation which was under the direct command of Supreme Commander Jace Malcom and SIS Director Marcus Trant. The mission was successful and the Ascendant Spear was destroyed and Darth Karrid killed.

The Hutt Cartel, under the leadership of Supreme Mogul Toborro, invades the neutral world of Makeb in order to harvest the Isotope-5 in the planet's core. The Republic lends the people of Makeb aid, while the weakened Empire undertakes a cover mission to secure isotope-5 reserves for themselves. The Empire manages to stabilize Makeb's core as it begins to tear the planet apart, saving the planet from complete destruction.

The Dread Masters are finally eliminated on the moon of Oricon. The Dread Masters were six powerful Human Sith Lords who served the Sith Emperor for centuries as prophets, generals, and advisors. Their name was earned when they studied the power of the Phobis devices, artifacts that had driven even the most depraved Sith mad with terror. This power allowed the Dread Masters to destroy entire Galactic Republic fleets during the Great Galactic War; they had mastered the art of battle meditation to the point that they would inflict an awful, mysterious terror upon members of any given Republic cruiser. In order to avoid being compromised, they kept in constant motion in an Imperial dreadnaught that roamed the galaxy. With the help of an elite Republic Special Forces Division team, Jedi Knight Jaric Kaedan infiltrated the dreadnaught and captured the Dread Masters. The Jedi Order publicly announced that the Dread Masters were killed, but secretly they were imprisoned on Belsavis. Later released by servants of the Sith Empire, the Dread Masters would eventually go rogue following the defeat of the Emperor on Dromund Kaas. After the slaying of one of their number on Darvannis, the remainder relocated to their Dread Fortress on Oricon, where they were defeated in 3640 BBY. Only one, Dread Master Calphayus, survived the downfall of the others, and was taken once more into Republic custody.

3500 BBY

Republic scouts discover the Moon of Iktotchon, home of the Iktotchi species, and are astonished to see the seal of the Republic carved into a high plateau on the moon's largest continent. The precognitive Iktotchi predicted the Republic's arrival by several weeks, and the Iktotchi leaders have gathered at the massive carving for their first contact with other species.

3350 BBY

The Centrality is founded as an independent territory. The Centrality was an independent government, a lengthy region of space nestled between Hutt Space and the Cron Drift, consisting of several dozen star systems. It was an empty region lacking many stable hyperspace routes, with areas so devoid of systems that some travelers would run out of fuel before finishing their journeys even halfway. The ruling body of this region of space was the Centrality Council. Inhabitants were referred to as Centrans.

3300 BBY

The environmental chaos on Sraato caused by the meteor storm finally comes to an end.

3200 BBY

The Yavin system is rediscovered by probe droids exploring the Perlemian Trade Route's spurs, but is cataloged as uninhabitable. The Yavin system was a three-planet star system in the Outer Rim Territories that contained the gas giant Yavin Prime and its twenty-six moons; only three of which were habitable: Yavin 4, Yavin 8, and Yavin 13. Discovered by Galactic Republic scouts during the Expansionist Era, this overall inhospitable star system went down in history millennia later during the Galactic Civil War, when it hosted the famous Battle of Yavin. In the decades following the end of the Civil War and the collapse of the Galactic Empire, the Yavin system was passed down from hand to hand, conquered by remnant Imperial warlords, recaptured by the New Republic and colonized by the extra-galactic invaders known as the Yuuzhan Vong. Despite its reputedly inhospitable environment, the Yavin system was home to at least four sapient native species, namely the Melodies, the Gerbs, the Sliths, and a race of humanoids that was wiped out by the Galactic Empire. Additionally, Yavin 4 became an adopted home for several other species, including the Critokians, the Massassi Sith, and some Humans.

3100 BBY

The Hapan Queen Mother seals the borders of the Hapes Consortium, beginning thousands of years of isolation. The Hapes Consortium was the ruling government and consortium of the Hapes Cluster. A hereditary monarchy based on the capital world of Hapes, it ruled over the region in isolation since before 3000 BBY, protected by the Transitory Mists. It spanned 63 closely positioned star systems, each with an inhabited world.

3053 BBY

Vandelhelm is discovered by two independent prospectors Vandel and Helm. Vandelhelm was a planet located in the Vandelhelm system, inside of the Vandelhelm Cloud within the Expansion Region. It was known for its starshipwrights, and manufacturing capabilities.

3025 BBY

Caretaker Varner Hilts coins the term "The Time of the Rot" to describe the period of upheaval and civil unrest on Kesh. Varner Hilts was a Human male who served as the mild-mannered caretaker of Sith lore for the Lost Tribe of Sith in 3000 BBY. He grew up during the tumultuous Time of the Rot which lasted almost a millennium and devastated much of the continent of Keshtah Minor. As a historian, Hilts hoped to use the wisdom of the ancients to reunite the Tribe. By that time, the Lost Tribe had descended into violent infighting, and the true origins of the Tribe had been forgotten. Unlike many of his Sith contemporaries, Hilts was very open-minded and forward-thinking. He even related to Keshiri, the purple-skinned humanoid beings indigenous to the planet Kesh, as his equals. Varner Hilts also developed a warm relationship with his Keshiri assistant Jaye Vuhld, who was a brilliant mathematician and theorist.

3017 BBY

The Seventeenth Alsakan Conflict, the last of such conflicts, comes to an end.

3000 BBY

The Gungan species on the planet Naboo undergoes a civil war that leads to their unification under Boss Gallo and the founding of the city of Otoh Gunga.

The Paecian Empire colonizes the planet Dathomir, using it as a penal colony. Dathomir was an obscure planet in the Outer Rim Territories, located in the Quelii sector. It was somewhat smaller than Coruscant in size, and had slightly-below-standard gravity, but the planetary day was close to standard, and the planetary year was long, lasting 491 days.

The Hapan Royal Guard, or Chume'doro, first begins service as the Queen Mother's protectors. The Hapan Royal Guard (Chume'doro in Hapan) was a military unit tasked to defend the Queen Mother of the Hapes Consortium and her family. Members of the Royal Guard included Major Moreem Espara. As was typical of Hapan women, they were generally attractive, but they were also generally very large and strong, sometimes carrying enormous shoulder-mounted weapons.

The planet Jabiim is colonized. Jabiim was a world deluged by torrential rains, experiencing less than five days per standard year without precipitation. Its muddy surface constantly shifted from the weight of the rains. Jabiim was also rich in ore, although by the time of the Battle of Yavin, the valuable ores were dwindling. During the Clone Wars, Jabiim was a world that the Galactic Republic ignored until it was too late. The world had a very unstable electric field, and electric storms were quite common. Due to this, repulsorcraft of any type were largely unusable on the planet.

2992 BBY

The Paecian Empire collapses.

2989 BBY

The Talecalle volcano chain erupts before entering a dormant stage that lasts for three thousand years.

2975 BBY

High Lord Edell Vrai's mission to the continent of Alanciar ends in failure as the Alanciari shoot down the Tribe's airships.

High Lord Korsin Bentado attempts to invade Alanciar, but is also repelled by the Alanciari. He and the remainder of his forces then assassinate the entire Alanciari War Cabinet. Edell Vrai and Alanciari allies halt Bentado's attempt to create a "Second Tribe" on Alanciar, and the Lost Tribe annexes Alanciar with minimal hostilities.

2974 BBY

After the Tribe discovers the polar continent of Eshkrene, a chain of events result in the release of the ancient Sith Lord Remulus Dreypa from his imprisonment. Baron Dreypa leads a revolt against the Lost Tribe and unearths his Leviathans from Sessal Spire, and then leads an invasion of the city of Tahv.

His invasion ends with the Sith Lord's death, and the Tribe reasserts control of Kesh.

2500s BBY

The "Battleship era" comes to an end thanks to economic strains, and tacticians largely start to prefer fleets of smaller cruisers.

2519 BBY

The main hall of the Jedi Archives is constructed. The Jedi Archives was a fathomless collection of ancient knowledge and research dating back thousands of standard years. Overseen by the Council of First Knowledge, the Archives served as a repository for journals and artifacts and was located in the First Knowledge quarter of the Jedi Temple on Coruscant. The Archives was open at all hours and were accessible to all Jedi in need of information. While Jedi were welcome to scan or copy most any data in the Stacks, removal of any material from the Archives was strictly prohibited. Remote access to the databases was near impossible, with eradicators built into the Temple's outer walls and firewalls in the database mainframes

---

2500 BBY

Prospectors discover that the core of Yavin Prime has fused hydrogen and carbon into Corusca gems, sparking a mining rush that dies out less than a century later.

2367 BBY

The first Priole Danna Festival is held on Lamuir IV. The Priole Danna Festival was a celebration of parades and music in Gryle City on the planet Lamuir IV in Tapani sector's Freeworlds Territory. Held annually one of the most popular attractions of the festival was the Anapolla Musical Splash. During the time of the New Republic, there was a hundred-thousand-being mass sighting of a Silentium at a Priole Danna festival

---

2320 BBY

The planet Taanab is settled as an agricultural outpost. Taanab was a planet of green meadows in the Taanab system. It was primarily used for agriculture and farming. Its populace was known for always maintaining an air of formality. Taanab had problems with seasonal pirate raids from bandits striking from the planet Norulac for millennia prior to the Battle of Taanab.

2219 BBY

The Saffa species begins a period that sees them create Saffa paintings.

2200 BBY

The Mining Guild claims the planet Ruusan along with a number of other worlds in the Teraab sector, but Ruusan's mineral deposits prove disappointing. The Mining Guild was one of the many galactic corporate entities operating during the time of the Galactic Republic. It survived the fall of the commerce guilds during the Clone Wars and continued into the Galactic Civil War.

2132 BBY

The Breath Stealing occurs on Alphoresis, an event that claims the lives of every child under the age of eight.

THE DRAGGULCH PERIOD

The Draggulch Period was an era of galactic history that coincided with the New Sith Wars, a galaxy-spanning conflict that lasted from 2000 BBY to 1000 BBY.

2000 BBY

The New Sith Wars begins with the Fourth Great Schism: The Jedi Master Phanius leaves the Jedi Order with fifty followers and takes the name Darth Ruin as he founds the New Sith, igniting a thousand years of conflict with the Sith.

A group of families and friends of members of the Jedi Order flee the early battles of the New Sith Wars, settling on the Outer Rim planet of Yanibar in hopes of establishing a temporary refuge. However, the colonists' relatives and allies are killed during the conflict, causing Yanibar to be forgotten; the colonists develop the Zeison Sha Force tradition.

A Near-Human species immigrates to the planet Bimmisaari, where they adopt the culture of the native Bimms and are integrated into Bimm culture, also becoming known as Bimms.

1989 BBY

Bespin is first colonized with the commissioning of Cloud City.

1960 BBY

The Amulet of Kalara is fashioned. The Amulet of Kalara was a Sith amulet infused with dark side energies and supposedly had the ability to make the possessor invisible in the Force. As a test by Lumiya around 2000 years later, Jedi apprentice Ben Skywalker was tasked with retrieving the amulet from the collection of art and artifacts found in Lando Calrissian's Tendrando Arms facility on Drewwa, a moon of Almania. However, before Ben got to it, the amulet had been stolen by Faskus Olvidan of Ziost. Ben successfully retrieved the artifact and brought it to Jacen Solo along with a Sith Meditation Sphere. When felt with the Force, it radiated a malicious glee.

1800 BBY

An orbital bombardment of the planets in the Uba system, a preemptive strike by the Republic to deter the native Ubese from continuing to build banned weapons, ignites superweapon caches that engulf the planets in radioactive firestorms. The native Ubese are nearly exterminated by the event, with the only survivors on Uba IV. Some are relocated to the Ubertica system, but the event sparks a deep-seated hatred of the Republic among the Ubese.

1750 BBY

The Dark Underlord seizes power and marshals his Black Knights, who raid space stations along the Zona Miki route. The Black Knights were an alliance of Sith forged together by the Dark Underlord. The Republic counter by hiring Mandalorian mercenaries who fight alongside the Jedi in battle at Malrev IV, where the Jedi Master Murrtaggh struck down the Dark Underlord.

1582 BBY

A military coup in the Tapani Empire brings down the Kappela Dynasty, and the region forms the Tapani Federation. The coup marks the transition from the Dynastic Era to the Federal Era of the region.[68]

1569 BBY

The end of the height of Saffa paintings.

1500 BBY

The Republic drafts a large number of soldiers and halts the Sith offensive at King's Galquek, Corphelion, and Hiit.

The Sayings, a collection of instructions about political strategy and conquest by Emperor Uueg Tching of Atrisia, are printed in a small run by the current Atrisian Emperor. The printing is a ploy by the Emperor to display his power to the Atrisian nobility, who are given the printed Sayings.

1486 BBY

The Tapani Federation sends its first representatives to the Galactic Senate, and the Tapani sector is established as a Republic sector.

1466 BBY

The Battle of Mizra occurs, ending with a Jedi defeat. It was one of the most crushing of Sith victories in the New Sith Wars. Sith forces were led by "scores" of Sith Lords, each riding a speeder named after an animal that personified the lord (such as Hssiss, Ng'ok, and Sleeth). During the Jedi retreat, a Sith sniper shot the Jedi Coordinator who was using Battle Meditation, turning the retreat into a full scale slaughter. Felloux later wrote a poem on the battle. The defeat at Mizra for the Republic led to the loss of control for much of the Outer Rim Territories and some believed that central control never returned.

1419 BBY

Dreypa's Oubliette is rediscovered on Jebble. Dreypa's Oubliette later nicknamed the Jebble Box was a stasis casket created by the Sith Lord Remulus Dreypa. Dreypa created the Oubliette in order to imprison and torture Karness Muur, and to contain the hypnotic influence of the Muur Talisman. The casket could theoretically preserve a living being for millennia, even beyond the death of the galaxy itself, according to the scientist Pulsipher. Neither conventional sensors nor the power of the Force could penetrate the Oubliette's skin.

1300 BBY

Republic scouts discover the planet Lan Barell in the ore-rich Lan system. Lan Barell was a dusty, dry backwater planet located on the Outer Rim of the galaxy near Breshkall. Heavy iron content in the soil gave the planet a faint blue sheen, and when combined with the red glare of its sun, gave the planet a garish and gloomy atmosphere.

1250 BBY

The Sith Lord Belia Darzu comes to power, beginning a period known as the Sictis Wars as she unleashes her technobeasts.

1230 BBY

The Sictis Wars end with Darzu's death on Tython.

1196 BBY

Hathrox III was an urban planet in the Hathrox system. Its civilization was destroyed in a biochemical civil war in about 1196 BBY. The planet was quarantined by the New Republic and all attempts by scouts to study the planet resulted in their deaths, as well as the deaths of the rescue team that came after them, and the quarantine staff that came after them.

1154 BBY

The Bengali Uprising begins, which sees the planets Bengali and Thyrsus revolt against the rule of the Echani Command over the Six Sisters. Bengali rejoins the Echani Command less than a century later.

1100 BBY

The Republic Dark Age begins.

1094 BBY

The city of Zehava is founded on the planet Melida/Daan.

1066 BBY

Calimondra began the Charge Matrica in 1066 BBY, to decide which of her seven children would become the heir to her holdings. She tasked them with expanding her empire, and planned to appoint as her heir the one that expanded her holdings the most. However, her daughter Xelian declared war on her sibling Chagras, causing all seven siblings to start fighting against each other. Since Vilia was unwilling to referee between her children, Sith conquests in the Outer Rim stalled due to infighting. Eventually, Chagras was the only one of Calimondra's children left, and she made him her heir. Thus, Chagras subsequently came to rule an empire known as the Chagras Hegemony. However, since Vilia lived, she still retained control of most of her holdings. Chagras was only guaranteed the cooperation of his multiple nieces and nephews in the reconstruction process. By 1042 BBY, Chagras had recovered his military resources sufficiently to launch an offensive against the Galactic Republic. Hegemomony forces under Lord Odion attacked Sanbra and Aquilaris Minor as part of a top-secret project to acquire the Helm of Ieldis, an ancient Sith artifact dating back to the Great Hyperspace War. In 1040 BBY, Chagras was killed, so Calimondra began a Second Charge Matrica, to determine which one of her grandchildren would become her new heir. However, her grandchildren Daiman and Odion went to war against each other, and soon the rest of her grandchildren began fighting against each other.

1058 BBY

The mercenary Aga Awaud returns to Mandalore and finds that the Candorian plague has killed his family and most of his clan, and that the Mandalorians are victims of raiders throughout Mandalorian Space. Appalled, Awaud leads a movement known as the Return in an effort to convince Mandalorians to defend their territory.

1057 BBY

The Sith Lord Xelian gives birth to her second son Daiman.

1052 BBY

The Sith Lord Mandragall is seduced and then killed by Xelian.

1051 BBY

Awaud claims the title of Mandalore the Uniter, and leads Mandalorian Space through the remainder of the New Sith Wars to become a regional industrial and military power.

1010 BBY

Jedi Master Skere Kaan abandons the Order with a group of like-minded Jedi, and within months his Brotherhood of Darkness emerges as the dominant Sith faction. The Brotherhood of Darkness was an organization of Sith that took the place of the fragmented Sith Empire after slaughtering many of its most powerful lords. Forming the Dark Army, a force of warriors and soldiers meant to rain fire upon Republic worlds, the Brotherhood existed under the leadership of the Sith Council of Lords, constantly warring with the Jedi Order's Army of Light until both armies were utterly decimated at the Seventh Battle of Ruusan.

Lord Hoth decides to take the offensive against the Sith, and gathers Jedi Lords and bands of Knights behind his banner. The Grand Council of the Order ultimately declares all of the Jedi baronies united as the Army of Light under Hoth, who bears the title of Seneschal.

1006 BBY

The Sith Academy on Korriban is reopened.

1004 BBY

The Brotherhood of Darkness lands armies on Dromund Kaas and Malrev IV, but are repelled by the Republic.

1002 BBY

The Army of Light clashes with the Brotherhood of Darkness at Ruusan, beginning the Ruusan campaign.

1000 BBY

The Seventh Battle of Ruusan ends when Kaan, influenced by Darth Bane, uses the thought bomb to eradicate his enemies, but the thought bomb kills all of the Sith as well.

FALL OF THE REPUBLIC/RISE OF THE EMPIRE ERA

Set in the time around the prequel trilogy this era takes place after the seemingly final defeat of the Sith. In the waning years of the Republic, the Senate was rife with corruption and scandal, and saddled with a bureaucracy so immense that effective governing was nearly impossible. The Sith Lord, Darth Sidious, secretly orchestrated his rise to Supreme Chancellor under the guise of Senator Palpatine and personally engineered the Clone Wars. He promised to reunite the galaxy under a New Order, and killed the majority of the Jedi. The Phantom Menace takes place in the year 32 BBY, Attack of the Clones and The Clone Wars film in 22 BBY, and Revenge of the Sith in 19 BBY.

1000 BBY

The Seventh Battle of Ruusan occurs when the remaining Sith are exterminated, with the exception of Darth Bane, who starts a new Sith Order with only one master and one apprentice at a time, also known as the Rule of Two. Each subsequent Sith would bear the title Darth.

Chancellor Tarsus Valorum presides over the Ruusan Reformation, which dismantles the Republic's central authority, abolishing the Republic's standing armed forces and reorganizing its millions of sectors into 1,024 regional sectors, each represented by a single Senator. This would draw to an end the Republic Dark Age.

---

980 BBY

Darth Zannah kills Darth Bane on Ambria and becomes the new Dark Lord of the Sith.

---

965 BBY

Chiss Ascendancy passes the Non-Aggression Law. It forbade any act of preemptive or aggressive military actions to be undertaken by the Chiss.

---

915 BBY

Sise Fromm is born. He later became a kingpin of organized crime in the galaxy.

896 BBY

Yoda is born on an unknown planet, and later begins his training with Hysalrian Jedi Master N'Kata Del Gormo on an unknown swamp planet.

867 BBY

Naboo joins the Galactic Republic. Naboo (pronounced /nə'bu/) was a planet that was the sector capital of the Chommell sector near the Outer Rim territories. It was a largely unspoiled world with large plains, swamps and seas. It was mostly known as the homeworld of notable historical figures who played major roles in the downfall of the Galactic Republic and the rise of the Galactic Empire, namely Padmé Amidala, Emperor Palpatine and Jar Jar Binks.

850 BBY

A box containing a 10,000 year old lightsaber is discovered on Ossus.

800 BBY

Yoda begins to train Jedi in the ways of the Force.

796 BBY

Yoda is granted the title of Jedi Master.

700 BBY

B'omarr monks arrive on Tatooine. The B'omarr Order, which consisted of the B'omarr Monks, was a mysterious religious order. They believed that cutting themselves off from all physical sensation would further their studies, and allow them to ponder the galaxy and achieve enlightenment. When a monk became enlightened, his brain was removed through a special procedure, and was placed in a nutrient-filled jar. The brains were held in very high regard by the lower, embodied monks, who saw to their every need, though the brains rarely did anything other than think and wonder. When they did need to travel around their monastery on Tatooine, the brains were transferred into specially modified BT-16 perimeter droids. On Tatooine they constructed a giant monastery, where they lived for centuries, though they were rarely the only inhabitants; over the years, many bandits and criminals occupied the palace, including Alkhara and Jabba Desilijic Tiure. After Jabba's death in 4 ABY, the monks took their palace back by force, recruiting new members without their consent. They then locked up Jabba's Palace and continued to practice their beliefs for many years.

An Alderaan Biotics operation is established on Borleias. Alderaan Biotics was an Alderaan-based hydroponics company. Their Borleias satellite facility, abandoned before the destruction of Alderaan due to lack of profit, was eventually reactivated by Evir Derricote and later co-opted by the forces of Ysanne Isard prior to the Bacta War. Rogue Squadron would soon recapture the facility. Through the Borleias facility, Alderaan Biotics would go on to become a large manufacturer of rylca.

---

620 BBY

The Antarian Rangers are established. They were a Paramilitary force established to assist the Jedi.

---

610 BBY

Dewlannamapia is born on Kashyyyk. Dewlannamapia, also known by the shortened name Dewlanna, was a female Wookiee who, at an old age, followed her mate Isshaddik in his exile from their homeworld of Kashyyyk. The two joined the crew of Trader's Luck, a starship captained by a Human named Garris Shrike and crewed with children who worked for him as thieves. Even after her mate was killed during a smuggling run, Dewlannamapia remained aboard Trader's Luck, working as a cook. During her days aboard the ship, she met a nine-year-old Corellian boy called Han. Dewlannamapia deeply cared for Han and essentially became a surrogate mother for him. She was responsible for discovering Han's last name, Solo, which Shrike had kept secret. Dewlannamapia oversaw Solo's education, and at one point she even saved him when he nearly died from Corellian Tanamen Fever.

---

600 BBY

The Jedi Knight Allya is exiled to Dathomir and would eventually found the Witches of Dathomir there.

Jabba Desilijic Tiure is born on Nal Hutta.

---

595 BBY

Gandle Ott is colonized by Humans. Gandle Ott was the fourth planet of the Ott system, located in the Kathol sector of the Outer Rim Territories. The terminus of the Trition Trade Route, Gandle Ott was considered to be the farthest major settled world in the sector.

571 BBY

The Clatear and the Nhoras begin a large-scale species-based feud.

550 BBY

The Bandit Alkhara moves into what would eventually become Jabba's Palace. His slaughter of a tribe of Sand people begins the centuries-long Tusken/Human blood feud.

532 BBY

Many Quarren and Mon Calamari are taken as laborers to Lamaredd.

529 BBY

The Atrisian Parliament is formed.

520 BBY

The Ark of Baron Auletphant is collected by the Baobab Archives on Manda. The Ark of Baron Auletphant was a barge of golden color encrusted with rose and azure colored mytag crystals. For over a century, it collected aquatic specimens from across the galaxy. It had been lost for over ten thousand years before it was retrieved in 520 BBY. That same year, it was placed in the Baobab Archives on Manda.

519 BBY

The Kallidahin, later known as the Polis Massans, begin to investigate the remains of the Eellayin civilization on Polis Massa. Polis Massans, were a race of sentient cetaceans native to the world of Kallidah, having obtained their misleading name due to their extensive century-spanning digs on their adopted home in Polis Massa. The Kallidahin lacked facial features and were commonly mute, resorting to signs and telepathy to communicate. Though they had little contact with other species and were considered hermetic, they were known for their extraordinary medical, archaeological and xenobiological skills, and were regarded as compassionate beings who understood the value of life. They were also known for their massive xenobiology database.

516 BBY

Jabba Desilijic Tiure forces the bandit Alkhara out of his own palace.

509 BBY

Yaddle is born. Yaddle, also known as "The One Below", was a renowned Jedi Master, who went on to serve the Jedi High Council for over a century before her death in 26 BBY during a peacekeeping mission to Mawan. A member of the same species as fellow Councilor Yoda, but about half his age, Yaddle trained dozens of Padawans in her time as a Jedi Master, including Oppo Rancisis, who would later join Yaddle on the Jedi Council, and the brash and overconfident Empatojayos Brand. After completing Brand's training, Yaddle did not take another apprentice, as she was almost five hundred years old when Brand passed the Jedi Trials for Knighthood.

500 BBY

The Jedi training vessel Chu'unthor, is built in orbit around the planet Abhean by Republic Fleet Systems.

The Federation of the Double Worlds is founded. The Federation of the Double Worlds (also called Fed-Dub) was the government of Talus and Tralus, the Twin Worlds of the Corellian system. It was independent of the central government on Corellia, and often maintained adversarial relationships with the other planets of the system.

Plagen is discovered. Plagen was a planet in the Expansion Region, on the Enarc Run, with high plateaus covered in lakes and grasslands; its lowlands were dry plains.

491 BBY

A civilization on Jandoon disappears.

490 BBY

The Corporate Sector Authority, a free-enterprise fiefdom of the galaxy, is founded to free the Galactic Senate and corporate moneymakers from each other.

---

470 BBY

Corellia unsuccessfully attempts to withdraw from the Galactic Republic, going so far as to utilize the Contemplanys Hermi clause for the first time in history. Corellia, Selonia and Drall ally in a failed attempt to takeover the Federation of the Double Worlds.

Yinchorr is first charted by the Galactic Republic. Yinchorr was the homeworld of the reptilian Yinchorri species which gradually organized themselves into rival city-states. According to ancient epochs, Tol-Kachorn was the strongest of these, with almost one hundred small communities providing it with resources and five lesser city-states serving as service centres. Several other polities tried to challenge the supremacy of Tol-Kachorn, confrontations that sparked wars of conquest that always ended in the defeat of the contender and the reign of chaos

---

439 BBY

Spore, a genetic construct, is created by Ithorian botanists, who had hoped to merge the DNA of a Vesuvague tree and a bafforr tree with other material to create a sentient plant. Instead, they created a creature which absorbed other minds to expand its thoughts and work its destructive tendencies. The entity used the minds of almost any living creature to augment its own power. It was thought that Spore could control several thousand minds at one time.

---

400 BBY

The elitist Nomad's Retreat in the Nomad Mountains on Corellia expands its membership to become a public resort.

Susevfi is settled by Corporate Sector expatriates. Its history is unknown until the arrival of Nikkos Tyris, an Anzat Dark Jedi and minion of Count Dooku. Tyris established the Jensaarai cult, with himself as first Saarai-kaar, but his death at the hands of Nejaa Halcyon would keep the Jensaarai hidden.

---

392 BBY

Kal'Shebbol is first settled by Twi'lek refugees.

380 BBY

K eiran Halcyon defeats the Afarathu cult.

378 BBY

I krit discovers the Golden Globe within the Palace of the Woolamander on Yavin 4. The Golden Globe resembled a massive, glowing, golden crystal sphere. As with many other dark side devices, it emitted a dark presence in the Force. Though no more than four meters when measured from the outside, its size within was infinite, allowing it to hold a large amount of captives. Within the Golden Globe was a realm filled with sand and dust. The Golden Globe was protected by a powerful energy shield which threw back anyone who attempted to touch it. The only way to break through this field was to weaken it with the Force. The Globe was also haunted by manifestations of the followers of Exar Kun who tried to dissuade visitors from going near the Globe and freeing the captives. The Golden Globe was bound by Sith magic that could only be destroyed by Force-sensitive children. If an adult tried to do so, the Golden Globe would shatter into dust along with the captives. Once inside, the only way to break the Golden Globe was to use the Force to weaken the field from within, allowing the captives to escape and shattering the Globe into sand.

365 BBY

N ear-Human colonists from supernova-threatened Hettitite settle the planet Sernpidal.

350 BBY

T he Trade Federation is created to regulate commerce in the Outer Rim.

The Great Cleansing occurs on Fyodos, devastating the planet.

Attichitcuk is born on Kashyyyk. Attichitcuk, also known as Itchy for short, was an influential male Wookiee Chieftain. He sired two pups, a female named Kallabow and a male named Chewbacca, the latter of whom became a fabled hero of the Rebel Alliance that fought the authoritarian Galactic Empire. A supportive father, Attichitcuk had allowed his only son to leave the household to travel all over the galaxy in search of adventure around the year 150 BBY. In his prime, Attichitcuk played a leading role on his homeworld of Kashyyyk, a planet covered in immense forests. It was he who represented his Wookiee brethren in the Galactic Republic negotiations for colonization rights to Alaris Prime, a moon of the gas giant Alaris. With the help of both his son and the Jedi Master Qui-Gon Jinn, the chieftain drove out invasion forces of the Trade Federation that occupied Alaris Prime illegally.

340 BBY

The Jedi training vessel Chu'unthor crashes on the surface of Dathomir. The ship was quite large: it measured two kilometers long, one kilometer wide, and at least forty meters tall. A command pinnacle in the center of the ship housed the majority of the non-Jedi crew, with the sublight and hyperdrive engine array mounted directly aft. The Chu'unthor could accommodate 10,000 Jedi students, and contained hundreds of exercise and lightsaber-sparring rooms to hone each student's concentration, form, and body. Workshops were provided for the construction and maintenance of lightsabers, while meditation chambers gave students and masters alike a place to contemplate the nature of the Force and further their mental discipline. A medical wing contained hundreds of rooms used to teach Jedi healing arts to young students, both for use in the aftermath of battle or accident and to aid the physically or mentally impaired. The ship contained its own extensive library with texts covering the myriad of Jedi teachings, advanced and theoretical science tomes, historical annals, literature from across the galaxy, and encyclopedias covering the galaxy's languages, art, and culture.

332 BBY

The Sheyfs of Clan Vos begin to rule Kiffu.

322 BBY

The Annoo-dat conquer Annoo (Gelefil). The original Annoo-dat were four-eyed reptiles indigenous to the original planet Annoo.

321 BBY

Ord Cestus becomes a prison planet. The planet's terrain was mainly arid, red desert with many mountain ranges and volcanic craters covering the span of the planet. The planet exported droids and fungi. Over 800 types of medical or edible mushrooms grew on the world. The planet's natural water was fine for the native species, but contained microorganisms that were lethal to offworlders. Kista could help them deal with the organisms, however.

319 BBY

An embezzlement scandal results in twelve Cybot Galactica executives being imprisoned on Ord Cestus.

312 BBY

Berethron e Solo establishes a democratic constitutional monarchy on Corellia, replacing the previous absolute monarchy.

300 BBY

The Techno Union claims Mustafar, recognizing an opportunity to collect rare ores in liquid form.

The Bothan Spynet is established. As an extension of the Bothan Way, the Bothan Spynet was a means to collect intelligence on potential political enemies, which to Bothans, included all individuals, species and governments (particularly the Empire). No other spy network in the galaxy could claim the level and expansion of Bothan Spynet. The Spynet consisted of thousands of spies, informants and data collection droids that fed into a centralized command structure. Using trade, bribery, espionage and observation, the Spynet obtained information from every corner of the galaxy. Despite many other species being active agents of the Bothan Spynet, positions of authority were filled almost exclusively by Bothans.

Myrkr, a forested world, located fairly close to the galaxy's major population centres, is discovered and settled.

Tall aliens called the Ho'Din begin to industrialize and move down from the trees.

The Nozho–Weogar War between the Bith city-states of Nozho and Weogar devastates Clak'dor VII. It originated from a competition between the cities over patent rights to a new hyperdrive that would be sold to other planets. As a Bith tradition, both cities submitted a patent claim to a neutral arbitrator. When the agent representing the city of Nozho found some unfavorable information on the arbitrator, he blackmailed him to choose Nozho as the preference in the decision. The mayor of Weogar received word of this shady deal; he refused to accept the arbitrator's decision and immediately began production on the hyperdrive unit. As a result, Nozho began production on their product as well. This rivalry eventually turned into a war of cutting prices and after a full standard year, Nozho unleashed a chemical weapon on Weogar, killing up to 90 percent of the population. Weogar retaliated with their biological weapons, which subsequently destroyed the ecosystem of Clak'dor VII, leaving it a poisonous and mutating wasteland. Bith were now forced to retreat to sealed cities, and rely on imported goods and machinery to keep their society functioning as the Bith industrial capacity was crippled. The aftermath also resulted in a strong pacifistic streak in Bith culture.

---

297 BBY

The Kian'thar begin developing strong ties with Black Sun. Kian'thar were humanoid nomadic people from Shaum Hii, most notable for their ability to sense emotions. Though they evolved from land-dwelling reptiles, their culture was based around the seas and oceans of Shaum Hii

---

296 BBY

The Tofs conquer the planet Nagi.

---

294 BBY

The star Carosi reaches the point where most of its hydrogen is consumed and begins an unusually rapid expansion into a red giant. Over the next three centuries, the star's expansion would destroy the five innermost planets of its system, including Carosi IV, the Carosite homeworld.

---

292 BBY

Oon Tien, in the Kathol Sector of the Outer Rim Territories, is colonized by the Republic.

---

282 BBY

The Houks colonize Sriluur. The Houk were a people with a reputation for raw strength and short tempers. They were very powerful due to their large bulk of pure muscle. They were among the largest and strongest humanoid sentients, rivaled only by species such as the Wookiees for physical power.

---

275 BBY

The Janguine language goes extinct, along with its users.

---

250 BBY

Human colonists from Salliche colonize Varonat, founding the settlements of Tropis-on-Varonat and Edgefields-on-Varonat.

Gelgelar, a cloud-covered cold swamp planet in the Outer Rim Territories, is colonized.

Adarlon, a planet in the Minos Cluster, is colonized by Alderaanians.

247 BBY

Bosbit Matarcher is born. Bosbit Matarcher was from the planet Delemede. After a relativistic shield malfunction during a brief hyperspace jump aboard a Delemedian starhopper in 212 BBY, found himself nearly two hundred years in the future. The unusual journey brought Matarcher brief fame, netting him a minor HoloNet News interview. However, Matacher was actually delighted at the mishap, when he had left in 212 BBY, Delemede was dilapidated, but by the time of his return in 22 BBY, the planet was flourishing.

232 BBY

The Jedi notice that the Force has begun to "flux", and fear that the dark side is growing again.

Worxer is destroyed when its sun goes supernova.

229 BBY

The Gardaji Rift, in the Outer Rim, is surveyed by the Galactic Republic.

222 BBY

A freighter from Geonosis crashes on Tatooine, leading to the domestication of the Massiffs by the Sand people.

220 BBY

The Academy of Carida is founded. The Academy of Carida was a private, and later state-supported, comprehensive military institution. It formed a triumvirate of elite military institutions along with the academies of Anaxes and Corulag. The institution was known by a variety of names such as Caridan Military Academy, Carida Academy, and Academy at Carida. It was located on the Spinara Plateau. It was considered a fairly prestigious Imperial military academy, and the planet's high gravity was used to train tougher, more resilient Stormtroopers.

The mining city of Tayana on Duro reaches its height.

Drongar is discovered by Nikto scouts. Drongar was a mostly uninhabitable tropical planet in the Outer Rim Territories, with the native airborne spores causing death to those who were not protected from them. The climate was characterized by common monsoons with devastating electrical storms, soaring temperatures, and humidity over 90%. There was also a large atmospheric oxygen content. The planet had two small moons and was located in its system with another three planets. Natural features of Drongar included the Sea of Sponges, Great Jasserak Swamp and the Qarohan Steppes.

219 BBY

Gowix Computers is founded. Gowix Computers was a computer-manufacturing company headquartered on the planet Corellia for much of its history. It was acquired as a subsidiary of the Tagge Company in the years before the Clone Wars, and Gowix became a staunch supporter of the Galactic Republic and later the Galactic Empire, under its new parent company. However, privateer raids sanctioned by the Alliance to Restore the Republic during the Galactic Civil War eventually forced Chief Executive Officer Gohn Danfeil to relocate the company to the planet Corulag.

212 BBY

Starting from his homeworld of Delemede, Bosbit Matarcher unintentionally time travels 190 years into the future, due to faulty relativistic shielding on his ship.

206 BBY

Oppo Rancisis is born on Thisspias. Oppo Rancisis, an adept strategist and tactician, was a Thisspiasian male who abdicated the throne of his homeworld in favor of becoming a Jedi Master. Offered to the Jedi Order as an infant by his mother, the Blood Monarch of Thisspias, Rancisis was apprenticed to Master Yaddle, training to become a Jedi Knight almost two centuries before the Battle of Yavin. In 186 BBY, Rancisis' sister was killed by terrorists, and he was offered the throne; he declined, instead preferring to continue on the path of the Jedi.

Quagga is born on Kashyyyk. Quagga was a Wookiee and former slave to an Imperial engineer. The engineer eventually bought Quagga's freedom, and the Wookiee set up a repair shop in the outskirts of Tatooine's Anchorhead. However, his methods were expensive, his location remote, and the local Jawas were fierce competition. With his business failing, Quagga resolved to enter Jabba the Hutt's demolition contests using a fully refurbished AAT in hope of securing a large enough fortune to set up shop in the center of Mos Eisley.

200 BBY

A Wookiee named Chewbacca is born on Kashyyyk.

The Jedi Order feels that the dark side of the Force is growing strong again.

The star Carosi destroys the innermost five planets in the Carosus system.

Yperio Baobab creates Bab-Prime, precursor to Bab-Neo and modern-day droidspeak.

Memory wipes become common droid maintenance following a personality virus unleashed by a member of the Baobab Merchant Fleet.

Competing scouts dispatched by Tor-Ro-Bo Industries and Eeook Mining and Reclamation simultaneously discover 244Core. The rival companies both claim the planet as their own.

195 BBY

Glova, a semi-tropical planet in the Glova system, is colonized.

194 BBY

Birth of the Bab-Prime language.

192 BBY

Recycling bacteria in a manner that revolutionizes waste management develops on Coruscant.

190 BBY

The natives of Fere are wiped out by a plague.

Vima-Da-Boda is born. Vima Da-Boda was the great-great-great-granddaughter of Vima Sunrider, daughter of legendary Jedi Master of ancient times Nomi Sunrider, and served the Force for over a century.

189 BBY

Vortex joins the Galactic Republic. Vortex was known for its violent weather, particularly sharp winds, which was caused by an abnormal tilt in the planet's axis. During the winter months, vast polar ice caps formed almost instantaneously by the freezing gases in the planet's atmosphere. The sudden change in air pressure made huge currents, which swept across the entire planet.

188 BBY

Kibh Jeen falls to the dark side of the Force.

Almas Academy is founded on Almas by the Jedi. The Almas Academy was an unorthodox Jedi training facility that was headed by the Almas Council. The academy was an experimental one. They accepted older students, a tradition which began with the local Tarasin. Eventually they accepted adults to begin training as Jedi, although those they accepted were carefully screened. The Almas Academy could never accept an applicant that had already been rejected by another praxeum. The Academy was kept under scrutiny of the Jedi Council on Coruscant because of this experiment. The Council yearly sanctioned Almas students, occasionally sent Jedi Knights to teach in Almas, and particularly kept an eye on the potentially dangerous situation of the Fortress. Ziveri, on his part, believed that the best place to study the dark side is near it, and so the nearby Fortress was a boon, not a hindrance. As the Cularin system was quite isolated, the Academy attracted some Jedi who thrived in meditation and introspection.

Jedi Master Qornah dies on Almas. A Force-sensitive raised in the ways of the Force, Qornah lived during the centuries of peace that marked the Republic's Golden Age. Trained by the Jedi Order and achieving the rank of Jedi Master, Qornah was responsible for crafting a famous holocron.

161 BBY

The Tarasin Revolt begins on Cularin. The Revolt began when the Tarasin tried to prevent certain off-world companies from entering the jungles to harvest rare trees, especially the ch'hala tree, which was sacred to the Tarasin. Violence erupted from this confrontation, and the situation escalated after that. Other reasons included the quick expansions of the twin urban cities Gadrin and Hedrett towards the surrounding jungle, which led to a deforestation the Tarasin were unable to accept. The companies hired armed guards, and eventually the Trade Federation sent in war droids to protect their assets on-planet. Eventually, the Tarasin wanted to remove all aliens from their world and launched a series of counter-attacks, using off-world weaponry and their own natural Force talent. Even after this use of the Force, the Jedi refused to take part in the conflict. However, the Federation droids took an aggressive stance and raided a Tarasin settlement (or "irstat"), killing a number of Tarasin. During the war, some Tarasins scouted and hid in the underground Ishkik caverns, storing military equipment. After years of not getting involved in the conflict, two Jedi from the Almas Academy came to Cularin to negotiate peace. The fighting continued, but after half a year, the negotiations proved successful, the Cularin Compact was drafted and the fighting came to an end. With that treaty, the Tarasin and their culture were recognized certain rights, and the off-worlds companies were forced to protect the ecology of Cularin whenever trying to harvest resources.

160 BBY

Orn Belden, future Bakuran senator, is born.

157 BBY

Chalmun is born on Kashyyyk. Chalmun was a male Wookiee proprietor of the most popular spacer's bar in Mos Eisley, Tatooine, the eponymous Chalmun's cantina. A distant relative of Chewbacca, he was a large tan-and-gray Wookiee, with a scar running from his left shoulder across the left side of his chest. This was a remnant of his days as a street thug.

155 BBY

Tojjevvuk dies after fighting Chewbacca on Kashyyyk.

154 BBY

The Tarasin Revolt on Cularin ends with the Cularin Compact.

150 BBY

The Bakur Mining Corporation under Arden colonizes Bakura, a rich, green and blue planet in the Bakura system of the Shiritoku Spur, located on the isolated edge of the Outer Rim, formally a part of Wild Space.

A coalition of corporations on Corellia overthrows its ruling constitutional monarchy, installing the office of Diktat to better steward business interests in the sector.

147 BBY

Incom Corporation and Subpro Corporation enter into a partnership.

145 BBY

Brath Qella is discovered by the Galactic Republic's Third General Survey. Brath Qella was the homeworld to the Qella and their predecessors, the Ahra Naffi. It was located five days from N'zoth and eight days from Coruscant with a standard hyperdrive. A thick atmosphere gave the planet a hazy, gray appearance from space. It was orbited by two natural satellites and positioned close to the system's asteroid belt.

142 BBY

The planet of Belasco begins a war with a neighboring planet.

140 BBY

Brath Qella enters a deep ice age.

132 BBY

The Republic first makes contact with the Elomin, horned humanoids from Elom who lived on the surface of the planet while another sentient species, the Elom, lived underground.

130 BBY

The Potentium first appears amongst younger members of the Jedi Order. The Potentium was the name of a sect of beings who had a particular way of viewing the Force used instead of the term "The Force."

128 BBY

Eppie Belden is born on Bakura. Eppie Belden, maiden name Eppie Antruse was a Human female member of the Antruse family, and was presumably one of the original Bakur Mining Corporation settlers of Bakura until she joined the Rebel Alliance during the Galactic Civil War.

---

124 BBY

The Senate approves two significant and related pieces of legislation. One declares the Outer Rim Territories a free-trade zone exempt from taxation, and the other extends the definition of functional constituencies entitled to representation in the Senate to guilds and corporations.

The Treaty of Trammis is orchestrated by Jedi Master Omo Bouri.

---

121 BBY

The armed conflict between the Human settlers and the Gungan natives of Naboo comes to an end.

---

120 BBY

Ugloste is born on Gentes.

---

119 BBY

The Galactic Republic discovers the planet Orax. Orax became known for its wondrous mineral formations. With the rise of the Galactic Empire, many Shard ambassadors operating off world were murdered, and their homeworld became a mining center using slave labor. Further, many Shard colonies were destroyed.

---

118 BBY

A war between Garos IV and Sundari ends with a treaty.

---

112 BBY

The 3PO-series protocol droid line begins production by Cybot Galactica. Manufactured by Cybot Galactica on the factory world of Affa, the 3PO-series protocol units were considered the most advanced Human-cyborg relations droids in the market for over a hundred years.

110 BBY

Batorine, a forested homeworld of the Blood Carver species, joins the Galactic Republic.

105 BBY

Durga the Hutt is born on Nal Hutta. Durga Besadii Tai, later calling himself "His Great Obesity; the Lord Durga", was a Hutt and the successor of Aruk as head of the Besadii kajidic. Durga served as a Vigo in the criminal organization Black Sun for a time, but after the death of the Underlord Xizor, he set out on his own. The ambitious Hutt created a plot to bring down the New Republic, using a superweapon called the Darksaber, a scaled-down version of the Death Star battlestation. However, his plan failed, thanks to the incompetence of his workers, the Taurill, and the efforts of New Republic General Crix Madine. The Darksaber was destroyed and Durga was killed, ending his short-lived rebellion.

102 BBY

Count Dooku is born to an aristocratic family on Serenno. He is discovered by the Jedi, and begins his training in infancy.

Lorian Nod is born. Lorian Nod was a male Human Jedi serving the the Jedi Order and the Galactic Republic as a member of the Agricultural Corps following his expulsion from the Coruscant Jedi Temple's academy in the decades preceding the Clone Wars. Nod eventually turned away from the Order to become a pirate on the Outer Rim of the galaxy before achieving elected office on the planet Junction V.

The Aqualish colonize Andosha II and the other Andoan Free Colonies. The Aqualish were tusked bipeds from the planet Ando whose appearance combined aspects of arachnids and pinniped aquatic mammals. Aqualish had a reputation for being nasty, crude and aggressive, and generally pursued off-world careers as mercenaries, bounty hunters, and pirates. One of the most infamous such Aqualish was the smuggler Ponda Baba.

100 BBY

The Dowager Queen crashes on Tatooine, which is subsequently colonized by miners and farmers. At the time of the Dowager's arrival at Tatooine, Mos Espa was small enough that the crew didn't notice it, and assuming that the planet was uninhabited they attempted to land, where a sandstorm wreaked havoc on the power, display, and guidance systems on the Queen, causing it to crash. Captain Lis Kaslan and the other survivors—the original "colonists"—built their first city, Eisley, out of the wreckage, while others who left went to found Bestine Settlement. The original inhabitants of Tatooine later renamed the city "Mos Eisley" to coincide with Mos Espa. The city of Mos Eisley grew up around the wreck. As buildings were constructed, the ship remained in its place, standing nearly vertically in the sand. It was later made into a first-class hotel, because of both its novelty and location at the intersection of Dune Street and Inner Curved Street. The hotel became popular during conventions and trade shows that came to Tatooine.

Fort Tusken is founded on Tatooine. Fort Tusken was the first settlement established in the northern sector of the temperate zone of Tatooine. The settlement was quite successful during its first two years because its extensive moisture vaporator array pulled enough water vapor from the atmosphere to allow the growing of healthy and bountiful crops. However, Sand people began attacking during the fort's third growing season, destroying several crucial pieces of farm equipment. Although the equipment was repaired, the harsh conditions and continued attacks caused the fort to be abandoned in 95 BBY. This incident resulted in the term "Tusken Raiders," which thereafter was synonymous with Sand People. Fort Tusken was briefly resettled by mercenaries and moisture farmers during the height of the Galactic Civil War, but a union of different clans of Tusken Raiders were able to recapture the fort. At some point during the war, some spacer artists briefly visited the ruins of Fort Tusken in order to paint up a panorama of the area across Tatooine, guided by various columns near certain landmarks.

The corporate wing of the Bakur Memorial Building is built on Bakura. The Bakur Memorial Building, also known as the Bakur Complex, served as the center of government on Bakura. Located slightly southwest of the center of the capital city of Salis D'aar, the truncated, wedge-shaped building overlooked Statuary Park at the city's center. It was first the headquarters of the Bakur Mining Corporation, before becoming the location of the Bakuran Senate.

Eixes Valorum is Supreme Chancellor. Eixes Valorum was a member of the Valorum family of Coruscant. His Chancellorship was first proposed at one of the annual elite gatherings on the Sojourn moon hosted by Caar Damask, and was known for a sense of style not seen again until the chancellorship of Thoris Darus.He was the last Supreme Chancellor to give a State of the Republic address prior to Palpatine.

Dreadnaught-class heavy cruisers vessels are first deployed. The Dreadnaught-class heavy cruiser, or simply the Dreadnaught, was a type of capital ship built for planetary occupation and space combat used by the Galactic Republic, Galactic Empire, New Republic, local governments, and various other organizations. It was one of the most ubiquitous ship designs in all of the galaxy. The keel of the Dreadnaught-class ran nearly 600 meters with the bow overlapping to produce a clamshell-like appearance. Each vessel had a cluster of weapons blisters spread across the hull. The ship was designated a heavy cruiser in standard classification and was considered a downscaled warship when compared to the ship-designs from the Core. The forward ventral portion of the Dreadnaught-class was used as a massive cargo hold, with a docking port located at the bow of the ship. Additional cargo holds were situated towards the center of the ship, in front of the areas housing the main reactor and secondary power generators. Docking ports were also located on either side of the ship. Weapon systems included twenty quad laser cannons (six bow, seven port, seven starboard), ten laser cannons (five port, five starboard and mounted in blisters), and ten turbolaser batteries (five bow, five stern). Some ships were later customized to feature a warhead launcher for anti-starfighter defense. Deflector shield projectors were also located inside some of the blisters flanking the hull, and the primary and secondary sensor transceivers were located towards the stern of the vessel, on the dorsal and ventral sides, similar to those on CR90 corvettes. While technologically advanced at the time of its construction, the Dreadnaught-class lacked in sublight and hyperspace speeds (a Class 4 rating), suffered computer failures, and could not compete with comparable designs in terms of firepower and shielding. Between three and five Dreadnaught-class cruisers could outgun one Imperial-class Star Destroyer. In addition to the technical drawbacks, Dreadnaught-class ships also required over 16,000 crewmembers to run at optimal performance, perhaps the highest crew per keel meter ratio of any modern starship. This high crew requirement put strains on recruitment efforts and turned supplying a Dreadnaught into a logistical nightmare. In comparison, slave-rigged Dreadnaughts reduced the complement requirements down to 2,200 crewmembers. The initial design was not focused towards carrier duty, but as the ships were upgraded and refitted, the center cargo holds were converted to hangar space, and a common complement of 12 TIE starfighters was added to the vessel. Unlike many contemporary warship designs, the Dreadnaught-class did not have an easily visible bridge section, opting to shelter the command decks and crew stations inside the main armored superstructure. These areas were located on the dorsal side of the bow.

The Prophets of the Dark Side colonize Kalakar Six from Dromund Kaas. The Prophets of the Dark Side, also called the Secret Order of the Emperor was an ancient dark side cult that arose on the planet Dromund Kaas in the Dromund system of the Outer Rim, a world once the capital of the Sith Empire. They were founded by a renegade Dark Lord of the Sith, Darth Millennial, and hence can be considered a splinter-faction of the Order of the Sith Lords. The Prophets were trained in the use of the dark side of the Force and used its power to delve into the possible future outcomes of any event. During the time of the Galactic Empire, they were led by Kadann, the Supreme Prophet. The prophets were all black-bearded individuals who wore gleaming black robes, and who obtained a great deal of power within the remnants of the Empire after the death of Palpatine. Among their many predictions, the Prophets supposedly foresaw the precise time and place for the destruction of both Death Stars by the Rebel Alliance. In order to retain their power, the Prophets used any means necessary to ensure the predicted outcome. When the group became part of the Secret Order of the Empire, the term became interchangeable with the title Emperor's Mage, used for a true Prophet of the Dark Side after they were recruited by Palpatine to serve him. The true Prophets should not be confused with their imitators, the false Prophets, who collectively comprised the Church of the Dark Side.

An unnamed Mandalore is assassinated by the bounty hunter Durge and a group of rogue Jedi Knights.

99 BBY

Survivors of the crash of the Dowager Queen found Bestine Settlement.

98 BBY

The first attacks by Tatooine's Sand people occur at Fort Tusken, lasting three years.

97 BBY

Droid Uprising occurs on Bakura.

Droid Uprising occurs on Tatooine.

Orn Belden and Eppie Antruse are married. A member of the Belden family, Orn was one of the original Bakur Mining Corporation settlers of Bakura. He was described as being tall in terms of both height and courage. He married Eppie Antruse in 97 BBY, the same year as the droid uprising on Bakura. Sometime afterward, they had their only child, Roviden. Along with his wife and son, Orn sympathized with the Rebel Alliance during the Galactic Civil War, but unlike them, he took no steps to help them. Thus, when the Galactic Empire occupied Bakura in 1 ABY, his son was executed and his wife slated to be so; however, he convinced Governor Wilek Nereus to save her life by giving up his voice box. Nereus still punished Eppie, however, by inserting a senility-creating parasite into her brain.

96 BBY

On Lwhekk, the Shreeftut seizes power over the Government and holdings, known as the Ssi-ruuvi Imperium, after years of internal fighting between his political allies and the factions that supported the previous ruler.

Danoor is colonized by scientists studying in the Kathol Rift.

95 BBY

Fort Tusken on Tatooine is abandoned after three years of Sand people attacks.

94 BBY

Famine on Telos IV.

The Twenty-First Battle of Zehava on Melida/Daan. It was one of the many struggles of the Melida/Daan Civil War on the planet of Melida/Daan and centered over control of the city of Zehava. In the battle, the Melida tried to recapture the city of Zehava that was captured by the Daan during one of the previous battles. During the battle, Captain Quintama was killed. It is possible that the Daan won that battle, because Pinani, the widow of Quintama, later participated in a raid on the city of Bin to avenge the Battle of Zehava.

---

93 BBY

A second group of colonists found Motesta and re-establish Anchorhead on Tatooine.

92 BBY

Qui-Gon Jinn is born on an unknown planet. He is discovered by the Jedi, and begins his training in infancy. He was later the Padawan to Count Dooku, and the mentor to Obi-Wan Kenobi and briefly Anakin Skywalker. Jinn often placed himself in conflict with the Jedi High Council. He was deeply attuned to the Living Force, which contributed to him frequently taking side trips to help seemingly weak and useless life-forms. Despite his opposition to the council, he was regarded by many Jedi as sharp-witted and possessing great wisdom. Jinn served the Galactic Republic and the Jedi Order his entire life, participating in the Stark Hyperspace War and actions against the Nebula Front, most famously during the Invasion of Naboo. It was Jinn who discovered the Chosen One, Anakin Skywalker, on Tatooine during this crisis and was largely responsible for championing his training. Even after his death at the hands of Darth Maul, he played a vital role in the legacy of the Jedi Order.

---

91 BBY

Finis Valorum was born on a planet in the Lytton sector. Valorum came from an ancient and distinguished family. He was later senator of the Lytton sector, a member of the Core faction of senators and Chancellor Kalpana's administration, and had been involved with negotiations to end the Stark Hyperspace War.

---

90 BBY

Coveway, a planet in the Koradin Sector, is colonized.

---

89 BBY

Dooku is apprenticed to Jedi Master Thame Cerulian. He later fell to the dark side of the Force and became a Dark Lord of the Sith, known as Darth Tyranus. Born into a noble family on the planet Serenno, he was the heir to vast wealth and the noble title of Count. Dooku was taken by the Jedi Order as a child and apprenticed to Thame Cerulian. As a Jedi Knight, he took Qui-Gon Jinn as his first Padawan, and later trained Komari Vosa. Dooku was a respected instructor in the Jedi Temple and one of the most renowned swordsmen in the galaxy, on par only with Masters Yoda and Mace Windu.

Followers of the discredited Jedi Potentium sect settle on Zonama Sekot.

Entrepeneurs intending to use ramjet mining ships to gather valuable gases from the Cauldron Nebula establish a settlement on Eol Sha, the only inhabitable world close enough to support the venture.

Lorian Nod is expelled from the Jedi Order after Nod and Dooku, eager to learn about the Jedi Master, discovered several documents and journals, including one which contained information drawn from a Sith holocron that was stored in the Holocron Vaults of the Temple Archives. Fascinated by the device, Nod attempted to convince Dooku to help in gain access to the device. Citing the regulations of the Archives and the Vaults, Dooku refused his friend and chastised him for broaching the subject. Undeterred, Nod slipped into the Vaults and stole the Dark Holocron in secret, accessing its hidden knowledge within his own chambers. Sickened by the dark side of the Force which was imbued in the holocron, Nod came to Dooku for help. As Dooku scolded his friend for stealing the ancient artifact, Jedi Councilor Oppo Rancisis was drawn to the darkness emanating from the room and confiscated the holocron. In the following days, the Council placed the two former friends on opposing teams during a group exercise through Coruscant. The teams, tasked with obtaining a muja fruit from the Old Galactic Market in the Senate District, eventually crossed paths and Dooku and Nod engaged in a fight. Upon returning to the Temple, the Council called the pair to a meeting, during which Dooku, who was infuriated with his friend's betrayal, explained that Nod was the only one to seek out the holocron and he alone bore the guilt. With this knowledge, the High Council deemed Nod unfit to continue along the Jedi Path at the Temple not for stealing the holocron, but for lying and implicating a friend. Following the High Council's decision, the Council of Reassignment placed Nod in the Agricultural Corps, a division of the Order's Service Corps, where the failed Jedi would stay for the next thirteen years. Eventually, Nod abandoned his post with the Service Corps and became the leader of a band of space raiders along the Outer Rim.

---

88 BBY

The Dark Woman, amysterious yet respected Master of the Jedi Order during the Clone Wars, takes Ki-Adi-Mundi to Coruscant for Jedi training.

Plett builds the city of Plett's Well between the cliffs of red-black rock on Belsavis.

---

87 BBY

Civil war breaks out between Garos IV and Sundari over the destruction of a Garosian grain-processing factory.

Tem Chesko is born.

86 BBY

Locus Geen, future General in the Army of the Republic, is born. He later became an informant for the Rebel Alliance. Around 0 ABY he established himself in the upper echelons of society on the planet Salliche and passed along sensitive information to the Rebels.

85 BBY

Mos Eisley, a large spaceport town, is founded around the wreck of the Dowager Queen.

83 BBY

Mos Espa is founded on Tatooine. It was the home of Anakin and Shmi Skywalker and also held the famous Mos Espa Grand Arena, at which the annual Boonta Eve Classic podrace was held, and the location of Watto's shop.

The Galactic Games are instituted. The Galactic Games became a galaxy-wide sporting event that occurred on a different planet every seven years. Planets all over the galaxy competed to host the Games. It included a number of different events with the fastest and skilled competing in races and contests, all of them exciting and dangerous, where betting on them was illegal. The Galactic Games Council organized the events with help from the Ruling Power, Euceron's governing body. During the games a representative from each planet played with each team playing against the other in 20 events. Those teams were Team Coruscant, Team Fondor, Team Fwillsving, Team Kinyen, Team Kothlis, Team Kubindi, Team Ord Mantell, Team Ralltiir, Team Tralus, and Team Yag'Dhul. During the reign of the Galactic Empire, the games were called the Imperial Games. An assassination attempt on Emperor Palpatine occurred when the Games were held on Coruscant.

82 BBY

Dooku passes the trials and is made a Jedi Knight.

Darth Sidious (Palpatine) is born on Naboo. He became Force-sensitive and would later serve as the last Supreme Chancellor of the Galactic Republic and the first Emperor of the Galactic Empire. A Dark Lord of the Sith in the Order of the Sith Lords, recorded by history as the most powerful who had ever lived, his entire life was the culmination of a thousand-year plan to overthrow the Republic and the Jedi Order from within.

Yoda takes Ki-Adi-Mundi as his Padawan learner. After he would serve on the High Council in the twilight years of the Galactic Republic and played a major role in several battles during the Clone Wars..Mundi was discovered at age four by the Jedi An'ya Kuro and became one of the few permitted by the Jedi Order to be trained starting beyond infancy. After more than two decades as a Padawan to Master Yoda, Mundi was named a Jedi Knight and returned to Cerea to liberate his home village from a gang of raiders. Assigned the Jedi Watchman of the Cerean sector, Mundi was granted a rare exception to the Jedi Order's ban on marriage due to his species' low birth rate and had a polygamous family of five wives and seven children, although he tried to avoid developing emotional attachments to them.

Cliegg Lars is born on Tatooine. The widower of Shmi Skywalker, He was the son of Gredda and Lef Lars and the elder brother of Edern Lars and would later become the step-grandfather of Luke Skywalker and Leia Organa, the stepfather of Anakin Skywalker, and the father of Owen Lars.

78 BBY

Rostek Horn is born on Corellia and was the step-grandfather of Corran Horn. Although Corran grew up thinking Rostek was his biological grandfather, he found out as an adult that Rostek was a friend of his real grandfather, Nejaa Halcyon. The two became partners in 32 BBY, and last saw each other when Nejaa was called away in 22 BBY.

Scerra is born on Corellia.

77 BBY

The Second Galactic Games are held.

Dooku, along with his apprentice Qui-Gon Jinn, is reunited with Lorian Nod, who is now the leader of a band of space pirates.

Ruwee Naberrie is born on Naboo. He was the son of Winama Naberrie, the husband of Jobal Naberrie, and the father of Sola Naberrie and Padmé Amidala. He was also the maternal grandfather of Ryoo and Pooja Naberrie, as well as twins Luke Skywalker and Leia Organa Solo.

Senator Blix Annon dies of a heart attack. He served as a Senator in the Galactic Republic Senate during the final decades of the institution. The subject of a secret Sith plot to replace him in the Senate with Eero Iridian, Annon died of a heart attack while being held for ransom by Lorian Nod.

76 BBY

Ronhar Kim is born on Naboo. He became a General in the Grand Army of the Republic during the Clone Wars. He was eventually betrayed by his close friend, Supreme Chancellor Palpatine, which led to his death.

132

75 BBY

Longwind is colonized by criminals released from Galactic Republic prisons.

Drewwa, the third moon of Almania, is colonized. It would become a heavily industrialized moon with companies from across the galaxy holding offices there, including Tendrando Arms, Trang Robotics, and Lyster Innovations.

74 BBY

Last civil war in Masterhome ends, being replaced by a harmless tradition.

73 BBY

The planet Kegan begins a period of isolation. Kegan was a planet located in the Outer Rim Territories. The planet was run by the Benevolent Guides, who isolated the planet from the rest of the galaxy after having visions of the destruction of Kegan.

72 BBY

Mace Windu is born on Haruun Kal. Mace Windu became Jedi Master of legendary status who was the Master of the Order in the days leading up to the Battle of Geonosis, after which he gave the title to Grand Master Yoda. Hailing from the world of Haruun Kal, Mace Windu served as one of the last members of the Jedi High Council before the Great Jedi Purge. Serving on the Council, Windu was often regarded as second only to the Grand Master Yoda, though Windu was eight centuries Yoda's junior. Windu's wisdom and power were considered legendary by many, as were the weight of his words.

Shmi Skywalker, mother of Anakin, is born on an unknown planet.

71 BBY

The Grand ChikatLik, the first prison built on the planet Ord Cestus, is converted into a hotel.

70 BBY

The Kira Run is founded, connecting the Lazerian system to the Ropagi system.

The space station Tatoo III is destroyed over Tatooine. It was built by the settlers of Tatooine, from metals and ores they were able to eke out of the desert. It was destroyed shortly after completion when the Obvious Nirvana suddenly rushed at the station during docking and collided with it. An investigation was launched, and it was discovered that the native Tatooinian metals used to construct the station had unusual magnetic properties. Thus, when the Obvious Nirvana approached it, Tatoo III suddenly became a huge magnet. This change in polarity drew the Obvious Nirvana into the station.

This one setback marked the beginning of the hardest years Tatooine had ever seen. Finding it too expensive to counteract this, the planet was abandoned as a mining colony. The original colonists remained, but Tatooine's prosperity came to an end

Jorus C'baoth is born on Bortras. C'baoth was a male Human from the planet of Bortras who served in the Jedi Order during the final decades of the Republic Classic era. Like fellow Jedi Master Dooku, C'baoth was arrogantly sure of his own skills and talents, believed himself to be a peerless warrior and philosopher, and viewed non-Force sensitives as inferior. A controversial figure among his own peers, C'baoth was regarded as the epitome of a Jedi Master by some, while others were distrustful of him. During his exemplary, if unorthodox, career, C'baoth settled a number of conflicts. He notably participated in the demobilization of Ando, defeated a band of Dark Jedi in the Elrood sector, put an end to the Ascendancy Contention of Alderaan, and helped his colleague Tra's M'ins mediate the Duinuogwuin-Gotal conflict. Above all that, he also found time to train a Padawan, the young Human female Lorana Jinzler.

69 BBY

Bail Organa of Alderaan is born. Bail Prestor Organa (formally styled as His Serene Highness, Prince Bail Organa, First Chairman and Viceroy of Alderaan) was a Human male who served as the First Chairman and Viceroy of Alderaan, and served in the Galactic Senate as the Senator of the Alderaan sector from 32 BBY to 19 BBY. Subsequently, he was Senator of the Alderaan sector of the Imperial Senate from 19 BBY to 1 BBY. He was Princess Leia Organa's adoptive father and a friend of Jedi Masters Obi-Wan Kenobi, Yoda and Rahm Kota. He was married to Queen Breha Organa of Alderaan and was, as Prince Consort, head of the royal house and ruler of Alderaan. One of the main founders of the Rebel Alliance, he was killed when the Death Star obliterated Alderaan. In the Alliance and its successor states, the New Republic and Galactic Federation of Free Alliances, he was respected as a martyr who died for his cause.

The ruins of Wiyentaah are discovered on Polis Massa. Wiyentah was one of the underground dwellings of the Eellayin on Polis Massa. It became known as the Local Dig when the Kallidahins uncovered the city's ruins.

The Third Galactic Games are held.

Clat'Ha is born. Clat'Ha was a Human female who worked as the chief operations manager for Arcona Mineral Harvest Corporation. She also had a deep rivalry with Jemba the Hutt and was a close friend to the Arcona miner Si Treemba. She was one of the first of the miners to befriend Obi-Wan Kenobi after his fight with Grelb the Hutt. She once saved Qui-Gon Jinn's life during a pirate attack on the transport they were traveling on, the Monument. A Togorian pirate captain was about to kill Qui-Gon, and failed to notice the presence of Clat'Ha, who shot him in the head. Along with Qui-Gon and Obi-Wan Kenobi, she later helped defend a cave in which crew and passengers of the Monument were hiding from draigons, after the Monument crash-landed on an Unidentified blue marble planet near Bandomeer.

68 BBY

Nejaa Halcyon is taken as a Padawan learner. Halcyon was a Human male who became a Corellian Jedi Master who served the Jedi Order and the Galactic Republic as a General in the Grand Army of the Republic during the Clone Wars. Unbeknownst to the Jedi High Council, Master Halcyon was married to a Corellian woman and was the biological father of Valin Halcyon. During his service to the Order, he befriended the Caamasi Jedi Ylenic It'kla, who remembered him as Spicewood in his memnii.

67 BBY

Ki-Adi-Mundi completes his Jedi training. He would eventually become a Cerean Jedi Master of the Jedi Order who served on the High Council in the twilight years of the Galactic Republic and played a major role in several battles during the Clone Wars. Born in 92 BBY, Mundi was discovered at age four by the Jedi An'ya Kuro and became one of the few permitted by the Jedi Order to be trained starting beyond infancy. After more than two decades as a Padawan to Master Yoda, Mundi was named a Jedi Knight and returned to Cerea to liberate his home village from a gang of raiders. Assigned the Jedi Watchman of the Cerean sector, Mundi was granted a rare exception to the Jedi Order's ban on marriage due to his species' low birth rate and had a polygamous family of five wives and seven children, although he tried to avoid developing emotional attachments to them.

Essara Till is born. Essara Till was a Human female pilot in the Naboo Royal Space Fighter Corps. In 49 BBY, on the eve of her nineteenth birthday, she had left Naboo to see the galaxy, eventually gaining work as a mercenary on such worlds as Agamar. Growing disillusioned with the corruption that pervaded the galaxy, she quit her job for the Garqi Agricultural Combine in 35 BBY and returned home, becoming leader of Bravo Squadron and, a year later, the lover of Dren Melne. She also served as flight instructor for Bravo Flight, Echo Flight, and Delta Flight. Two years later, Melne was killed during a pirate raid on Station TFP-9 that he had helped coordinate and the following year Till became Rhys Dallows's superior in the Bravo Squadron mission to protect Queen Padmé Amidala during a rendezvous with the Trade Federation. She was killed by a mercenary hired by the Trade Federation.

Darth Plagueis kills his master Darth Tenebrous and becomes the sole Dark Lord of the Sith.

66 BBY

Jango Fett is born on Concord Dawn. He was a renowned Mandalorian bounty hunter, assassin, mercenary, and the "father" of Boba Fett, a genetic clone of his, whom he raised as a son. A Human from Concord Dawn, Fett was adopted by Mandalorian warriors following the murder of his parents and the disappearance of his older sister Arla in 58 BBY. Years later, he would go on to lead them through much of the Mandalorian Civil War as Mandalore. After being imprisoned by Jedi, Fett was responsible for destroying the Death Watch, a Mandalorian group who killed Fett's mentor, Jaster Mereel. Following the conclusion of that conflict, Fett became a bounty hunter, quickly establishing a reputation as being one of the best in the galaxy. Later on, Fett agreed to serve as the genetic template for the clones that would form the bulk of the Grand Army of the Republic during the Clone Wars. When Master Obi-Wan Kenobi located Jango and Boba on Kamino, Fett fled to join Count Dooku. Though struck down by Mace Windu in combat, Fett's legacy would live on through his son Boba, as well as his cloned brethren, who would have a profound impact on galactic history.

Radiant VII is built and launched over Corellia. The Radiant VII was one of many Consular-class space cruisers that were used by the Galactic Republic to provide transport to the government's diplomats.

Dooku and Qui-Gon Jinn embark on their last mission as Master and Padawan.

Shmi Skywalker is sold into slavery.

Dorja is born on Coruscant. Captain Dorja of the Imperial Navy was a career military officer who commanded the Imperial I-class Star Destroyer Relentless in the fleet of the Galactic Empire and later the Imperial Remnant. A Human male, Dorja embraced the tenets of Emperor Palpatine's New Order and took command of the Relentless prior to 4 ABY, during the Galactic Civil War between the Empire and the Rebel Alliance. He was known for a cautious command style that saw his ship suffer no casualties, and he held his Star Destroyer back from the main combat lines at 4 ABY's Battle of Endor, an engagement with the Rebels that saw the Emperor killed and the Empire splinter into warlordism. Over the next five years, as Imperial Space was greatly diminished by the Alliance's successor state, the New Republic, Dorja plotted to seize control of the fleet from Captain Gilad Pellaeon. His plans were foiled, however, when the tactically gifted Grand Admiral Thrawn returned from the Unknown Regions in 9 ABY and was given control of the Empire. Dorja and the Relentless were put in command of the navy's secondary force, and Dorja saw his exclusion from the Grand Admiral's primary armada as a personal slight against himself.

65 BBY

The Hutts take control of Tatooine, seeing it as a useful point for transferring smuggled goods between the Corellian Run and the Triellus Trade Route.

The Dark Jedi Maw is born. Maw was a Boltrunian male Jedi Shadow who fell to the dark side of the Force and joined Inquisitor Jerec's cadre of Dark Jedi, assisting him in his search for the fabled Valley of the Jedi, which Jerec hoped to use to help rebuild the Galactic Empire. In 5 ABY, in an effort to learn about the location of the Valley, Jerec attempted to capture the Jedi Master Qu Rahn on the planet Dorlo. Maw and fellow Dark Jedi Sariss and Yun were assigned to capture Rahn on the surface of the planet, but failed their mission. Although Rahn escaped from the planet aboard a CR90 corvette, the ship was captured in the tractor beam of Jerec's personal Super Star Destroyer, the Vengeance. Aboard the Vengeance, Jerec ripped the information he needed from Rahn's mind, but immediately afterward, the Jedi stole Yun's lightsaber and attacked Jerec's darksiders. Before Rahn was killed by Jerec, Maw's legs were severed from his body by the Jedi Master. Maw survived and replaced his legs with a repulsorlift carriage, but eventually mastered the art of Force flight and appropriated the Trispzest form of lightsaber combat. Due to his injury, he also came to be known as the Half-Man. Eventually, Jerec located the Valley of the Jedi on the planet Ruusan, and his forces occupied the planet. However, Jerec was tracked down by an aspiring Jedi, Kyle Katarn, who tried to stop the Dark Jedi. Maw confronted Katarn on a landing pad near the cargo freighter Sulon Star and was defeated. Immobilized and defenseless, he taunted Katarn with remarks of his father's death, trying to goad him into the dark side. Katarn succumbed to his anger and murdered Maw, but was ultimately able to resist his dark thoughts and remained with the light.

Palpatine becomes Plagueis's apprentice, becoming Darth Sidious.

---

64 BBY

Qui-Gon Jinn passes the Trials and becomes a Jedi Knight.

Tahl passes the Trials and becomes a Jedi Knight.

The H'kig arrive on Rishi. The H'kig was a religious sect based on the teachings of H'kig.

---

62 BBY

The Flash speeder is developed on Naboo and was a small landspeeder used by the Naboo Royal Security Forces.

The Fourth Galactic Games are held.

The R3 series astromech droid is developed around this time. The R3-series astromech droid was an astromech model developed and sold by the droidmaker Industrial Automaton (IA). The R3 came at the heels of IA's blockbuster launch of the R2-series astromech droid as the company rushed to capitalize on their new dominance of the maintenance and repair droid market. The R3's designers copied the R2's general aesthetic, including the bright, contrasting color trim on a white metal chassis. The obvious difference in the factory unit was its head: the R2's opaque dome was swapped for a clear dome of plastex or transparisteel. The transparency gave the droid's internal sensor package greater range and showcased the R3's other major distinction, its newly updated Intellex V computer brain. Over time, however, some units' original domes were replaced with opaque ones or painted over carelessly

Jocasta Nu joins the Jedi Council. Jocasta Nu was a female Human who served as the Chief Librarian of the Jedi Archives during the final days of the Galactic Republic, with a penchant for being a bit overconfident in the completeness of her Archives. Her patterned robes bore the symbols of the Ansata, representing her devotion to knowledge and learning.During her career, Nu served as a member of the Jedi High Council and trained many Padawans, including the future Emperor's Hand, Jerec, Olee Starstone, whom she tutored in the years prior to the Clone Wars, and Jin-Lo Rayce, founder of the Agents of Ossus. Jocasta Nu died when the 501st Legion ransacked the Jedi Temple at the end of the Clone Wars.

61 BBY

Followers of the H'kig religion, fleeing from persecution on their homeworld, settle the planet Rishi.

60 BBY

A massive wave of religious refugees from Galand arrived on Rishi. These settlers, who were members of the strict H'kig sect, took up residence in the planet's lowlands and ignored the native Rishii.

The Millennium Falcon is constructed over Corellia. The Millennium Falcon, originally known as YT-1300 492727ZED, was a modified YT-1300 light freighter with a storied history stretching back to the decades before the Clone Wars and the rise of the Galactic Empire. Manufactured by the Corellian Engineering Corporation, the light freighter was first owned by Corell Industries Limited and underwent several name changes before being bought by the smugglers Kal and Dova Brigger in 48 BBY, and the ship eventually ended up as the property of the secretive Republic Group under the name Stellar Envoy by 29 BBY. The Envoy was destroyed in a collision with a bulk freighter above Nar Shaddaa, but it was rebuilt and served various owners under different names before Quip Fargil named it after the bat-falcon, and it eventually fell into the hands of Lando Calrissian after a game of sabacc, but Calrissian himself lost the ship in another game of sabacc to the smuggler Han Solo several years later. Solo and his Wookiee copilot, Chewbacca, became the ship's most famous and permanent owners, flying the Falcon during their smuggling careers and their subsequent work with the Alliance to Restore the Republic; a fateful trip to the planet Alderaan from Tatooine, ferrying Ben Kenobi and Luke Skywalker there, saw Solo and the Falcon embroiled in the Alliance's affairs and participating in the historic Battle of Yavin, during which Solo and Chewbacca flew the Falcon to save Skywalker from Imperial TIE fighters and allowed him to fire the shot that destroyed the Death Star. Despite Solo's insistence that he did not work for the Alliance, his misadventures continued to draw him back to the Rebels and Princess Leia Organa, and the Falcon was present for many pivotal battles of the Galactic Civil War such as the Battle of Hoth and the Battle of Endor, where Lando Calrissian and his copilot Nien Nunb flew alongside Wedge Antilles into the second Death Star's superstructure and fired the shots that spelled the massive battle station's destruction.

The Corellian Security Force, or CorSec, is formed on Corellia. It would become the primary law enforcement agency on the planet.

Nejaa Halcyon becomes a Jedi Knight.

The Mandalorian Civil War begins The conflict erupted prior to the Clone Wars, following a schism in the Mandalorian clans that stemmed from a fundamental difference in ideology over the Mandalorians' place in the greater galaxy. Fought between Mand'alor Jaster Mereel's True Mandalorians, who believed that the Mandalorians should act as honorable mercenaries, and Tor Vizsla's splinter group known as Death Watch, which advocated that the Mandalorians return to their savage roots as raiders and brigands, the war lasted over a decade with victories and losses on both sides. Jaster Mereel would fall on Korda Six as a result of a comrade's betrayal, while Jango Fett succeeded him as the new Mand'alor and leader of the True Mandalorians until the devastating defeat at the Battle of Galidraan against the Jedi Order. There, a Death Watch scheme unfolded that brought a contingent of Jedi Knights led by Master Dooku to the planet under the false pretenses that the True Mandalorians were murdering civilians. When the Jedi attempted to take them into custody, fighting broke out that left eleven Jedi and every True Mandalorian on Galidraan dead, save for Jango Fett.

Raith Sienar is born. He became a prominent engineer during the closing years of the Galactic Republic and early days of the Galactic Empire, producing countless highly advanced designs, most well-known among them the TIE fighter; he was also the originator of the concept for the Death Star. Ambitious and keen, Sienar was raised inside the Sienar family, which had run the prominent shipbuilding concern Santhe/Sienar Technologies for thousands of years. Sienar struck off to prove himself as a teen before returning to the fold, where his father Narro Sienar trained him to take over the company. When Narro was killed by assassins seeking Raith, the younger Sienar, only in his twenties, took over the company. For the next decade, Sienar lived an aristocratic lifestyle, designing unique and cutting-edge ships on Coruscant for wealthy and secretive clients, among them the Scimitar for Darth Sidious.

---

59 BBY

Nejaa Halcyon and Scerra have a secret wedding on Corellia.

Qui-Gon Jinn's first apprentice passes the Trials and becomes a Jedi Knight. Qui-Gon becomes a Jedi Master and takes Xanatos as his second Padawan learner.

---

58 BBY

Jango Fett is orphaned when his family of simple farmers is murdered by the Mandalorian Death Watch. He is picked up by former Journeyman Protector Jaster Mereel.

Jabba Desilijic Tiure is sent to Tatooine to represent the Desilijic Clan.

Mace Windu is sent to Hurikane to negotiate with the insectoid-rock humanoids. He makes peace with them and receives purple Hurrikaine crystals that he uses to build his lightsaber.

The Yinchorri gain representation in the Galactic Senate. The Yinchorri were a species of sentient, corpulent, turtle-like, green-skinned reptilians with an inherent immunity to telepathic uses of the Force, including mind tricks. They were born from eggs and had a great endurance when facing pain or heat. Native to the planet Yinchorr, the Yinchorri were divided into two castes: the Intelligentsia, who governed through the Council of Elders of each city-state, and a highly aggressive warrior caste. They were also known to value family ties. They had strong willpower that allowed them to resist attempts by slavers to enslave them. They also had the skill to develop specialized technology. However, they were poor strategists. Yinchorri culture was best characterized by the expression, "might makes right"; they considered anything they were able to take and hold by force to be rightfully theirs and anything they disliked was to be destroyed. They were commonly found as pirates, mercenaries or in other violent jobs.

Garen Muln is born on an unknown planet. Garen Muln was brought to the Coruscant Jedi Temple at an early age where he entered a clan of other Initiates and was taught the ways of the Force. A restless adolescent, Muln was a contemporary of Obi-Wan Kenobi and maintained a good friendship despite arguing over trivial things. When a dark sider infiltrated the Temple in 44 BBY, Initiate Muln worked to thwart the intruder by disguising himself as Padawan Kenobi to help throw off the intruder's plan. While Muln and Master Ali-Alann posed as Kenobi and Master Qui-Gon Jinn, the pair were able to capture the Dark Jedi and protect the Temple from destruction.

57 BBY

The Yinchorri join the Galactic Republic but, being a potential threat, they were not provided with starships. Secretly motivated by Darth Sidious through his minion Vilmarh "Villie" Grahrk, they unleashed a pan-galactic uprising that was only stopped when the Jedi Order became involved. Afterward, an embargo was placed on their homeworld. That was Sidious' plan. He had felt that both the Force-resistant Yinchorri and the Jedi could become a menace to his plan; by fighting each other, both sides would be weakened as a result. Later, the Galactic Empire took control of the Yinchorri system. Local Imperial Governor Marcellin Wessel betrayed the Yinchorri, killing their elders in a failed scheme to capture Princess Leia Organa. Enraged, the Yinchorri rebelled against the Empire. The galactic government answered their uprising by destroying the reptilians' civilization. Although the New Republic later helped the surviving Yinchorri retake control of their planet, the species refused to join another galactic government. Their planet eventually came within the area of control of the Empire of Darth Krayt.

Bruck Chun is born on Telos IV. A Force-sensitive Human male with ice-blue eyes and white hair, Bruck Chun, the brother of Kad Chun, was born to Vox Chun. Given to the Jedi Order for training in the ways of the Force, Initiate Chun was enrolled in the academy at the Coruscant Jedi Temple. Befriending fellow Initiate Aalto, Chun and his friend often taunted their peer Obi-Wan Kenobi, whom they called "Oafy-Wan" after Kenobi had lost his balance on one occasion, colliding with Chun. He also attempted to impress the attractive Initiate, Siri Tachi, many times, but to no avail; he eventually moved on.

Garen Muln begins training in the Jedi Temple under Master Yoda.

Cerasi is born on Melida/Daan. In later years, and during the civil war, Cerasi met a Daan youth, Nield, and together, the two decided to unite the Daan and the Melida orphans. They created an organization which would fight for peace, and were known as the Young. During the war, the group helped the Jedi, Qui-Gon Jinn, and his Padawan, Obi-Wan Kenobi, to rescue their fellow Jedi, Tahl. Later, Kenobi chose to stay and fight with the Young. Cerasi became very close friends with Kenobi during his stay on Melida/Daan; Kenobi would later say to Bant Eerin that he had loved her

Obi-Wan Kenobi is born on Stewjon. Obi-Wan Kenobi was born the first son of a moderately wealthy family, and was taken to Coruscant to begin his Jedi training while still in his infancy. His homeworld was Stewjon, from which Kenobi himself believed that he had once visited, possessing vague, pleasant memories of playing with his brother, Owen. In reality, Kenobi would later conclude that these memories were visions from the Force of Owen Lars. The fraternity he felt between himself and Owen was true, from a certain point of view. As Kenobi felt a brotherly bond with his former student, Lars too would be his brother. As a Jedi Initiate, Kenobi trained under Grand Master Yoda alongside other Jedi hopefuls of his age; later he would be placed into a clan under the tutelage of Master Vant. Bant Eerin, Garen Muln and Quinlan Vos became Kenobi's friends, and he eventually fell in love with fellow Padawan, Siri Tachi. Others would become rivals, and even enemies, such as Bruck Chun and Aalto. His lightsaber instructors included Anoon Bondara and Cin Drallig. As a youngling, Kenobi had been fascinated by machines, building models of ships and even dreaming of becoming a pilot. Ironically, as he grew older, Kenobi came to despise flying. His ability to repair machinery and reprogram computers would serve him well in the future, but because of his ability to learn quickly, Kenobi became arrogant and was often impatient. Under the careful guidance of Master Yoda, however, Kenobi became more humble and reserved. Despite his rapid growth as a Jedi, by the time Kenobi reached the age of twelve, it seemed that his chances of becoming a Jedi Knight had all but passed him by; Younglings who weren't selected to be Padawans by the age of 13 would be shifted into one of the divisions of the Jedi Service Corps. One day, Jedi Master Qui-Gon Jinn visited the Jedi Temple to watch the matches. Kenobi dueled one of his competitors, Bruck Chun, to draw the attention of the maverick Jedi Knight. Kenobi fought valiantly to the point of exhaustion. The final offensive against Chun was carried out so fiercely that Jinn thought Kenobi too dangerous and declined training the boy. Kenobi was sent to the mining colony of Bandomeer to work as a ploughman for the AgriCorps. Strangely enough, Jinn happened to be sent on a mission to the same place. The youngling and the Jedi Knight had to work together if they wanted to survive the mission, which was a trap set for Jinn by his former Padawan, Xanatos. Kenobi showed Jinn that he was worthy to be taken as a Padawan learner en route, when they were attacked by members of Xanatos' criminal organization, the Offworld Mining Corporation. After putting an end to the tense situation, the two arrived on Bandomeer, where Jinn received a letter signed by Xanatos. It turned out that Bandomeer was not in need of Jedi assistance; it had all been organized by Xanatos, who was revealed to be the leader of Offworld, a company whose ruthless business practices and mining operations terrorized all of the citizens on the planet. Jinn sent Kenobi off to his AgriCorps duties while he planned to meet with Xanatos, not as old adversaries, but as ambassadors, working to find an agreement between Offworld and Bandomeer. Xanatos, however, planned all along to sabotage their meeting and kill Jinn. With the help of Kenobi, Jinn once more attempted to end Xanatos' acts of terror. Jinn dueled with his former apprentice, and though they ended Offworld's business on Bandomeer, Xanatos was able to escape. During their altercation with Xanatos, Jinn discovered Kenobi's true potential, and took him as his new Padawan learner. Their relationship got off to a bad start, as the pair's personalities were constantly at odds; Jinn was headstrong, while Kenobi was more practical. As time went on, however, their opposing natures blended them into an effective duo. For his thirteenth birthday, Kenobi received a river stone from Jinn, something that came from the River of Light on the Jedi Master's homeworld. The stone was later revealed to be Force-sensitive. It had helped Kenobi save his memories when he was almost erased by the Syndicat, a criminal organization on Phindar. During his time with Jinn, Kenobi temporarily left the Jedi Order. Caught up in the civil war on Melida/Daan, Kenobi elected to stay and help the children, otherwise known as the Young, who were fighting against their tradition-obsessed elders. The planet's residents had been fighting a pointless war for generations, and had actually forgotten what had started the feud. Kenobi befriended a boy within the Young called Nield, and possibly developed an attraction for another of the Young named Cerasi. Soon after Kenobi's decision to stay, Cerasi was mortally wounded and died in Kenobi's arms. For a time, Kenobi remained on the planet to continue helping the war effort, but soon enough felt that his place was with the Jedi and was taken back by Jinn, though it took a long time for them to fully trust each other again. Jinn and Kenobi eventually caught up with Xanatos when the Dark Jedi was planning an attack on Master Yoda. The two were able to find and engage him before his plans went into effect, though. It would be while foiling Xanatos that Kenobi was forced to fight his long time rival, Bruck Chun. Chun had kidnapped Kenobi's friend Bant Eerin while working with Xanatos, and Kenobi engaged the misguided youth in a lightsaber duel. Kenobi won the duel when Chun fell off a ledge and died, though he would carry the guilt for many years. After he escaped, Xanatos returned to his homeworld of Telos. Kenobi and Jinn went after him. On Telos, however, they were not very welcomed. They were astonished to find out that Xanatos wielded significant financial and political power there. He was considered a hero to his people. What the people of the planet did not know is that while Xanatos and the government had been distracting them with a form of gambling called Katharsis, Offworld had been pillaging the planet's resources. The two Jedi were then framed and wanted for a crime they did not commit. Xanatos captured them, but the two Jedi managed to escape. Xanatos committed suicide by diving into a pool of acid after Jinn stopped his plans. It was during this time that Kenobi first spoke to Siri Tachi, whom he had met during lightsaber training at the Temple. They started off on rocky terms, as she was angry at him for leaving the Order, but would later forge a friendship that would last the rest of their lives, and even develop into something more. Kenobi and Tachi were together sent on a mission with their respective masters, Qui-Gon Jinn and Adi Gallia, to the planet Kegan. A simple mission to test a child for Force-sensitivity quickly devolved into a non-violent uprising to overthrow Kegan's Benevolent Guides after Kenobi and Tachi were mistakenly captured for truancy and sent to the planet's Learning Circle. Unable to slip away, the Padawans had to withstand brainwashing at the hands of the Teaching Guides, who sought to enforce The Learning curriculum upon them to teach the two the value of the General Good. After being reassigned to the Re-

Learning Circle for lack of discipline, Kenobi and Tachi, having learned to work together and with a little help from their Masters, soon escaped with their new friend Davi and O-Lana, the child they had originally come to the planet for. The Keganites, upon discovering what really went on in the Re-Learning Circle, quickly voted out their leaders while Kenobi and his fellow Jedi were still on-planet. Soon after, Kenobi would travel with Jinn to Ilum to make his first lightsaber. While there, Jinn and Kenobi were sent to Ord Sigatt to investigate the disappearance of a Republic refinery ship. After noticing the the low attitudes and that no one had any weapons (except for guards), Kenobi met the Besalisk Dexter Jettster, who was selling weapons to the people of Ord Sigatt. Jettster was told to wait for Kenobi as a fight had broken out between a boy who threw a rock at a guard. The Jedi jumped in and sliced the guards weapons before returning to Jettster, who commented on how a lightsaber could stand for danger and for hope. Jettster and Kenobi would soon become friends. Jinm soon came back with information that a senator from Denon, Denon-Ardru Mutual, had sent a small army to put a monopoly on the mining business there. Kenobi fought alongside his master in the Stark Hyperspace War, one of the last of the many small-scale conflicts that plagued the Galactic Republic in its final days. It was during the Fourth Battle of Qotile when Kenobi's enduring friendship with fellow Padawan Quinlan Vos truly began. Kenobi would later recall fondly a training mission the two Padawans undertook on Ragoon VI and missions the both of them would undertake with Dexter Jettster on the Outer Rim. When Kenobi was nearly fourteen years old, he and Jinn traveled to a planet once devastated by turmoil and currently under a temporary truce. The rulers of each planet temporarily exchanged children when they reached the age of seven and raised them in an effort to get the future leaders to appreciate each other. The plan backfired after hundreds of years of success, however, when the heir of Rutan decided he wanted to remain on Senali, forsaking his royal title and home planet. This infuriated his father, King Frane, who believed his son had been brainwashed by the Senali, and he threatened to declare war on Senali. Kenobi and Jinn arrived to mediate the dispute, and after meeting with King Frane, they went to the ocean world of Senali and attempted to convince Leed to return to Rutan, thus avoiding war. In later years, Kenobi and Jinn were sent on an extended mission to Mandalore, which was engulfed in the the Mandalorian Great Clan Wars. They were tasked with serving as bodyguards to the Duchess Satine, leader of the pacifist New Mandalorians, whom the Senate supported against the belligerent Mandalorian clans. Together, the two Jedi spent a year on Mandalore protecting the Duchess from the hostile insurgents threatening her world. Kenobi fell in love with Satine during his stay on Mandalore, but despite his feelings toward her, he continued with his training and was reassigned. Kenobi regretted leaving her, but ultimately followed the Jedi Code he had sworn to live by. During his training, Kenobi and a Jedi strike team were sent to Corellia to stop a group of Rodian terrorists from destroying a Spaceport outside of Coronet City. Prior to the Battle of Naboo, Kenobi and Jinn participated in the colonization of Alaris Prime, where they battled the Trade Federation for control of the moon. During this time, Chewbacca had his first recorded encounter with Jedi, as Jinn and Kenobi had been assigned by the Galactic Republic to end the conflict on Alaris Prime. Under Jinn's tutelage, Chewbacca was able to successfully lead the colony to military and economic success. Kenobi and Chewbacca would eventually meet again in 0 BBY, though it is unclear whether the two recognized each other after not seeing each other for nearly 40 years. In 33 BBY, Kenobi would assist his master in missions to Yinchorr and Dorvalla. After the Incident at Dorvalla, Kenobi and Jinn were also involved in the attempt to mediate relations between the Trade Federation and the Nebula Front, an attempt that would sadly fail with the disaster at the Eriadu Trade Summit. Kenobi would later investigate the mysterious disappearance of a fellow Padawan, Darsha Assant. He found a few tantalizing clues to her fate, but galactic events caught up with Kenobi before he could track down the missing Alderaanian. Shortly after being given the assignment, he and Jinn were dispatched by Supreme Chancellor Finis Valorum to resolve the Blockade of Naboo.

56 BBY

Nerra Ziveri turns control of the Jedi academy on Cularin to Lanius Qel-Bertuk and disappears.

55 BBY

The Fifth Galactic Games are held.

The Neimoidians become the leaders of the Trade Federation. Neimoidians were a species of humanoids that were distant genetic relatives of Duros. They were native to the planet of Neimoidia and also lived on colony worlds in the same sector like Cato Neimoidia, Deko Neimoidia, and Koru Neimoidia. They had a reputation for greed and cowardice. Neimoidians placed tremendous value on wealth and material possessions, and would go to great lengths to gain money and power; however, they were very easily intimidated, and hated combat

Siri Tachi is born on an unknown planet. Siri Tachi was a female Human Jedi Master, apprentice of Adi Gallia and Master to Ferus Olin. She was a talented pilot who participated in the First Battle of Geonosis, fighting alongside Master Gallia guarding the Galactic Republic transports in space above the planet. She was one of Obi-Wan Kenobi's closest friends, and at one point they were romantically involved. During the Clone Wars, she met an early death on Azure while on a mission with Kenobi.

Bant Eerin is born on Dac. As a Force-sensitive female Mon Calamari, Bant Eerin was trained in the ways of the Force. A contemporary of Obi-Wan Kenobi, Darsha Assant, Reeft, and Garen Muln, Eerin excelled in her classes at the Temple academy, though she often took breaks throughout the day to visit the Room of a Thousand Fountains. Due to her aquatic nature, her dormitory was filled with moisture to keep her skin moist and cool.Though two years younger than him, Eerin was a close confidant of Kenobi's. She attempted to console him when he was at first assigned to the Agricultural Corps, then welcomed him back to the Temple after Jedi Master Qui-Gon Jinn accepted Kenobi as his Padawan.

54 BBY

Darth Maul is born on Dathomir, and given to Darth Sidious by his mother to escape the fate of becoming a Nightbrother. Darth Sidious trained him in the ways of the dark side of the Force as his secret apprentice on a secret Mustafar training facility, along with the help of a split personality droid. Maul became a master of Juyo, Ataru, Jar'Kai, and Teräs Käsi, with training in Niman, and chose to wield a red-bladed saberstaff in combat. Though well trained in the ways of the Sith and a Sith assassin rather than a full apprentice, Maul was technically a violation of the Rule of Two because his own Master was at the time apprenticed to another, the Muun Sith Lord Darth Plagueis. Plagueis however, was fully aware of Maul's existence, and supported Sidious's decision to train him. The primary reason for Plagueis's support, despite the violation of the Rule of Two, was that Maul was trained to be expendable. As an assassin, he could perform high priority, boots-on-the-ground missions for the Sith without running the risk of exposing either Plagueis or Sidious should he fail.

53 BBY

Xanatos leaves the Jedi Order after Qui-Gon Jinn is forced to kill the boy's father, Crion, on Telos IV. The opera, The Brief Reign of Future Wraiths, leaves Coruscant to tour the galaxy.

Padawan Jorus C'baoth attends Mirnic University.

Bossk is born on Trandosha. The son of Cradossk, the leader of the Bounty Hunters' Guild. After hatching, Bossk devoured each of his unhatched siblings, which made his father proud. As was customary for a Trandoshan, Bossk began his career by hunting Wookiees, typically considered suicidal if attempted by any other species. During this time, Bossk made a name for himself and began accepting bounties on non-Wookiees as well, becoming one of the galaxy's most feared bounty hunters.

Aurra Sing is born on Nar Shaddaa. Aurra Sing was born in the slums of Nar Shaddaa to a spice-addicted mother named Aunuanna and a father she never knew. It was also rumored she was once owned by Sennex slavers. She was brought to the Jedi Order as a candidate for Jedi training. In an attempt to control the young woman's overtly aggressive instincts, the Council assigned her to the Dark Woman, a mysterious and secretive Jedi Master with a track record of training difficult apprentices. However, the two did not get along well and Sing never progressed past the stage of Padawan. Around the age of nine, she was kidnapped by Sennex pirates on Ord Namurt, who played on her deep-seated fears of abandonment and betrayal to shake her trust in the Jedi. They raised the conflicted young woman as a fellow pirate. Tragedy struck again when she was eventually captured by the Hutt crime lord Wallanooga, who in turn lent her to a group of Anzati assassins. The Anzati trained her to be a remorseless killer, even equipping Sing with a bio-computer that fed her additional sensory data. Her training was paid for by the family of Hutt crime lord Urdruua, something which set his family back a generation in debt.

52 BBY

Palpatine's predecessor as senator of Naboo, Vidar Kim, is assassinated on Coruscant. Palpatine is elected to the Galactic Senate as Senator of Naboo and the Chommell sector.

Oppo Rancisis begins teaching at the Jedi Temple on Coruscant. Oppo Rancisis, an adept strategist and tactician, was a Thisspiasian male who abdicated the throne of his homeworld in favor of becoming a Jedi Master. Offered to the Jedi Order as an infant by his mother, the Blood Monarch of Thisspias, Rancisis was apprenticed to Master Yaddle, training to become a Jedi Knight almost two centuries before the Battle of Yavin. In 186 BBY, Rancisis' sister was killed by terrorists, and he was offered the throne; he declined, instead preferring to continue on the path of the Jedi.

The Galactic Correctional Authority is formed, and establishes prisons on several worlds including Oovo IV.

Jaster Mereel is killed at the Battle of Korda Six when he is ambushed by the Death Watch and betrayed by his second-in-command, Montross, Mereel was killed by Vizsla. His body was carried back to the Mandalorians' landing zone by Fett, where Montross was exposed as a traitor and Fett succeeded his adoptive father as the new Mand'alor, in accordance with what Mereel would have wanted.

Jango Fett becomes leader of the Mandalorians.

Jedi Master Dooku mediates an end to the Sevarcos Dispute.

Jocasta Nu steps down from the Jedi Council.

Jar Jar Binks is born on Naboo. Jar Jar Binks was the first Gungan to represent his people in the Galactic Senate, first serving as a Junior Representative along with Senator Padmé Amidala, and then, after her death, serving as full Senator himself. Like most Gungans, Binks was lanky and spoke Basic with a unique accent. Despite being naïve and clumsy, Jar Jar Binks contributed greatly to the fate of the Galactic Republic, both for good and ill. He was a General, Representative, and later a Senator

Bolabo Hujaan is born on Sullust. Drifting from ship to ship in later life, Hujaan learned first hand the operations of hundreds of starships, and eventually settled down on Byblos to establish her own facility, Bolabo's Garage. To maintain security and secrecy, Hujaan paid off a number of contacts in Byblos Starport Security. Hujaan earned a reputation for expert repairs and creative modifications, particularly amongst smugglers and Rebel Alliance agents, but she never did anything for free and demanded payment up front. When parts were unavailable, Hujaan called on her skills as a smuggler to acquire them. Some of Hujaan's most impressive work was on Dash Rendar's Outrider, although if any modification proved a failure, she claimed it was Rendar's work.

Owen Lars is born on Ator. Owen Lars was the son of moisture farmer Cliegg Lars and the stepbrother of Anakin Skywalker. He married Beru Whitesun, and after his father's death, inherited his moisture farm. In 19 BBY, Beru convinced Owen to adopt Anakin's son, Luke Skywalker, as Anakin had turned to the dark side and become the infamous Darth Vader. Owen and Beru raised their nephew as well as they could, and Owen instilled into Luke the values of his own childhood. Fearful of Luke's potential, and distrustful of the outside galaxy, Owen attempted to keep Luke isolated and ignorant of his true parentage

51 BBY

Jorus C'baoth begins his service as the personal advisor to Senator Palpatine of Naboo.

The Dark Woman brings Aurra Sing to Coruscant for Jedi training.

Silya Shessaun is born on Thesme. Silya Shessaun was a female Human from Thesme who represented the Thesme sector in the Galactic Senate during the waning years of the Galactic Republic. Coming from a working-class family, she was one of the few non-upper class citizens of Thesme able to make a name for herself in the political arena. Due to her origins, Shessaun consistently championed the causes of the poor and underprivileged. During her time as a Galactic Senator, she often confided in her close friend, fellow Senator Padmé Amidala of the Chommell sector. Shessaun received only minor criticism in her tenure, since she seemed to focus on her sector as a whole more than her native Thesme. Shessaun was forced back to her homeworld when the Separatist Crisis threatened it circa 22 BBY. During the Clone Wars, Amidala asked her to join the Delegation of 2000, but the Thesme native believed that such actions were little better than those of the Confederacy of Independent Systems. When the New Order rose in 19 BBY, and Amidala apparently died during the "Jedi uprising," Shessaun launched an inquest into her friend's death, but the now-Emperor Palpatine barred it. She was later asked to step down as Senator due to her lack of enthusiasm for the Galactic Empire, and lived out her early retirement on Alderaan. Shessaun would later return to her native Thesme, where she peacefully died in 4 ABY.

Gilad Pellaeon is born on Corellia. Gilad Pellaeon was a dedicated Human male naval officer, serving for seven decades in the fleets of the Galactic Republic, Galactic Empire, Imperial Remnant, and Galactic Alliance, and rose to the position of supreme commander for the latter two governments. Pellaeon began his career in the Republic's Judicial Forces, where he ascended the ranks and captained the assault ship Leveler during the Clone Wars. Pellaeon developed a strong attachment to the navy as an institution, and when the Republic became the Empire, Pellaeon continued serving aboard the Star Destroyer Chimaera.

50 BBY

The Moddell sector is admitted to the Republic as a freestanding subsector. The Moddell sector and the Zuma Region were considered part of the Unknown Regions until the Old Republic's final centuries, and later admitted as a freestanding subsector. The Empire eventually made the Zuma a regional sector and the Moddell sector one of its subsectors.

Galladinium founds Galladinium's Galactic Imports on Lenthalis.

Salt is introduced to the Arcona, scaleless reptiles with humanoid bodies that hailed from the tropical desert planet of Cona in the Teke Ro system.

Annaj joins the Galactic Republic and becomes the Moddell sector capital.

Young Anomids develop a nonconformist subculture.

Galactic Republic scouts discover Bosph and the Bosph species. The Bosphs were a mammalian species from the planet of Bosph in the Outer Rim Territories' Bosph sector. They had six limbs, no neck and a pair of multiple-lensed eyes that also functioned as auditory sense organs. The Bosphs were a fiercely independent and isolationist species who preferred seclusion from both the rest of the galaxy and each other. The homeworld, where most Bosphs remained, was controlled by a hierarchical government made up of various factions each consisting of Force-sensitive Bosphs. These Bosphs were the only individuals who had the right to claim ownership of any object, though any unclaimed object was equally owned by all Bosphs. The Bosphs also kept a tradition of recording the history of their travels, both on Bosph and in the galaxy by tattooing star maps on to their skin.

The Galactic Republic makes first contact with the Eloms. Eloms were short, stocky, bipedal sentients, with a thick pelt of oily, dark fur, native to the frigid and mineral-rich desert planet of Elom, located in the Borderland Regions. The primitive species had extremely tough skin, several layers of fat, and their hands and feet were coated by thick calluses. As a result of living in dark caves, where the only light was created by phosphorescent crystals, Eloms had exceptional eyesight, though they could not tolerate bright light. Rarely leaving their underground habitats, Eloms were pacifistic and peaceful herbivores, despite their savage and fearsome appearance. Although they were highly ambitious and intelligent, Eloms were often manipulated into becoming involved with illegal activities, due to their underestimation of the capacity for wrongdoing exhibited by other species. With an average lifespan similar to Humans, Eloms remained undiscovered for thousands of years by Galactic Republic scouts, although the species they shared the planet with, the tall humanoid Elomin, had made contact with the scouts long before they had even discovered the Eloms.

Quarg and his pirates are exiled from the Korteen Belt to Drexel. During the time of the Galactic Republic Quarg's father had been the governor of the Korteen asteroid belt, an area whose residents posed as miners but were actually scavengers. Soon this activity caught the attention of Jedi Knights who forced the scavengers from their residence and sent them limping to the remote, water covered planet Drexel. There, the scavengers were divided, and rebels became the Dragon Lords, against Quarg's portion.

The Arkanian Revolution is fought over the re-engineering of the Yaka. It was a fierce and bloody civil war between the planet's Dominion government and the Arkanian Renegades. Known for their genetic and cybernetic expertise, Arkanian scientists began to experiment on the unintelligent local Yaka species, despite the objections of a group of more socially conscious scientists. After several centuries of injustice, these scientists formed a faction known as the Arkanian Renegades, and launched a coup against the Dominion, after forming a powerful mercenary army of warriors who were part cyborg and part organic. In the process of fighting what they saw as injustices to the Yaka, the Arkanian Renegades became much like their opponents by committing similar atrocities. The Renegades' army, whose number included Gorm the Dissolver, butchered the Dominion's forces in early skirmishes. The desperate Dominion appealed to the Republic and Jedi Order to intervene on their behalf. Republic police squads were eventually deployed to Arkania, supplemented by Jedi forces including Mace Windu, Aqinos, and the Iron

Knights. The Renegades were soundly defeated by the reinforcements, and those not killed in battle were executed for their treason. Some of their cyborg creations, including Gorm the Dissolver, survived, becoming bounty hunters and hired killers. The Arkanian Revolution, although unsuccessful, contributed greatly to the escalating public fear of droids.

Jorj Car'das is born on Corellia. Early in his life, Car'das would join the crew of the smuggling ship Bargain Hunter, working mainly as a bootlegger for the Hutts. In 27 BBY, Car'das, Dubrak Qennto, and Maris Ferasi became the captives of Commander Thrawn of the Chiss Expansionary Defense Force. Thrawn wished to learn the language of the Republic from the smugglers and they stayed in his base on Crustai for several weeks, teaching him Basic and learning the Chiss language, Cheunh. Car'das assisted Thrawn in defeating the alien Vagaari, before being allowed to return to the Republic.

Gorm the Dissolver is born. He was a cyborg assembled by the Renegades of the Arkanian Revolution. One of the few beings to survive the Arkanian battlefield, Gorm went on to a long and tumultuous career as a bounty hunter, surviving multiple encounters with the Jedi Knights, including one particularly brutal fight with Mace Windu himself.

Schennt is born on Corulag. Later, Governor Schennt ruled the planet Gellefon from his domicile in the center of Kig Dannen Spaceport.

Sayer Mon Neela is born. She later joined the Alliance to Restore the Republic during the Galactic Civil War.

---

49 BBY

Lorana Jinzler is born on Coruscant. Lorana's parents were both employees at the Jedi Temple on Coruscant. When she was born and taken in by the Jedi Order, her parents were dismissed in accordance with the Jedi Code regarding emotional attachments and relationships. Her parents kept track of her progressive Jedi training from a friend who still worked at the Temple. The third of four Jinzler children, Lorana was accepted for Jedi training at the age of 10 months, and was taken to the Temple, only meeting her jealous, hurt brother Dean at the initiation of Outbound Flight

Rorworr is born on Kashyyyk. He was a male Wookiee who would later live on Naboo with his father, an ambassador. With help from his translator droid TDo-2, Rorworr studied at the Royal House of Learning in Naboo's capital city, Theed, and often explored the wilderness areas surrounding the city. The Wookiee had a penchant for adventure, and assisted the Jedi Rann I-Kanu with the investigation and defeat of a group of veermok smugglers.

Deel Surool is born on Ryloth. In 32 BBY, he played a minor role as a member of the Naboo Underground in defending the planet from Trade Federation forces.

Sylvn is born on Cerea.

Pter Thanas is born. was a male Coruscanti Human Imperial Navy commander who defected to the Rebel Alliance after the Bakura Incident during the Galactic Civil War. Thanas was noted as a diplomatic officer of the Imperial Starfleet, known for his ability to rule successfully without using fear as a motivator. Early in his career, he led an Imperial task force against the Crimson Nova pirates on F'Dann IX.

48 BBY

Arani Korden is born on Naboo. She was the daughter of a Theed noble and later served as Senator to represent Naboo in the New Republic during the Galactic Civil War.

Mon Mothma is born on Chandrila. She would grow up to serve as an important political figure from the waning days of the Galactic Republic, one of the founders of the Alliance to Restore the Republic, and the first Chief of State of the New Republic. When the foundation of the Galactic Empire replaced the Republic that had existed for many millennia, she met with her allies in the Senate, such as Senators Padmé Amidala and Bail Prestor Organa. In 2 BBY, she signed the Corellian Treaty, along with Organa, Garm Bel Iblis, Rahm Kota, and Galen Marek, in order to form the Alliance to Restore the Republic. She, along with the others, were taken captive aboard the Death Star I, although they were rescued. She played an important role in the ensuing Galactic Civil War, and after the decisive Rebel victory at the Battle of Endor, she became the first Chief of State of the newly founded New Republic. She also had a daughter, Lieda, and a son, Jobin. In 24 ABY, she passed away peacefully on Chandrila.

Toba is born on Naboo. Toba would fly the hyperlanes near the Naboo system as a smuggler during the Great Peace of the Republic. An adventurous spirit from an early age, Toba was born to influential parents in the city of Otoh Gunga—his mother the former Rep Neesada Bari, and his father, the powerful bongo manufacturer Bullba. The Gungan enjoyed his youth, embarking on dangerous excursions of his own design and living as a playboy until the Invasion of Naboo, during which he entered service in the Gungan Grand Army and fought in the Battle of the Great Grass Plains. Inspired by the combat prowess and offworld exploits of his Bombad General, Jar Jar Binks, Toba aspired to a life away from Otoh Gunga and Naboo

Imperial Navy Officer Gaen Drommel is born on Oplovis.

Sola Naberrie is born on Naboo. She was the elder daughter of Ruwee and Jobal Naberrie, the sister of Padmé Amidala, as well as the mother of Ryoo and Pooja Naberrie. She would later become the maternal aunt to twins Luke Skywalker and Leia Organa Solo.

47 BBY

Sharad Hett leaves the Jedi Temple. Despite his fame and prestige within the ranks of the Jedi Order, Hett had grown weary, recognizing that the acclaim of his peers ran counter to the humility taught by the Jedi Code, and desired nothing else but to be with his family, whom he had all but lost contact with over the years. After completing another dangerous mission and arriving back at the Temple, Hett turned his back on the cheering crowds of his peers and sought out Master Koth. In a corridor of the Temple, Hett confessed his desire to leave the Order to the Zabrak. With a tearful goodbye, Master Koth accepted Hett's resignation and the Human departed from the Temple for the last time. In a tragic twist of events, the long-awaited reunion between Hett and his family would never occur. When Hett arrived on his homeworld, he returned to death and ruin. An alliance of offworld rivals had attacked his homeworld in the time he had been gone. Every major city on the planet was razed. Millions were killed, including every member of Sharad's family.

A'Sharad Hett is born on Tatooine.

Sia-Lan Wezz is born. Discovered to be Force-sensitive during infancy, Wezz was taken to the Coruscant Jedi Temple for formal training in the ways of the Force at the Temple's academy. After years of training, Wezz was selected by Jedi Master Lo-Jad as a Padawan and was destined to travel the galaxy with him to continue her studies down the Jedi Path. A year after her thirteenth birthday, Wezz was assigned to investigate the Coruscant-based terrorist organization known as the Flail. Teaming with a Wookiee, Wezz was forced to engage members of the group and went on to complete her mission. In 32 BBY, Master Lo-Jad assigned Wezz to Naboo where she was to study for a semester at the Royal House of Learning in Theed. Becoming close with headmaster Lucos Dannt, Wezz was on planet when the Trade Federation blockaded the planet. During the invasion, Wezz joined the Naboo Underground, a resistance movement that attempted to topple Federation control. During her time in the resistance, Wezz became well acquainted with the likes of Deel Surool, Rorworr, and fellow Padawan Rann I-Kanu. While Wezz would leave Naboo shortly after the Federation was defeated, she kept in touch with her new comrades and would involve them in several missions in her future career

Beru Whitesun is born on Tatooine. The wife of Owen Lars, Beru Whitesun would later raise Luke Skywalker after the fall of the Galactic Republic. Coming from a long line of moisture farmers, she grew up near Mos Eisley on Tatooine. On a trip to Anchorhead, she met Owen Lars, the son of another moisture farmer, Cliegg Lars. Beru and Owen fell in love, and Beru later became part of the Lars family.

---

46 BBY

Padmé Amidala (Padmé Naberrie) is born to Ruwee and Jobal Naberrie on Naboo. Padmé Naberrie of Naboo (publicly known by her regal name, Padmé Amidala, and also known as Her Royal Highness, Queen Amidala of Naboo from 33 BBY to 25 BBY and as Her Excellency, Senator Padmé Amidala of Naboo from 25 BBY until her death) was the younger daughter of Ruwee and Jobal Naberrie, and the sister of Sola Naberrie. Later in her life, Amidala became the secret wife of Jedi Knight Anakin Skywalker and the mother of Luke Skywalker and Leia Organa Solo, two of the most important figures in galactic history. She was also the grandmother of Jaina, Jacen, and Anakin Solo, as well as Ben Skywalker. This relationship made her great-grandmother of Allana Solo, Jacen Solo's daughter, and an ancestor of Nat, Kol, Cade Skywalker, and Ania Solo. Amidala was the democratically elected Queen of Naboo before representing the Chommell sector as a Senator in the Galactic Senate. As Queen of Naboo, Amidala fought bravely to liberate her people during the Trade Federation's invasion in 32 BBY, thus becoming one of the most respected political figures in the galaxy. In 22 BBY, following the Military Creation Act, Anakin Skywalker was assigned to protect her, and following the Battle of Geonosis, the two secretly married on Naboo after the pair fell in love. Senator Amidala participated in many events of the Clone Wars, both political and military, while also becoming pregnant to her husband. Around the end of the war, she doubted the motives of the Galactic Republic. In 19 BBY, appalled by the dissolution of the Republic and the creation of the Galactic Empire, she signed the Delegation of 2000 along with Bail Organa, Mon Mothma, and other Senators. After Anakin slaughtered many Jedi, including younglings, Obi-Wan Kenobi came to tell Padmé about Anakin's transformation to the Sith Lord Darth Vader. She refused to believe him, and went to Mustafar to find her husband. Unknown to her, Kenobi had hidden aboard her ship in order to find his former apprentice. When Kenobi revealed himself, the newly christened Sith Lord assumed she had betrayed him, and he strangled his wife using the dark side, knocking her unconscious. After Kenobi defeated Vader, and left him for dead, he took Amidala to a medical facility on Polis Massa, where she gave birth to fraternal twins and named them—the boy, Luke, and the girl, Leia. Unfortunately, her husband's fall to the dark side had broken her heart, causing her to lose the will to live, which, coupled with the strain of giving birth to her children, resulted in her death. Before death took her, she spoke her final words to Kenobi, stating her strong belief that there was still good within Anakin. At her state funeral, thousands of Naboo gathered in the streets of Theed to pay their respects to their beloved former Queen and Senator. Throughout her relatively short life, she played a vital role in the politics and events surrounding the Clone Wars. Amidala and other Senators were responsible for creating the foundation for any chance of rebellion against the Empire. Eventually, Padmé's children would play a major role in the fragmentation of the Empire and the redemption of Anakin.

Airen Cracken is born on Contruum. Cracken would become a resistance fighter from Contruum who became a general in the Alliance to Restore the Republic and the New Republic.

---

45 BBY

The Katana fleet is lost. The Katana fleet, also known as the Dark Force, was a starfleet launched by the Galactic Republic several years before the Clone Wars as part of its attempt to restore the Republic Navy to its long-gone glory. Highly advanced for its time and equipped with state of the art automation systems, it was lost in its first hyperspace voyage. The fleet consisted of 200 modified Dreadnaught-class heavy cruisers, all carrying experimental AT-PT walkers. The ships' controls could be slaved to the controls of Katana. This slave circuit system reduced the crew required from 16,000 to 2,200 per ship, allowing larger numbers of craft to be fielded. The fleet may have been a "showcase" of the slave-circuit and/or Dreadnaught design, as the ships' interiors were in a comparatively flamboyant blue color scheme rather than the standard gray; indeed it was this distinctive feature that partially alerted the New Republic to the fleet's continued existence. The fleet fell victim to a hive virus (possibly caused by carsunum spice) that wiped out the crew after driving them insane. In their insanity, the captain ordered a jump to random hyperspace coordinates before his death. Because of the slave circuits, every other vessel in the group followed suit, and the Katana fleet disappeared, presumably making no further communication with either the Republic or the galaxy at large. The loss of the fleet was a huge scandal that contributed to the growing dissatisfaction with the Galactic Republic, and also to a shift in starship systems from slave-circuitry and computer control to vessels with substantial crews and human control of vital systems.

A pair of comets struck and poisoned Toong'l. Many of the survivors relocated to Tund and other planets. Others chose to rebuild on their homeworld under King Kikipi.

Qui-Gon Jinn chooses a young Obi-Wan Kenobi as his Padawan.

Byss is first charted by the Galactic Republic, a planet in the Deep Core, near the center of the galaxy. Byss itself was somewhat of a myth, seeming to be the perfect place to live. Its eerie blue-green glow, caused by its sun, also added to the strangeness of the world. Despite this outward appearance, however, Emperor Palpatine's dark side energies were everywhere, corrupting not only the inhabitants, but the planet itself.

Veruna becomes King of Naboo. A relation to the Earl of Vis and a member of House Veruna, King Veruna succeeded Bon Tapalo as King of Naboo. He was the confidant of Tapalo before Tapalo's rise to the throne in 65 BBY. Veruna contacted Hego Damask, secretly the Muun Sith Lord Darth Plagueis, and Damask Holdings for the possibility of an alliance regarding the plasma reserves. Sometime later, Damask and his fellow men came to Naboo to formalize their agreement. Damask Holdings also ensured that Tapalo became the King of Naboo with Veruna as governor.

Raymus Antilles is born on Alderaan. He was a male Human and the captain of the Corvette Sundered Heart at the time of the Clone Wars and the Galactic Civil War. He served the Royal Alderaan Civil Fleet under Senator Bail Prestor Organa. During the early stages of the Civil War, he served the Rebel Alliance in the fight against the Galactic Empire. He captained the Alderaan Diplomatic Cruiser Tantive IV before his death in 0 BBY at the hands of Darth Vader.

Brandei is born on Mantooine. He would later serve the Imperial Navy of the Galactic Empire during the Galactic Civil War.

44 BBY

Xanatos commits suicide on Telos IV by jumping into a pool of acid, rather than be captured by his former master, Qui-Gon Jinn.

The Stark Hyperspace War is fought. This was a small regional military conflict and was fought almost entirely in the Qotile system. The Galactic Republic, with the aid of the Jedi, fought against the Stark Commercial Combine, a group of pirates, mercenaries, bounty hunters, and assassins united together under the charismatic leadership of fellow pirate Iaco Stark. The Combine had received some aid from the Trade Federation and the bacta-supplying company, Xucphra. The entire affair was orchestrated by Darth

Sidious as part of his larger scheme to control the galaxy.

Tyvokka is killed by Trade Federation droids. Tyvokka was a Wookiee Jedi Master who served the Galactic Republic during the Republic Classic era. A revered and respected member of the Jedi High Council, Tyvokka trained several Padawans, including the Kel Dor Plo Koon. The Wookiee was renowned for his ability to "sense the future," and assess the best possible course of action in any given situation, so he was chosen to help Senator Finis Valorum broker peace between the Stark Commercial Combine and the Trade Federation during a bacta shortage. At the peace summit, which took place on Troiken, Tyvokka and Valorum were accompanied by four other Jedi: Koon, Qui-Gon Jinn, Obi-Wan Kenobi, and Valorum's advisor, Adi Gallia. At Troiken, they rendezvoused with the Federation's representative, Nute Gunray, and were in turn met by the head of the Stark Commercial Combine, Iaco Stark. Upon arrival, however, Stark had his men draw their weapons on Tyvokka and his companions, and demanded their immediate surrender. Tyvokka literally turned the tables on Stark and his men, but in the ensuing skirmish, he was accidentally gunned down by Gunray's hunter-killer droid escort. Eventually succumbing to his wounds, Tyvokka's role in the mission was taken by Koon, who was able to secure victory over Stark. Koon would in time take Tyvokka's place on the High Council.

Plo Koon joins the Jedi Council. Plo Koon was a Kel Dor male from the planet Dorin held this position from after the Stark Hyperspace War to the end of the Galactic Republic in 19 BBY. During the Clone Wars, Koon served as a Jedi General in the Grand Army of the Republic, leading soldiers in campaigns, fighting on Geonosis and at Kaliida Shoals amongst others. Koon was also an accomplished starfighter pilot.

Kol Huro Unrest. At the urging of Darth Sidious, Mustag Olus, the dictator of the Kol Huro system used his battle droids to attempt to rise up against the Galactic Republic, but was defeated by Jedi Knights.

Tap-Nar-Pal is born on Cerea. Later nicknamed "Tap", Nar-Pal would later serve the Jedi Order and the Galactic Republic as a Commander in the Grand Army of the Republic during the Clone Wars.

---

43 BBY

The planet of Kegan ends its thirty year isolation. Kegan was a planet located in the Outer Rim Territories. The planet was run by the Benevolent Guides, who isolated the planet from the rest of the galaxy after having visions of the destruction of Kegan.

Dean Jinzler is born on Coruscant. As a young child, Dean loathed his elder sister, Lorana. Lorana was a Jedi, and Dean's parents were truly proud of her, causing Dean to feel jealous and unloved. In actuality, his parents offered him the same love and encouragement as they gave Lorana, but Dean blocked this out and created a false belief that grew with him over the years. Lorana and Dean parted on bad terms, just before Lorana embarked upon the ill-fated Outbound Flight mission, which led to her death.

Ferus Olin is born. Ferus Olin was the Human Jedi Padawan of Jedi Master Siri Tachi. Considered very mature for his age by many Jedi, Olin was well-respected for his dedication to the Jedi Order. He often clashed with fellow Padawan learner Anakin Skywalker, who disagreed with his strict adherence to Jedi rules and protocol. The two and their masters, Tachi and Obi-Wan Kenobi, often worked together on missions, traveling to such varied worlds as Radnor, Euceron, Andara, Typha-Dor, Romin, Falleen, and finally, Korriban. Many of these missions were orchestrated with the goal of capturing the escaped scientist and criminal Jenna Zan Arbor, who the Jedi later discovered was working with Granta Omega, the murderer of the Jedi Council member Yaddle. However, Zan Arbor consistently eluded them.

42 BBY

Omo Bouri dies. Omo Bouri was a male Wol Cabasshite Jedi Master serving the Jedi Order and the Galactic Republic. During his tenure in the Order, Bouri sat on the Jedi High Council. After his death, Bouri was remembered by his fellow Jedi for his years of service to the Order. Tiin had a difficult time with Bouri's passing, spending much of the next twenty years attempting to contact the spirit of his departed Master through the Force, but was never successful. Thus preoccupied, Tiin never took a Padawan of his own, and his usefulness on the Council was sometimes questioned prior to the Clone Wars

41 BBY

Anakin Skywalker, the Chosen One who will bring balance to the Force, is born to a slave named Shmi Skywalker on an unknown world.

Jedi Master Tahl dies on New Apsolon. Tahl was a female Noorian Jedi Master, a librarian of the Jedi Archives, and was also a close friend of Qui-Gon Jinn, with whom she fell in love. She was also the master of Padawan Bant Eerin. During a mission on Melida/Daan, she was blinded in a prison. However, her improved hearing and Force-sensitivity helped her get back on her feet. In 41 BBY Tahl received a call of help from the twins Eritha and Alani of New Apsolon, as their father Ewane was murdered after being reelected Supreme Governor. She answered the call for help and went alone to the world, despite Master Jinn's objections. Upon arriving on the world she accepted the twins' request to go undercover in the former secret police called the Absolutes, now outlawed and trying to coup the planet's democratic government. As Tahl didn't report back to the High Council after several weeks, Master Jinn grew concerned and decided to go looking for her, despite the disapproval from the Council. The Jedi Master and Padawan Kenobi managed to find Tahl and helped her complete the mission. During their struggles, Master Jinn pledged his life to her, and she did the same to him, speaking aloud the feelings they had long held for each other. Little time had passed before Tahl's undercover status was discovered and she was kidnapped by Balog, the Chief Security Controller who had pretended to assist the Jedi. Chief Balog kept her in a sensory deprivation containment device, injecting a drug that slowly drained her of her strength. Upon discovering their betrayal, Jinn and Kenobi began a full-scale chase of Chief Balog in the process of rescuing Tahl. When they finally found her, she was still alive, but the injuries she had suffered while in captivity were too severe, and she soon succumbed to her fatal injuries. This loss, magnified by Jinn's close relationship to her, drove him to the edge of the dark side. Bent on seeking revenge, Jinn hunted down

Balog and was prepared to execute him for his heinous acts. However, before Jinn could deliver the fatal blow to Balog's chest, Tahl's voice came to him warning him not to. He regained control of his emotions and didn't kill Balog, instead he delivered Balog and the twins to the authorities

Kit Fisto takes on Tahl's apprentice, Bant Eerin, as his own apprentice.

Shea Sadashassa is born on Herdessa. Shea Sadashassa was a Human female who served in the Galactic Senate as the Senator of Herdessa. At the end of the Clone Wars, she was also one of the members of the Delegation of 2000.

Darra Thel-Tanis is born. Darra Thel-Tanis, also known as Darra Haariden, was a female Human Jedi Padawan of Master Soara Antana in the waning years of the Republic Classic era. In 27 BBY, she and her master joined fellow Jedi Masters Obi-Wan Kenobi with his Padawan Anakin Skywalker, Siri Tachi with Ferus Olin, and Ry-Gaul with Tru Veld on a mission to the planet Radnor, where some deadly toxins were accidentally released into the atmosphere. The Jedi were briefed and tasked by the Jedi Council to aid the evacuation of the surviving Radnorans from the Twin Cities Tacto and Aubendo.

Kitster Chanchani Banai is born on Tatooine. Kitster Chanchani Banai was a Human slave boy on Tatooine, and the best friend of Anakin Skywalker. After not seeing his smuggler father, Rakir Banai, in many years, Kitster gave up hopes of becoming rescued from Tatooine and instead hoped to one day be a majordomo for a wealthy Mos Espan estate.

40 BBY

Finis Valorum is elected Supreme Chancellor of the Galactic Republic.

Barriss Offee is born on Mirial. She would soon become a talented Jedi healer who ascended to Jedi Knighthood during the Clone Wars.

Sien Sovv is born on Sullust. Sien Sovv was the male Sullustan Supreme Commander of the New Republic/Galactic Alliance Defense Force from roughly 23 ABY to 29 ABY, commanding the Defense Force just prior to and throughout the whole Yuuzhan Vong War, and again from 29 ABY to 36 ABY. Partially responsible for the disastrous loss of Coruscant to the Yuuzhan Vong armada, Admiral Sovv nevertheless retained the confidence of the Jedi and Galactic Alliance leadership and was allowed to remain on his post. A fleet under his command narrowly defeated the Yuuzhan Vong at Ebaq 9, an event that marked the turning point of the war, and he regained some of his former prestige. Sovv also served on Cal Omas' first High Council from 27 ABY to 29 ABY.

39 BBY

Shmi and Anakin Skywalker come to live on Tatooine when they are purchased by Gardulla the Hutt. However, the Hutt ultimately loses her prize to a junk dealer named Watto.

The Galactic Republic makes its first known survey of the swamp world, Dagobah, on the Outer Rim planet in the Dagobah system. A remote world of swamps and forests, it would later serve as a refuge for Jedi Grand Master Yoda during his exile, but otherwise had no notable intelligent life.

38 BBY

A Galactic Republic survey team crash-lands on Dagobah and begins a one-way battle to survive.

Professor Murk Lundi, a male Quermian from the planet of Ploo II and an expert on the history of the Sith, takes a sabbatical to scour Kodai for a lost Sith Holocron.

W. Wald is born on Tatooine. Wald was a friend of Anakin Skywalker in their childhood years. He lived on Tatooine with his family, which had moved to Mos Espa only shortly before the Invasion of Naboo, and helped Anakin as he built a podracer. Wald was known as a petty thief and vandal, and graffiti proclaiming Watto to be a "dirty old bird" was attributed to him. Wald always managed to share his illicit earnings with his friends, and his friendship with Anakin was strong.

Diric Wessiri is born. Diric Wessiri was a Corellian Human who was married with Iella Wessiri. After escaping from Corellia, he settled on Coruscant with his wife. In 6 ABY, he was captured by Imperials and sent to the Lusankya prison where he was brainwashed into one of Ysanne Isard's sleeper agents

Narro Sienar dies when his starship is destroyed near Dantooine. Narro Sienar was the father of Raith Sienar and CEO of Santhe/Sienar Technologies. Despite being the owner of one of the Corellian Engineering Corporation's primary competitors, Sienar helped the Corporation design the successful YT-1300 light freighter. He died when his starship was destroyed near Dantooine by a bomb planted by the Xi Char, in an attempt on his son's life.

37 BBY

The Yam'rii are enslaved. The Yam'rii, also known as the Huk, were a sentient species of insects who hailed from the planet Huk. They had mantis-like bodies, with large, mutifaceted eyes, thin torsos, knobby carapaces, and pointed feet. Some members of the species had large, clipper-like forelimbs that could be used as weapons, while others featured two fingers instead. They stood two meters or more in height and walked about on two legs. Members of the species were known as stealthy predators who were easily angered. They loved meat and eggs and had no compunctions about eating the eggs of other sentient species.

Liberal revolution on Pergitor. Pergitor was a planet in the Minos Cluster settled by Jesa Corporation miners. Overmining resulted in volcanic eruptions that poisoned the atmosphere and destroyed the ecosystem. The inhabitants were forced to retreat to sealed cities. After having been ruled as a despotism for years a group of young liberals overthrew the government, resulting in a disorganized democracy. However, just before the start of the Clone Wars, the Church of Infinite Perception launched a counter-coup, installing a theocracy. Due to its nebulous affiliation with the Galactic Republic, the Republic could do nothing to stop the bloody revolt.

Bene is born. A Force-sensitive Human, Bene was discovered by the Jedi Order and inducted into their ranks, learning the ways of the Force at the Coruscant Jedi Temple. Selected by a Jedi Master at the start of the Clone Wars, a conflict between the Republic and the Confederacy of Independent Systems, Bene constructed a blue-bladed lightsaber and took up the rank of Commander in the Grand Army of the Republic.

Orman Tagge, future head of the House of Tagge, is born on Tepasi.

---

36 BBY

Finis Valorum is re-elected Supreme Chancellor.

The Yam'rii uprising. Eventually, the Yam'rii had joined the Galactic Federation of Free Alliances. By this time, they were still commonly referred to as the Huk and when the Swarm War broke out in 36 ABY, disgruntled Yam'rii on Huk received overtures from the Killiks encouraging them to overthrow their government and side with the Colony against the Galactic Alliance. Some Yam'rii responded and became Joiners, addicted to the Dark Nest's black membrosia. Alliance operatives Han Solo, Leia Organa Solo, and C-3PO saw them among other targeted insectoid species in the nest known as Lizil. Knowing that such a coup, if it came along with others around the galaxy, would spread the Alliance forces thin, Jedi arrived to stymie any rebellion. In 137 ABY, after the fall of the Galactic Alliance to the forces of Sith Lord Darth Krayt, the Yam'rii were once again isolated and outside the reach of extraplanetary governments.

Nenevanth Tion is born on Lianna. She would become a citizen of the Galactic Republic and one of the earliest members of SAGroup, the youth chapter of the political lobbyist organization known as COMPOR.

Horton Salm is born on the planet Norval II in the Calaron sector. He would become a military officer of the Alliance to Restore the Republic and its successor, the New Republic.

35 BBY

The Great Resynchronization occurs, in an attempt to harmonize different Galactic calendars. The Great ReSynchronization was a 60 year long notation system that was established by the Republic Measures & Standards Bureau to recalibrate the disparate dating systems used by the Galactic Republic. Later in 25 ABY, it was disbanded and reorganized by the New Republic into the GSC. It was since used as a zero year for the dating system; thus, the Battle of Geonosis takes place in the year 13, the Great Jedi Purge in the year 16, Battle of Yavin in the year 35, and the Battle of Endor in the year 39. The Seventh Battle of Ruusan occurred in the year 965 BrS. Dates using the ReSynchronization were written in the following format: [Year]:[Month]:[Day] (ex. 13:5:21). Dates after ReSynchronization did not include trailing characters. Dates occurring before the ReSynchronization were followed by "BrS", for Before ReSynchonization. (ex. 4,965 BrS). The dating system introduced with the Great ReSynchronization was still used during the Imperial period, although some Imperials preferred to use the establishment of the Galactic Empire (19 BBY) as the starting point. The Great ReSynchronization system eventually became obsolete under the New Republic and was replaced in 25 ABY with the current Galactic Standard Calendar, centered around the Battle of Yavin (0 ABY).

Padmé Naberrie, also known as Her Royal Highness, Queen Amidala of Naboo, is made an Apprentice Legislator at the age of 8. The Apprentice Legislature was an organization for politically-minded youth and had offices on many different planets, including Alderaan, Naboo and Thesme.

Jedgar is born. Jedgar started his life as a Jedi youngling in the Jedi Temple on Coruscant. While there, he was troubled by his dark dreams which had a frightening habit of coming to pass. He had many nightmares of the Clone Wars and Great Jedi Purge long before they even happened. Though he was filled with a talent for foreseeing the future, Jedgar frightened all the other students and couldn't find a single Jedi Knight or Master who would even accept him as a Padawan and start training him. When his thirteenth birthday came in 23 BBY he was assigned to the Agricultural Corps, but he refused to accept such a menial occupation and fled the Jedi Order forever to follow his dreams to the dark side of the Force.

Ahsoka Tano is born on Shili. Ahsoka Tano, nicknamed Snips by her master, was a Togruta female from the planet Shili who trained as a Jedi apprentice during the Clone Wars, the conflict between the Galactic Republic and the Confederacy of Independent Systems. Tano was assigned to Jedi Knight Anakin Skywalker by Jedi Grand Master Yoda, and she demonstrated an eagerness to prove herself worthy to be his apprentice. Tano was involved in the defeat of the Separatist army on the planet Christophsis and was important to Republic efforts during the Battle of Teth. Along with Skywalker, Tano was instrumental in acquiring the Republic's safe passage through Hutt Space, due to her part in rescuing the son of Jabba the Hutt, which ensured an alliance between the Republic and the Hutt clans.

---

34 BBY

The Mandalorians are destroyed by a Jedi task force led by Count Dooku in the Battle of Galidraan. Jango Fett is the only survivor.

Mandalorian Myles dies on Galidraan. Myles was a male Mandalorian and member of the True Mandalorians under Mand'alor Jango Fett. Myles would follow Jango to the planet Galidraan when the Mandalorians under Fett had been hired by the Governor of Galidraan to put down a planetary insurrection. There, he would serve as Fett's aide-de-camp during the battle. When Fett found that the Mandalorians had fallen prey to a Death Watch trap, in which they were framed as murderers killing "political activists" and a Jedi strike team sent to arrest them, Fett frantically attempted to contact Myles and warn him to evacuate the camp. However, Fett was unable to get advanced warning to the camp, arriving the same time as the Jedi, under the leadership of Jedi Master Dooku. In the ensuing clash between the Jedi and Mandalorian forces, Myles attempted to use his jetpack to provide air support for Fett, but was killed by a Jedi who used force jump to get to Myles and cut him in half at the waist with his lightsaber. Myles' death would drive Fett to brutally kill the same Jedi and five others with his bare hands in vengeance.

Anakin Skywalker begins to build C-3PO out of the pieces of several broken protocol droids.

---

33 BBY

The Yinchorri Uprising begins.

Ki-Adi-Mundi joins the Jedi Council.

In response to a wave of Nebula Front attacks, the Galactic Senate grants the Trade Federation the right to arm its ships, in return for trade route taxation.

Eriadu Trade Summit occurred. This was an event proposed by Senator Palpatine, ostensibly to gather all parties affected by Supreme Chancellor Finis Valorum's proposal to allow the Trade Federation an increase in standing permissible armament in exchange for Galactic Senate taxation of free-trade zones. The Nebula Front, a radical political group that opposed the Trade Federation, was specifically not allowed to attend the event. This decision culminated in an attempt on Valorum's life by the spurned Nebula Front. The event was held on the planet of Eriadu, an important trade world in the Outer Rim. The event itself resulted in disaster. The majority of the Trade Federation Directorate was assassinated by its own security force in a plan orchestrated by Darth Plagueis and Darth Sidious, who made the Nebula Front appear responsible for the murders. No consensus was reached regarding the taxation of trade routes, and the Trade Federation was placed under the leadership of Nute Gunray, who would proceed to blockade trade on the planet of Naboo in protest.

Padmé Amidala becomes Princess of Theed.

Republic exploration ship Pathfinder III rediscovers Yashuvhu.

R2-D2 is created. R2-D2 was an R2-series astromech droid manufactured by Industrial Automaton Resourceful and spunky, the droid developed an adventurous personality during his many decades of operation. Inside of his cylindrical frame were many arms, sensors, and other tools that could be extended to fulfill various needs, such as slicing computers, extinguishing fires, projecting holograms, repairing starships, and flying. Along with his counterpart, the protocol droid C-3PO, R2-D2 constantly found himself directly involved in pivotal moments of galactic history. His bravery, coupled with his many gadgets, played large roles in saving the galaxy time and time again. Like other astromech droids, R2-D2 could walk on two legs or use a third leg to roll across the ground.

32 BBY

The Blockade of Naboo.

Padmé Amidala, former Princess of Theed, is elected Queen of Naboo.

The Invasion of Naboo

The Trade Federation, under the influence of Darth Sidious, blockades, and eventually invades, Naboo at the behest of the Dark Lord of the Sith.

Obi-Wan Kenobi and Qui-Gon Jinn free Queen Amidala along with her political entourage and personal security force.

R2-D2, an astromech droid aboard the Queen's Yacht, repairs the shield generator in the midst of danger while the ship attempts to escape the blockade. After the ship eludes the Trade Federation and lands on the remote world Tatooine, R2-D2 begins a longstanding relationship with the protocol droid C-3PO built by Anakin Skywalker.

Anakin Skywalker is discovered by Qui-Gon Jinn on the planet Tatooine. Qui-Gon wins Anakin's freedom by betting against Anakin's owner Watto in a podrace Anakin himself participates in.

Queen Amidala returns to Naboo and ends a period of disdain between the two predominant species on the planet: Humans and Gungans. The Gungans engage the droid army while the Queen and her security force capture the leaders of the Trade Federation. In the battle, Qui-Gon Jinn is killed by Darth Maul, who, in turn, is bisected by Obi-Wan Kenobi, but survives. Daultay Dofine is killed when the Droid Control Ship is destroyed by Anakin Skywalker.

Darth Plagueis is killed by his apprentice, Darth Sidious, who then becomes the new Dark lord of the Sith.

Following the Battle of Naboo, Senator Palpatine is elected Supreme Chancellor of the Republic, replacing

Finis Valorum.

Count Dooku leaves the Jedi Order and disappears, secretly joining Darth Sidious.

The creation of a secret clone army begins on Kamino, under the order placed by Jedi Master Sifo-Dyas. Jango Fett a bounty hunter whose DNA is the specimen for replication, requests an unaltered clone be made for him; he names him Boba Fett.

Count Dooku murders Sifo-Dyas and becomes Darth Tyranus, the second Sith apprentice of Darth Sidious.

The Yuuzhan Vong reach the galaxy.

31 BBY

Lando Calrissian is born. Lando Calrissian was a Human male professional gambler, entrepreneur, smuggler, and general throughout various points in his life. Born on Socorro, he became a gambler and con man early in his life and acquired his own ship, the Millennium Falcon, in a game of sabacc with a man named Cix Trouvee. He went on to have numerous adventures with the Falcon and its piloting droid, Vuffi Raa, during which he ran afoul of a Sorcerer of Tund named Rokur Gepta, whom Calrissian eventually killed. After a series of events led to him losing the Millennium Falcon to a Corellian named Han Solo on Bespin, Calrissian eventually became the Baron Administrator of Cloud City for a time—a position he once again gained through sabacc.

The Nightsisters succeed in capturing a Star Temple and slaughter many Kwi during their attempt to access the secrets of the Infinity Gate. The remaining Kwi disappeared into the deserts and would form tribes including the Blue Desert People and the Blue Mountain People, as well as the Rhoa Kwi. The Kwi also migrated every dawn and every dusk.

30 BBY

Adi Gallia, Ki-Adi-Mundi and A'Sharad Hett begin the hunt for Aurra Sing. Aurra Sing, also known as Nashtah, had been a female Jedi Padawan, but following a series of tragedies and misfortunes, she left the Jedi Order to become a vicious bounty hunter specializing in Jedi and political assassinations. She even became an associate in the posse of Cad Bane, a brief mentor of the orphaned Boba Fett, a commander for the Confederacy of Independent Systems during the Clone Wars, and later an Imperial Agent under the Sith Lord Darth Vader.

The Jedi Knight Vergere traveled to Zonama Sekot and encountered an advance scouting force of Yuuzhan Vong, which she then left with to prevent any conflict from harming the world.

Kh'aris Fenn, the son of Ro Fenn and leader of Clan Fenn, attempts a coup on the Twi'lek Clan Council.

Professor Rynalla, sometimes known as "Profex Rynalla" and a female Human dark side adept archaeologist and scholar affiliated to the University of Sanbra, attempts to excavate the Bracers of Najus on Leritor.

Anzati released from stasis by Aayla Secura overrun Kiffex. The Anzati (singular: Anzat) were a dangerous and mysterious Force-sensitive near-Human species with two tentacle-like proboscises that curled out and extended from their cheeks, with which the Anzati were able to feed upon the brains of their prey. With the tentacles retracted into seams along each side of their nose, Anzati were indistinguishable from any other humanoid species in the galaxy.

---

29 BBY

Raith Sienar presents the original concept for the Death Star to Wilhuff Tarkin. The Death Star was a moon-sized Imperial military battlestation armed with a planet-destroying superlaser and the concept had been explored even before the Clone Wars. It was the first in a long series of superweapons developed to execute the Tarkin Doctrine. The Death Star was designed to allow Emperor Palpatine to more directly control the Galactic Empire through fear. In most instances, a Death Star was to be commanded by a Moff. One Death Star was completely built by the Empire, with a second and third one never reaching full completion, as well as a prototype being in existence. In addition, a scaled-down version, the Tarkin, and a Hutt knockoff, the Darksaber, would be created by the Empire and Durga the Hutt, respectively. Both Death Stars were destroyed by the Rebel Alliance shortly after they became operational. The first Death Star was destroyed by Luke Skywalker, with the help of Han Solo, and the second Death Star was destroyed by Wedge Antilles and Lando Calrissian. Prior to the second Death Star being built, the Galactic Empire tested out a planetary superlaser for protecting its installations on the planet of Dubrillion. At some point after the second's destruction, the Rebel Alliance also attacked and destroyed a third Death Star. Following their destruction, other planet-devastating superweapons followed, including the Galaxy Gun, the Darksaber, the Sun Crusher, and the World Devastators.

Han Solo is born on Corellia. Solo would become a smuggler who would achieve galactic fame as a member of the Rebel Alliance and later the New Republic. Born on Corellia, he was orphaned at an early age and taken by the pirate Garris Shrike to serve on his crew. He was treated cruelly, and served Shrike for many years before escaping while in his teens. Solo became a smuggler, and fell in love with Bria Tharen, though she left him due to her duties to the Rebel Alliance. Solo then entered the Imperial Academy at Carida, serving with distinction. He was kicked out, however, when he stopped an Imperial officer from beating a Wookiee named Chewbacca with a neuronic whip for resisting capture. In gratitude, the Wookiee swore a life debt to Solo, protecting him with his life and a bond of friendship formed between the two that was unbreakable. Solo became a smuggler once again, with Chewbacca at his side. Piloting the upgraded and customized the Millennium Falcon, which he won in a game of Sabacc against Lando Calrissian, his future ally, he became known as one of the best smugglers in the galaxy.

Thracia Cho Leem leaves the Jedi Order. A Force-sensitive Human, Thracia Cho Leem was educated in the ways of the Force by the Jedi Order; eventually attaining the rank of Jedi Master. After achieving the rank of Knight, Leem undertook independent study as a Jedi Consular, becoming a renowned healer and well respected by many of her peers.

Preparations begin for the Outbound Flight Project. Outbound Flight was an expeditionary project, led mainly by Jedi Master Jorus C'baoth, that sent a mission of six Jedi Masters, twelve Jedi Knights, and 50,000 men, women, and children beyond the borders of the Galactic Republic into the Unknown Regions where they hoped to pierce the edge of the galaxy and seek out extragalactic life. Despite bureaucratic complications during funding and construction, Outbound Flight was eventually launched in 27 BBY as a central fuselage surrounded by six Dreadnaught-class heavy cruisers. It set out from Yaga Minor, and after visiting several worlds on the Outer Rim, Outbound Flight headed off into the Unknown Regions. Problems arose when the Jedi leader and project creator Jorus C'baoth took command of the vessel and imposed severe restrictions on its civilian and military population. In the Unknown Regions, the ship was almost destroyed by the forces of Commander Mitth'raw'nuruodo, at the request of Darth Sidious, though it was the Sith Lord's minion Kinman Doriana who dealt the final blow. It crashed on a world in The Redoubt, where it stayed for 49 years until it was rediscovered by the Chiss in 22 ABY. Along with Luke and Mara Jade Skywalker, they led a mission to recover it and encountered the survivors of the crash and their descendants, who had formed their own society amidst the wreckage

The Jamaane Coup occurs. The Jamaane coup was a coup against Supreme Overlord Quoreal by Domain Jamaane which made Shimrra Jamaane the Supreme Overlord of the Yuuzhan Vong.

---

28 BBY

The Vagaari, a race of nomadic conquerors and slavers that ruled a considerable area in the Unknown Regions, are defeated by the Chiss Ascendancy.

The Chancery election occurs. Palpatine is re-elected Supreme Chancellor.

The Colicoids take over spice processing on Nar Shaddaa. Spice was slang for a variety of mind-altering drugs. These included ryll and the strongest (and most expensive), Glitterstim.

Aayla Secura is knighted on Coruscant. Aayla Secura, born Aaylas'ecura, was a female Rutian Twi'lek Jedi Master in the later days of the Republic, who served with distinction as a General during the Clone Wars. She served as a Padawan under the tutelage of Quinlan Vos, and later, Vos' own master Tholme. Both Secura and Vos survived a brush with the dark side early in their Jedi training, though she later proved herself worthy of knighthood.

Quinlan Vos is promoted to Jedi Master on Coruscant. Quinlan Vos, nicknamed Quin by those closest to him, was a Kiffar male Jedi Master who, despite walking perilously close to the dark side of the Force throughout his life, served the Jedi Order and the Galactic Republic in their final days. Born into Clan Vos, the ruling bloodline of the planet Kiffu, Vos possessed a strong sensitivity to the Force, one that nurtured in him an exceptional talent for psychometry. After Jedi Master Tholme discovered his Force sensitivity, Vos underwent initial Jedi training on his homeworld instead of at the Jedi Temple on Coruscant, as his people hoped to one day make him a Guardian of Kiffu. Yet everything changed for Vos after his power-seeking great-aunt, Tinté Vos, secretly sacrificed his parents, Guardians Quian and Pethros Vos, to Anzati vampires and then tricked him into psychometrically experiencing their murders. To master his subsequently acquired fear of Anzati, Vos began proper Jedi training as Tholme's Padawan learner, though the memory of his parents' deaths spawned in him a darkness that he would never be able to vanquish.

27 BBY

Radnor, a small, sea–covered planet with a small main landmass, is struck by a bio plague; the nearby Avoni attempt to conquer it. The plague first struck the city-state of Aubendo. The city-state of Aubendo was called the Isolation Sector because no one could exit Aubendo once they entered. Tacto was called the Clear Sector because there weren't any plague cases there. The ministers of Tacto fled creating a panic among the healthy population, and causing looting and unrest.

Mon Mothma is elected Senator of Chandrila. Mon Mothma was born in 48 BBY into a wealthy and influential family living on Chandrila. Her mother, Tanis Mothma was the governor of the planet, and her father was an arbiter-general for the Republic, so it came as no surprise when she would follow in their influential footsteps and become a Senator and later on lead a Rebellion against the Empire.

The Outbound Flight Project departs from Yaga Minor, but is destroyed shortly after by Mitth'raw'nuruodo.

The Sepan Civil War begins between the Ripoblus and the Dimok. It had raged for several decades and become sufficiently violent to draw the attention of the Galactic Republic. In an attempt to diffuse the war, three different Jedi missions were dispatched to negotiate a peace. The final mission was staffed by Jedi Knights Empatojayos Brand, Bultar Swan, and Chellemi Chuovvick. Unable to mediate the dispute, questions surrounding a potential Sepan secession from the Republic became common.

Reija Momen becomes administrator of the Intergalactic Communications Center. During the Clone Wars, the Intergalactic Communications Center, located on Praesitlyn, played a vital role in communication for the Core Worlds.

Master Yarael Poof is slain by Ashaar Khorda while protecting Coruscant from the Infant of Shaa.

Firmus Piett is born on Axxila. Firmus Piett was a Human male who was the last admiral of the Imperial Navy's Death Squadron, Darth Vader's personal fleet of Star Destroyers. Coming from humble beginnings on the backwater Outer Rim world of Axxila, Piett began his naval career with the Axxila antipirate fleet. Though his posting was not notable, Piett's creativity, dedication and integrity made his home sector the safest in the Outer Rim. Piett made an extraordinary number of arrests and suppressions of smugglers and pirates, and his record earned the attention of high-ranking officers on Imperial Center.

26 BBY

Yeorg Captison is elected to the Bakuran Senate. Yeorg Captison was a member of the notable Bakuran Captison family of politicians. His grandfather or great-grandfather may have been Deredith Arden.

Maxo Vista wins the Galactic Games. In an exhibition, he forced Obi-Wan Kenobi to race him on a holographic obstacle course. He also made a deal with Doby Tyerell and Deland Tyerell to supply advanced track information in an illegal podrace, but he also programmed the Podracer, which Anakin Skywalker was flying for Doby and Deland, to crash into a stadium once it appeared above it. Anakin, however, was able to regain control of his podracer and finish the race. Later, Maxo Vista was exposed by the Jedi for attempted murder and disruption of the events and was arrested. He was later set free because all of Obi-Wan Kenobi's evidence was destroyed.

25 BBY

The Yuuzhan Vong establish an advance base on the planet Bimmiel.

The Jedi begin a campaign against the Pirates of Iridium. The Pirates of Iridium were a group of bloodthirsty thieves who roamed the galaxy's spaceways, preying on hapless spice haulers and freighters during the Separatist Crisis. Utilizing their shield-penetrating power gems, the bandits would plunder any ships coming through the Atrivis sector. the Jedi Order took it upon themselves to rid the Republic of this threat and launched a campaign to destroy the marauders, led by Kit Fisto. The pirates, being paid as profiteers by the burgeoning Confederacy of Independent Systems, had attracted Jedi attention by raiding grain and spice convoys. In their traditionally non-violent way, at least six Knights (including Fisto, Belsed-Qan Idan, Dovish Hokken, Yrada Soludisan, and Aruden Kej) had intended to begin peaceful negotiations; however, that plan was abandoned once the pirates opened fire and a skirmish broke out.

Alderaanian scouts find the planet Isis, but keep it a secret. Isis was a crystalline world and its surface was covered with large translucent crystalline mountains and spires. The crystals refracted the incoming sunlight and filled the skies with countless rainbows. The canyons had an average width of 750m and a height of 12,500m. The crystal were rich in minerals and ores, but also disrupted all communications and sensors, even from orbit. Despite its unusual environment, the planet was hospitable to most sentient life.

Yaddle sacrifices herself to save the people of Mawan by using the Force to absorb a deadly chemical weapon. She, along with Obi-Wan Kenobi and his Padawan Anakin Skywalker, were sent to Mawan to attempt to restore peace to the lawless world. Yaddle sacrificed her life to save the people of Mawan, using the Force to absorb a deadly chemical weapon unleashed by Granta Omega. She was then given a traditional Jedi funeral back at the Jedi Temple on Coruscant and was succeeded by Shaak Ti on the Jedi High Council.

Shaak Ti joins the Jedi Council, replacing Yaddle. Shaak Ti was a female Togruta Jedi Master, hailing from the planet Shili, serving the Galactic Republic as a member of the Jedi Order in the final decades of the Republic Classic era. Joining the Jedi High Council in the years before the Clone Wars, she took up the ranks of General within the Grand Army of the Republic and was tasked with the oversight of clone trooper training on the ocean world Kamino.

24 BBY

Count Dooku reappears on Raxus Prime and alleges that the Republic has become too corrupt and pushes for citizens to break from the Republic and form a new government of their own.

Granta Omega plots two assassination attempts on Palpatine and though they are averted by the Jedi, 21 Senators are killed.

Ferus Olin resigns from the Jedi Order. He eventually ends up living on the world of Bellassa where he starts a good friendship with Roan Lands.

Palpatine reaches the end of his second term as Supreme Chancellor. The passage of the Emergency Powers Act allows him to stay in office until the crisis is dealt with. The Act eliminated term limits for Supreme Chancellors, giving each Chancellor the option of when to stand down for new elections. The act also granted powers for chancellors to make instant decisions without the need for full senate approval, giving Palpatine all necessary authority to attempt to end the Separatist Crisis, including declaration of martial law on local systems. The senate granted Palpatine special powers for the duration of the emergency, yet Palpatine himself was the only person who had the authority to declare the emergency over.

Amidala, after serving two terms as Queen, is appointed by her successor Jamillia to be Naboo's Senator.

Start of the Virgillian Civil War. This was an internal conflict between the revolutionary Virgillian Free Alignment and the ruling Aristocracy government. Because the Virgillian sector was nominally a part of the Galactic Republic, the Galactic Senate attempted to negotiate peace. A diplomatic team of four Jedi Knights, Ludwin Katarkus, Danyawarra, Everen Ettene, and Halagad Ventor, were dispatched to the sector. However, the Jedi transport was destroyed and it was believed that all four were killed. That, combined with the advent of the Clone Wars shortly after, ended any attempt by the Republic to mediate the war. It later became apparent that Halagad Ventor and Danyawarra survived, and continued to serve the Republic.

The Commerce Guild takes control of Korriban. The Commerce Guild was a trade conglomerate made up of major commercial entities, such as the SoroSuub Corporation. The Guild was known for pressuring smaller companies to join.

Ister Paddie assumes Lanus Wrede's former seat in the Galactic Senate after Wrede committed suicide.

Senator Paddie was a member of the Loyalist Committee established prior to the start of the Clone Wars.

23 BBY

Ludi Billane is born on Ord Thoden. Aris-Del Wari, born Ludi Billane, was a Jedi youngling who lived in the era known as the Great Peace of the Republic. Separated from her mother, Jonava Billane, during a quake that wracked the city of Domitree on Ord Thoden, the child was recovered by the Jedi Order, who discovered that she was Force-sensitive. The Jedi brought the infant into their ranks and gave her the name of "Aris-Del Wari," before introducing her to the power of the Force.

Judder Page is born on Corulag. Judder Page was a Human male from Corulag who throughout his life served as a commando in the Galactic Empire, Rebel Alliance, New Republic, and Galactic Alliance. He was a nondescript-looking man who could easily blend into any crowd, traits that served him well on many missions that required stealth. Page was born to a wealthy Imperial senator and spent his youth training himself in various combat techniques before being sent to the Imperial Academy. After graduating with honors, Page briefly served in the Imperial Army, but had no love for the Empire and quickly defected to the Rebellion after hearing a passionate speech given by the Rebel leader Leia Organa to the Council of Galactic Rights. In his first years as a Rebel, Page served on the ground at the Battles of Hoth and Endor. Following the latter battle, he was given command of the Katarn Commandos, and he trained them to be an irregular and independent unit that was given a great deal of freedom in completing its mission objectives.

22.5 BBY

Battle of Antar 4.

22 BBY

The Military Creation Act. The Military Creation Act was a bill proposed in the Galactic Senate during the Separatist Crisis, in the years leading up to the Clone Wars. Created in response to increasing secessions from the Galactic Republic, the Act authorized the creation of an Army of the Republic, to aid the local security forces, Judicials, and Jedi that made up the Republic's peacekeeping forces. The Act remained in limbo for two years until, on 13:3:6, a vote was at last set for it two months hence. Over the following weeks, vociferous debate and intense campaigning ensued as Senators and many others sought to either advocate or oppose the measure.

The First Battle of Geonosis occurs. The First Battle of Geonosis, known most commonly as simply the Battle of Geonosis, was the first battle between the Confederacy of Independent Systems and the Galactic Republic in the conflict that would become known as the Clone Wars. It would be the first major combat of the Grand Army of the Republic, as well as the first major battle the Jedi would fight in years.

Anakin Skywalker returns to his homeworld of Tatooine and meets his step brother Owen Lars and his girlfriend Beru. Shmi Skywalker is captured by the Tusken Raiders. Anakin Skywalker finds her but, unfortunately, it is too late and his mother dies in his arms. Driven by anger and rage, Anakin massacres the entire village of Tuskens while the Force ghost of Qui-Gon Jinn tries to stop him.

Obi-Wan Kenobi discovers that Nute Gunray has been attempting to have Padmé Amidala assassinated as revenge for the Battle of Naboo. He also discovers that separatists under the leadership of Count Dooku are forming the Confederacy of Independent Systems.

Palpatine is given emergency powers by the Senate and authorized the creation of the Grand Army of the Republic to "counter the increasing threats of the separatists." The Grand Army of the Republic (GAR), also known as the Grand Army and the Clone Army, was a major branch of the Galactic Republic Military composed entirely of clone troopers, an army of elite soldiers created from the genetically altered template of the Mandalorian bounty hunter Jango Fett. Bred in secret within the cloning facilities of the planet Kamino, the Grand Army was officially formed by Supreme Chancellor Palpatine at the behest of the Galactic Senate in response to the Separatist Crisis which threatened to divide the galaxy between the Republic and the newly born Confederacy of Independent Systems. The members of the Jedi Order were commissioned as high-ranking commanders and generals in the Grand Army, second in authority only to Chancellor Palpatine, who held the rank of Supreme Commander. Under the leadership of their Jedi officers, the Grand Army engaged the Separatist Droid Army on many worlds during the Clone Wars, suffering heavy casualties for three years while restoring Republic sovereignty to numerous rebellious areas throughout the galaxy.

Anakin Skywalker and Padmé Amidala marry in secret on Naboo.

---

22 – 19 BBY

The Clone Wars begin. The Clone Wars, also known as the Clone War and the Great Clone War, was the name given to the major galactic conflict fought between the Galactic Republic and the Confederacy of Independent Systems. The war was named after the clone troopers utilized by the Republic against the battle droid forces of the Separatists. These armies, the Grand Army of the Republic and the Separatist Droid Army, were two of the largest ever pitted against each other in galactic history, and the fighting between them rapidly spread to countless inhabited worlds. Beginning with the First Battle of Geonosis, both sides scored significant victories over the other, and at different times during the war either seemed likely to triumph. The death of the Confederate Head of State Count Dooku during the Battle of Coruscant and that of the Confederate General Grievous during the Battle of Utapau, coupled with the issue of Order 66 and the deactivation of the droid army, brought an end to the fighting. At the time, it was the largest galactic conflict to date. Unbeknownst to most of those involved, the conflict was started, maintained, and eventually ended by the Dark Lord of the Sith Darth Sidious, whose ultimate goal was the transformation of the Republic into the Galactic Empire with him as Emperor as well as the eradication of the Jedi Order through the Great Jedi Purge. The conflict led to the Order of the Sith Lords controlling the dominant galactic government.

---

21 BBY

Wedge Antilles is born on Corellia. Wedge Antilles, a Human male, was a famed Corellian pilot and general, known as a hero of the Rebel Alliance and New Republic. Orphaned at age seventeen, he joined the Rebellion after Imperial forces killed his girlfriend, Mala Tinero. A standout starfighter pilot, he was one of the few to survive the Battle of Yavin, after which he founded Rogue Squadron with his friend Luke Skywalker. Antilles and Skywalker built Rogue Squadron into a renowned unit, and after the Battle of Hoth, Antilles took command. He flew as Red Leader in the Battle of Endor, striking the blow that destroyed the second Death Star alongside Lando Calrissian and becoming the only pilot to survive both Death Star runs.

Second Battle of Geonosis.

IMPERIAL PERIOD

The Imperial Period took place from the Declaration of a New Order in 19 BBY, the transition of the democratic Galactic Republic into autocratic Imperial rule, until the death of Emperor Palpatine at the Battle of Endor in 4 ABY. The era was characterized by the beginning and later rule of the Galactic Empire, giving the period its name. It was also known by such nicknames as the Imperial era, the Dark Times, or the Birth of the Rebellion.

---

19 BBY

Birth of the Galactic Empire. The Galactic Empire, also known as the New Order, the Old Empire, the First Galactic Empire, Palpatine's New Order, the Imperium or simply the Empire, was the galactic government established by Supreme Chancellor Palpatine to replace the Galactic Republic in 19 BBY and bring Sith rule to the galaxy. The Republic, which had lasted for at least 25,034 years, ended following a period of intense political turmoil and the subsequent devastation of the Clone Wars. After the death of Count Dooku above Coruscant, the death of General Grievous on Utapau and finally the massacre of the leaders of the Confederacy of Independent Systems on Mustafar, Chancellor Palpatine (by then ruling with near-absolute power), began a purge of the Jedi Order, and then proclaimed himself Emperor of the galaxy and reorganized the Galactic Republic into "the first Galactic Empire" on the galactic capital, Coruscant.

The Clone Wars end, Count Dooku is killed by Anakin Skywalker during the Battle of Coruscant and General Grievous is killed by Obi-Wan Kenobi on Utapau. Chancellor Palpatine, revealed to be the Sith Master Darth Sidious, kills Masters Kit Fisto, Saesee Tiin, Agen Kolar and, with Anakin's help, Mace Windu.

Anakin Skywalker turns to the dark side of the Force and becomes Darth Vader, Palpatine's ruthless second-in-command and third apprentice.

The Great Jedi Purge is orchestrated by Sidious and Vader and almost all Jedi are hunted down and killed. The Great Jedi Purge, later also known as Palpatine's Purge, was initiated by the Sith Lord Darth Sidious, upon his creation of the Galactic Empire. It resulted in the near-annihilation of the Jedi, as it had been with the First Jedi Purge that occurred after the Jedi Civil War. The purge officially began with Order 66, following a botched attempt by Mace Windu and three other Jedi to arrest Sidious, who was the Supreme Chancellor. The Jedi were declared the enemies of the Republic, and the Grand Army of the Republic was ordered to turn on them. Sidious, now Emperor of the Galactic Empire, used his new apprentice, Darth Vader, and other agents of the Empire to hunt down and kill the remaining Jedi. Some Jedi fought the Empire until their deaths, like Roan Shryne, and those at the Conclave on Kessel. Others hid from the Empire, like Obi-Wan Kenobi and Yoda. In the nineteen years that followed Order 66, many Jedi fell to

Vader, Inquisitors, Emperor's Hands, and even bounty hunters. By 1 BBY, so small a number of Jedi remained that the Emperor, considering the Jedi to be no longer a threat, put an end to the Purge.

Darth Vader kills all the Separatist leaders on Mustafar,[143] then is defeated and severely wounded in a duel by Obi-Wan Kenobi.

Luke Skywalker and Leia Organa are born to Padmé Amidala on Polis Massa. Padmé Amidala dies in childbirth. Obi-Wan Kenobi, who survives the Purge, leaves Luke with Anakin's step brother Owen Lars and Leia with Bail Organa, in order to protect them from Palpatine and their father.

Mon Mothma and Bail Organa along with other senators loyal to the Galactic Republic, discuss in secret plans for a Rebellion. This eventually leads to the Galactic Civil War.

Galen Marek is born on the Wookiee homeworld of Kashyyyk. Galen Marek, codenamed Starkiller, was a male Human apprentice of the Sith Lord Darth Vader. A powerful Force-user who lived during the era of the Galactic Empire, Marek originated from the Wookiee home planet of Kashyyyk as the sole offspring of two Jedi Knights—Mallie and Kento Marek—who deserted the Jedi Order during the Clone Wars. Following the death of his mother, the young Marek's father was killed in battle by Darth Vader. Though only a child, Marek possessed an exceptionally strong connection to the Force that the Dark Lord of the Sith sought to exploit. Thus, Darth Vader abducted Marek in order to train the orphan in the ways of the Sith Order. Although the Sith were limited to only two members at any given time, Vader nonetheless trained Marek as a secret apprentice during his own apprenticeship to Darth Sidious, the Sith Lord who ruled the galaxy as Emperor Palpatine. The physical and psychological trauma of Vader's unforgiving training regimen resulted in Marek's immersion within the dark side of the Force as his Master intended. With his childhood memories suppressed and his original identity forgotten, Marek only knew himself as the Dark Lord's apprentice; a Sith assassin who operated under the codename "Starkiller" and a living weapon to be deployed against the enemies of Darth Vader.

---

18 BBY

The Ghorman Massacre occurs when a group of activists were protesting Imperial taxation on the planet Ghorman in the Sern sector. Wilhuff Tarkin's vessel was blocked by peaceful protesters who stood on the ship's landing pad and refused to move. With implied permission from Palpatine, Tarkin landed the ship right on the protesters. An overwhelming majority were killed instantly, while hundreds were severely injured, many of them later dying from the resulting injuries. Only a lucky few escaped the ordeal with their lives intact, but almost all sustained horrific psychological damage.

Jedi Master Plett turns his fortress in Plawal on Belsavis into a sanctuary for fugitives from the Emperor's Jedi purge. Plett was a male Ho'Din from the planet Moltok who served as a Jedi Master during the final decades of the Galactic Republic. A talented botanist and ecologist, he settled on the remote Outer Rim world of Belsavis, in an isolated valley that came to be known as Plett's Well. There, he practiced his botanical skills for seventy years, genetically tailoring plants to the unique environment. At the time of the

Great Jedi Purge, he provided refuge to dozens of students from the Jedi Temple within his compound.

Emporor Palpatine constructs the Eye of Palpatine, a colossal, asteroid-shaped super dreadnaught. The deadly warship was the Emperor's first superweapon. It was referred to as both a "dreadnought" and a "battlemoon." As part of its secretive origin, the vessel was made to look similar to an asteroid, including the implementation of impact craters under Palpatine's direct input. The reason for this was officially stated as a means of protection from detection by enemy vessels and worlds, although it was speculated to have either been done as a means to ensure its development remained a secret due to potential outrage, or possibly even converted from a large space rock in order to save on material resources. Akin to a Torpedo Sphere in role (ie an enormous siege platform intended to target sections of planet with myriad weapons) the Eye was armed with much more weaponry and built on a much larger scale. Its firepower rivaled and possibly exceeded that of an entire fleet carrying out a Base Delta Zero-type orbital bombardment, i.e. it could reduce the upper crust of a planet to molten slag while acting alone and using only its own weaponry.Its overall size surpassed that of the Torpedo Spheres as well as several Super Star Destroyers, although its length was on par with the Executor-class Star Dreadnoughts and the Vengeance-class dreadnoughts.

Callista Ming transfers her spirit to the Eye of Palpatine's computer system when the automated Imperial dreadnaught came to demolish the settlement. Masana, and her lover Geith Eris, launched a desperate mission to sabotage the ship. They were successful, but in the process, Masana shed her physical body, remaining embedded in the ship's computer as a spirit. Many years later, Luke Skywalker and several other Jedi were brought onto the ship as it resumed its mission. Masana, in spirit form, communicated and began to fall in love with Skywalker. She later took the body of one of the other Jedi, Cray Mingla, after Mingla gave it up to stop the superweapon once and for all. However, in the process, Masana, now using the surname "Ming," lost her ability to touch the Force.

Han Solo meets his cousin Thrackan Sal-Solo, who sells him back to Garris Shrike.

Obi -Wan Kenobi finds Ferus Olin on Bellassa and foils an Imperial plot to mass murder the residents of Bellassa's capital city, Ussa. Ferus Olin had been the Human Jedi Padawan of Jedi Master Siri Tachi. Considered very mature for his age by many Jedi, Olin was well-respected for his dedication to the Jedi Order. He often clashed with fellow Padawan learner Anakin Skywalker, who disagreed with his strict adherence to Jedi rules and protocol. The two and their masters, Tachi and Obi-Wan Kenobi, often worked together on missions, traveling to such varied worlds as Radnor, Euceron, Andara, Typha-Dor, Romin, Falleen, and finally, Korriban. Many of these missions were orchestrated with the goal of capturing the escaped scientist and criminal Jenna Zan Arbor, who the Jedi later discovered was working with Granta Omega, the murderer of the Jedi Council member Yaddle. However, Zan Arbor consistently eluded them. Shortly before the onset of the Clone Wars, Olin resigned from the Jedi Order due to the guilt he felt over the inadvertent death of fellow Padawan Darra Thel-Tanis on Korriban, where Omega was finally killed in battle with Kenobi present. Eventually, he befriended Roan Lands on Bellassa, and the two started a business together— Olin and Lands. Olin and Lands would produce fake, brand-new identities for anyone that wanted to escape from the empire. Olin grew fond enough of Bellassa to adopt it as his homeworld.

Ferus Olin finds Jedi Master Garen Muln in the Crystal Caves of Ilum.

Obi -Wan Kenobi stops Inquisitor Sancor from finding information about Padmé Amidala's death on the asteroid Polis Massa.

Ferus Olin and Trever Flume find Jedi Master Fy-Tor-Ana, now going by the name of Solace, in the underlevels of Coruscant, with the help of Dexter Jettster.

Ferus Olin is captured by Imperial stormtroopers in the Jedi Temple, and then interrogated by Inquisitor Malorum.

Ferus Olin, with the help of Queen Apailana and Boss Rugor Nass, defeats Malorum and temporarily rids Naboo of its Imperial presence.

In the aftermath of the Battle of Naboo, in which Apailana is assassinated, the Empire installs Kylantha as the new Queen of her people. Although Queen Kylantha was outwardly loyal to the Empire, she refused to dissolve the Naboo Royal Advisory Council and, unlike other Imperial-held worlds, had only implemented a few changes to Naboo's democratic government. This led many Imperials, including Chief Inquisitor Loam Redge, to believe she was actually a Rebel Alliance sympathizer. Kylantha's personal view towards the Empire remained ambiguous. During her reign, Kylantha appointed Pooja Naberrie, the younger niece of the beloved Naboo politician Padmé Amidala, as Naboo's representative in the Imperial Senate, a position Naberrie held until Emperor Palpatine dissolved that governmental body in o BBY

17 BBY

Darth Vader defeats all of the Sa Cuis clones and defeats the rebellious Dark Jedi Sheyvan in a lightsaber duel.

Rodia experienced an internal coup when Navik the Red of the Chattza Clan conquered his rivals. Under its new leadership, the planet would become a free trading port and an emerging economic power. Navik the Red was a male Rodian warlord who served as the Grand Protector of Rodia during the Galactic Civil War. He gained his nickname from the red birthmark on his face. His given name, "Navik," was Rodese for "dark", and was considered to be a prophetic name

16 BBY

Skee, a portly Rodian who was a member of the Tetsu Clan, and his family flee to the jungle planet of U-Tendik, during the Rodian Clan Wars. There Skee discovered a predatory species of animal known as a Manka cat and became a prosperous Manka Cat hunter. He particularly enjoyed hunting them late in the year during mating season and would hang Manka pelts from the limbs of the Tendril trees as a testament to his skill.

15 BBY

The Rego Mineral Company discovers the planet of Altor 14. In return for a trade agreement with the native Nuiwit, the Rego Mineral Company gained rights to the planet's mineral deposits.

The Fromm Tower Droid is created. The Fromm Tower Droid, also known as a guardian droid and sentry droid, was a heavily armed droid designed by Tig Fromm, the son of the noted Annoo-dat crime lord Sise Fromm, and manufactured at his secret base on the planet Ingo. Four meters tall, with a cylindrical tower extending from an armored chassis, the Tower Droid could travel at speeds up to 100 kilometers per hour on six large pneumatic wheels. The Tower Droid was fitted with numerous sensors, and could respond to nearby threats with its arsenal of four laser cannons and two repulsor ball launchers. Tower Droids were primarily used by the Fromm Gang as perimeter sentries, but they were also used by the Confederacy of Independent Systems at the Battle of Xagobah during the Clone Wars. In 15 BBY, many Tower Droids were destroyed during the rescue of the captive speeder racer Jord Dusat from Tig Fromm's base, leading Fromm to increase production to cover the losses. Soon after, both Tig and Sise Fromm were captured by the bounty hunter Boba Fett. The Fromms' rivals seized their assets, and the remaining Tower Droids were dispersed around the galaxy.

14 BBY

Syal Antilles runs away from home and changes her name to Wynssa Starflare. She was a human actress and was connected to two of the most famous starfighter pilots of the day, Soontir Fel was her husband, while Wedge Antilles was her brother, and was the mother of Galactic Emperor Jagged Fel.

13 BBY

The Renatasia system is re-discovered. The Renatasia system contained the medium-sized yellow star Renatasia and eight planets, including Renatasia III and Renatasia IV. It was one of the many lost Human colonies founded by Grizmallt under the Old Republic. The colony was rediscovered by the Centrality. Osuno Whett and Vuffi Raa were assigned by the Centrality and the Galactic Empire to win the trust of the Renatasians to make them easy targets for the armed forces to subdue. Covering the droid Vuffi Raa with an organic exterior, Whett posed as Vuffi's assistant and presented them as representatives of a galactic civilization eager to welcome the Renatasians. Whett and Vuffi Raa toured the world and helped the Renatasians form a unified world government. Then after 700 days, Whett transmitted all his data, beginning the invasion by the Imperial and Centran forces. Because of the massacre that followed, Vuffi Raa was nicknamed the "Butcher of Renatasia" since none of the Renatasians realized he was a droid and that Whett was the true butcher. In response, a group of the survivors had commandeered twelve aging starfighters and vowed to hunt down and kill Vuffi Raa.

12 BBY

A joint Imperial/Centrality invasion force conquers the Renatasia system after a brutal conflict.

The Kamino Uprising occurs on the aquatic planet Kamino, the origin world of the Grand Army of the Republic during the waning days of the Old Republic. After having spent the better part of the last couple decades growing clone troopers for the Old Republic and stormtroopers for the Galactic Empire under Emperor Palpatine, a group of Kaminoans went rogue, using their cloning resources to grow an army with the intent of combating Palpatine's New Order. The Kaminoan resistance once again utilized the Grand Army of the Republic's template, Jango Fett's DNA and equipped their soldiers with phase I clone trooper armor.

11 BBY

Maridun is discovered by the Galactic Empire; slaving and mining operations are quickly established. Maridun was the grassy and forested homeworld of the Amanin species. Maridun went unnoticed for many millennia, and so was considered a haven by those who knew of of its existence. The planet would come to support a colony of Lurmen who sought to escape the Clone Wars, and was the site of a battle when Confederate General Lok Durd arrived on the planet to test an experimental weapon.

Soontir Fel is blackmailed from Corellia and enlists in the Academy of Carida. Soontir Fel was considered among the best starfighter pilots in the galaxy, becoming an Imperial hero, but his journey to those heights was anything but easy. Born on Corellia to a farming family, Fel developed his piloting skills over the fields before gaining entrance to the Imperial Academy and beginning a career as a TIE fighter pilot. He served dutifully, demonstrating a strong sense of responsibility for his men. After a series of events out of his control tarnished his career, Fel was exiled to the lackluster 181st Imperial Fighter Wing, which he revived, eventually gaining its command and the title of Baron of the Empire, winning Fel a reputation as the Empire's most deadly pilot and the 181st as its most elite starfighter unit. During that time, Fel met and married the famous actress Wynssa Starflare, who he discovered was actually the sister of Rebel ace Wedge Antilles.

10 BBY

Han Solo escapes from Trader's Luck and begins life on his own, away from Garris Shrike's band of space gypsies.

9 BBY

Following the fallout from the Battle of Kamino, a key campaign of the Clone Wars, the Empire begins to employ clones from different templates and non-clones into the Stormtrooper ranks.

Dash Rendar enters the Imperial Academy. Dash Rendar was born into a wealthy Corellian family during the final years of the Galactic Republic and he chose to pursue a career as an officer in the Imperial Navy rather than joining the family shipping business. When his parents refused to sell their business to Prince Xizor, owner of Xizor Transport Systems and leader of the Black Sun crime syndicate, the Dark Prince sabotaged a freighter flown by Rendar's older brother, Stanton, killing him as his ship crashed into the Imperial Museum. Emperor Palpatine blamed the Rendar family, exiling them from the Core Worlds and dismissing Rendar from the Imperial Academy on Carida. Fleeing to the Outer Rim Territories, Rendar gained a reputation as a hot-shot pilot, smuggler, and mercenary. His success gained him his own ship, the YT-2400 light freighter Outrider, and the services of the Nautolan navigator Eaden Vrill and the Cybot Galactica LE-series repair droid LE-BO2D9.

A groundquake crumbles the civilization of the Chadra-Fan, short, rodent-like humanoids, usually no more than one meter tall, with bat-like faces, converting those that survived into spacefaring nomads.

The HWK-290 light freighter that would become Moldy Crow is manufactured. The HWK-290 was a light freighter manufactured by the Corellian Engineering Corporation during the decades leading up to the Battle of Naboo, in an effort to break into a new market for fast, small cargo ships. Unlike YT-series of ships for tramp captains, the Hawk line was aimed at more upscale clients, like wealthy merchants and noble politicians. The series saw modest success, but never reached the amount of sales of YT-series, and was discontinued during the Clone Wars to make way for military production.

Sienar Fleet Systems (owned by the massive company Santhe/Sienar Technologies) purchases the patents and production rights to the Eta-2 Actis-interceptor and Alpha-3 Nimbus V-wing from Kuat Systems Engineering.

Luke Skywalker contracts a case of Tatooine dust fever.

An entire village of settlers on Coveway is killed by the new Imperial garrison's commander.

8 BBY

Han Solo earns the nickname "Slick" from Lieutenant Badure when he safely lands a malfunctioning LU-33 orbital loadlifter.

Emporor Palpatine discovers a method of transferring his consciousness into a new body in a Holocron retrieved from Jedi Master Ashka Boda.

The Mount Tantiss storehouse on Wayland completes construction. Its architects, V'Droz brothers are killed to keep it a secret. Mount Tantiss was originally the site of an Old Republic fort that was reactivated by Palpatine during the Clone Wars. The storehouse contained both objects and trinkets of unspeakable evil, as well as mementos from the conquests of the Empire. His most private treasures were hidden in a massive labyrinth designed by Garrbo V'Droz in the mountain's bottom chamber. The mountain and its storehouse were guarded by a Dark Jedi referred to as "the Guardian" until he was (presumably) killed by the insane clone Joruus C'baoth. The mountain also held the twenty-thousand Spaarti cloning cylinders which were used by Grand Admiral Thrawn to create a crew of clones for his new fleet of Dreadnaughts, and the schematics for the cloaking devices that he would install on those very same ships and would make their way into much of the Imperial Fleet as time went by.

Venthan Chassu's Selonian nudes are displayed in the Coronet City Museum of Fine Art on Corellia.

Eib sells Gryseium Incorporated to Rigis Corazon. Gryseium Incorporated was a ranch founded by Huegu Eib, a Sullustan and was located in the clouds of Tyed Kant, a planet in the Mid Rim. Corazon attempted to use Gryseium Incorporated to corner the food market on Demophon, but failed due to a lack of a contract with the Demophonian government or the Galactic Empire. Sabel Corazon later took control over the company.

The Mecetti government nationalizes its key industries.

Ken is delivered to the Lost City of the Jedi. Ken was a male Human who was the son of Triclops and a "Jedi Princess" named Kendalina, therefore supposedly making Ken the grandson of Emperor Palpatine and a "Jedi Prince." There was some ambiguity regarding Ken's true origins, as accounts of Palpatine fathering offspring were generally discounted and all records of the Emperor's family disappeared shortly after he ascended to the Imperial throne.

---

7 BBY

On Falleen, two hundred thousand Falleen perish in a controlled Imperial bombardment of a city ruled by Xizor's father to quarantine the spread of a biological weapon.

Soontir Fel is assigned the 6th Squadron of the 37th Imperial Fighter Wing.

Flirry Vorru, a famed Corellian Human male who served as a politician and criminal underlord, is sent to Kessel after being framed by Prince Xizor.

---

6 BBY

Pooja Naberrie, a human female who was the younger daughter of Sola Naberrie and Darred Janren Naberrie and the niece of Padmé Amidala, becomes Senator of Naboo at age 20.

Loka Hask is expelled from the Imperial Academy just as Han Solo graduates from the same institution. Hask showed little skill as a fighter pilot. Arrogance and being openly corrupt ended his days as a cadet. As he went back to his home, he found his criminal father executed. Using his deceased parent's hidden stash of credits, Hask funded a pirate gang that grew in power during the Galactic Civil War.

Xizor seizes control of Black Sun. Xizor was a ruthless competitor and charismatic public figure in high society with his headquarters in the city planet Coruscant. Close to the Imperial Palace, but less splendid, was Xizor's Palace: his home outside Falleen. Following the Battle of Hoth, Xizor was considered one of the most influential beings in the galaxy, on a par with Emperor Palpatine and Darth Vader, due to his exceptional wealth and influence through his criminal activities.

Lando Calrissian visits Trammis III.

Captain Hoffner and Talon Karrde discovers the Katana Fleet.

---

5 BBY

Han Solo, now in a military academy, saves Chewbacca, now a slave, and is subsequently drummed out of the Imperial Navy. Chewbacca pledges a life-debt to Han Solo and remains his partner for the next three decades.

Lando Calrissian wins the Millennium Falcon in a game of sabacc.

Kyle Katarn enters the Imperial Academy of Carida. Kyle Katarn was a famous Human male Rebel operative from Sulon and later a Jedi of the New Jedi Order. He was a former Imperial stormtrooper who defected to the Rebellion. Often paired with fellow Rebel agent and smuggler Jan Ors, he performed many covert missions for the Rebel Alliance and later the New Republic, including the sabotage of the Dark Trooper Project. Katarn was later informed of his Force sensitivity, and taught himself to become a Jedi while in search of the Valley of the Jedi. During this journey, he confronted the dark side within both himself and in the form of the Dark Jedi Jerec and his minions. After defeating them, Katarn went on to become a Jedi Master, teaching at the Jedi Praxeum. He participated in the offensives against the Yuuzhan Vong and became a part of the Jedi High Council in the New Jedi Order.

---

4 BBY

Lando Calrissian discovers the Mindharp; its accidental activation causes massive changes in the Rafa system. The Mindharp was a fork-shaped tool about a meter in length, with a continually altering number of tines. According to legend, the Mindharp was the tool that the Toka could use to recall the Sharu. Legend says the Mindharp would call the Sharu back to aid the Toka in an emergency. However, the true purpose of the Mindharp was to unlock the hidden knowledge of the Sharu and reestablish their intelligence networks which were hidden eons ago, awaiting the day when the danger of the Celestials had passed and they could reemerge. It was kept in a hidden chamber of the Great Pyramid accessible only to the Toka priests by use of a mystical key passed down through the generations. An entity inhabited the hall in which the Mindharp was kept, guarding and watching over the artifact.

Jorj Car'das's starship is commandeered by a Bpfasshi Dark Jedi. The vessel crashes on Dagobah, where Yoda kills the Dark Jedi and heals Car'das.

The Service Special blaster pistol is developed. It was a small blaster used by Imperial law enforcement agency officers. Developed only half the size of most blasters but possessing six times the power, the Service Special blaster was a secret even from some elements of the Imperial military. Its power was roughly equal to one of the four cannons in the Millennium Falcon's quad-guns. Corrupt officer Waywa Fybot used this weapon to kill Bassi Vobah during the raid on Bohhuah Mutdah, literally disintegrating her head.

Slyder moves onboard the Star of Empire. A Rodian male, Slyder operated as a bounty hunter before, during, and in-between the years 4 and 1 BBY, who based his entire operation out of the luxury cruiser Star of Empire. As opposed to tracking down wanted criminals, he simply looked for anyone who should have a price on their head, and reported them to whoever may have wanted that individual the most. During 1 BBY, Slyder discovered, with the help of a porter droid, that a fledgling officer working for the Galactic Empire, Kyle Katarn, was going to defect to the Empire's enemy, the Rebel Alliance, with the help of several Rebel agents. The Rodian reported them to Governor Dol Donar II, who dispatched Slyder, along with Imperial troopers, to capture or kill the Rebels. Although the Rebels avoided the bounty hunter, Slyder was able to secure their protocol droid, A-Cee. When the Rebels escaped the Star, Donar decided to chase them with his own yacht, and brought Slyder and A-Cee along. However, the droid announced its self-destruction aboard the starship at the sight of Nathan Donar's Imperial uniform. Slyder, furious, executed the Imperials for their lack of precautions, before he patiently awaited his demise.

Navik the Red attempts to slaughter Greedo's family, forcing them to flee to Nar Shaddaa. Greedo, son of Greedo the Elder, was a male Rodian bounty hunter. He lived in Mos Espa alongside the young Anakin Skywalker and W. Wald circa 32 BBY.

On Zelos II, an attack on the capital city of Kryndyn by a horde of nocturnal predators resulted in the death of the planet's leaders. In response, general Galleros Nul declared a state of emergency and launched a successful counterattack. However, Nul, who had no intention giving up his power, did not lift the state of emergency.

---

3 BBY

Gallofree Yards, Inc. goes bankrupt. Gallofree Yards, Inc. was a small manufacturer known for their transports and freighters. The company's vehicles were not as innovative or reliable as those made by Corellian Engineering Corporation. Even with continued product overhauls and slick marketing, the company rarely turned a profit. Gallofree Yards eventually filed for bankruptcy several years before the

Battle of Yavin, though many of their starships remained in active use as a part of the Rebel Alliance fleet.

Canna Omonda becomes senator of Chandrila, replacing Mon Mothma. Canna Omonda was a female Human senator of Chandrila and the Bormea sector after Mon Mothma was branded a traitor by Emperor Palpatine's New Order. Senator Omonda was a political firebrand who was public about her disdain for the Galactic Empire. After the dissolution of the Imperial Senate, she returned home to Chandrila, refusing the request of some senators to intercede on their behalf to Palpatine. For her vocal lashings of the Empire, Senator Omonda was arrested and tortured into giving false confessions of "crimes" against the Empire. She was to be publicly executed on Coruscant during the Emperor's festive new year celebrations, but her appearance was removed from the celebratory schedule and executed in private.

Lando Calrissian saves the Oswaft people. The Oswaft were a species that developed outside of the confines of a planet. Instead, they "swam" through space as if it were a great body of water. These massive creatures had brains that took up approximately two-thirds of their immense volume, and found tasks like deciphering encrypted Imperial communications codes trivial. They used an intense, information dense language, which was "spoken" by emitting microwaves. Oswaft also had the ability to travel through hyperspace without a starship to carry them. In 3 BBY, Emperor Palpatine tried to exterminate the Oswaft because of his distrust of an intelligent alien species of significant population that could make hyperspace jumps at will. An armada of 500 capital ships under the command of his local ally, Sorcerer of Tund and Centran Scrivinir Rokur Gepta, blockaded the ThonBoka Nebula. The armada's Carrack-class light cruisers were modified to contaminate the interstellar plankton that inhabited the nebula. Help came in the form of Lando Calrissian and a mysterious droid species known as the Silentium, who led the Oswaft against the Imperial fleet during the Battle of ThonBoka.

Tavell Geen becomes Scrivinir of the Centrality. Little is known of Geen. Prior to becoming Scrivinir, he earned the prestigious title of Ottdefa from the University of Lekua V. Geen was outed from office in a bloody military coup by Centrality Fleet Admiral Sris Lehhett in the galactic turmoil not long after the beginning of the Yuuzhan Vong invasion. He managed to flee with his life to Coruscant where he tried to drum up support among the New Republic for his reinstatement.

The Rebel spy post, Ghost Base, is discovered and captured by the Galactic Empire. Ghost Base was a Rebel Alliance base operated by Rebel spy Utric Sandov on the planet Krant. It was captured by Moff Yittreas and Strike force Alpha around 1 BBY, but the Rebel staff escaped to the nearby Le'Roche island. The Imperials established a base of their own there, which consisted of a Command center at least two troop centers, a war center, and a gate along with some remanents of the Rebel base. The Imperials, after creating their base, protected the base with laser turrets. A Rebel strike force, led by Leia Organa and Echuu Shen-Jon later retook the base and drove the Imperials out. Sandov then contacted Organa and sent transports to bring her to Le'Roche.

The first recorded encounter with a Yarkora. The Yarkora were bipedal, anthropomorphic beings resembling cameloids. They hailed from an unknown desert world in the Outer Rim[4], and were rarely seen amongst the galactic populace.

Narg is taken over by the Galactic Empire. Narg was an isolated planet in the Rayter sector of the Outer Rim Territories. Its Human inhabitants were known to be xenophobic. During the Galactic Civil War, the planet was controlled by TransGalMeg Industries, Incorporated.

Tsoss Beacon constructed. Tsoss Beacon was an asteroid in the Tsoss Beacon system of the Deep Core, containing an Imperial communications relay station built in 3 BBY.

---

2 BBY

Meant to eventually overthrow the Emperor, Darth Vader sends a secret apprentice, Starkiller, to hunt down and eradicate the last of the Jedi.

Shaak Ti is killed on Felucia by Galen Marek.

The apprentice, Galen Marek, under orders from Vader seeks out the opposers and secret enemies of the Empire and convinces them to organize to actively fight the Emperor.

The apprentice, Galen Marek ultimately turns against both Vader and Palpatine and is killed. Rejecting the codename "Starkiller", Darth Vader's former apprentice reclaimed his birth name, Galen Marek, and for the first time, considered himself as a Jedi. Opting to save the Rebel Alliance by tracking down both Vader and the Senators, Galen entered into deep meditation in an attempt to provoke a Force vision. Although successful in his attempt, he was almost overwhelmed by a plethora of possible futures. Focusing on one of the common elements, he discovered the location of the incomplete Death Star. Travelling to the Horuz system, they used the Rogue Shadow's cloaking devise to approach the massive battle station, entering the thin atmosphere maintained for the workers and slaves building the behemoth. Standing on the open boarding ramp of the Shadow, Galen and Juno exchanged their last words. When inquired as to whether or not he would survive, Galen reluctantly answered that he would most likely die in the attempted rescue. Juno then rushed forward and kissed him on the lips. At first, Galen was surprised by Juno's sudden action, but then he returned the embrace. After their first and last kiss, Galen said farewell and leapt into the Death Star's extensive superstructure. Landing on the exterior hull in a clear patch between two construction sites, Galen attempted probing about for the Rebels, but found their Force signatures obscured by both the widespread suffering and despair within the Death Star, and especially by Palpatine's presence. Darting cover to cover, Galen advanced on two Imperial stormtroopers on a scaffold, overseeing a string of Wookiee slaves. Telekinetically choking one into unconsciousness, he manipulated the other into providing him with information before inducing him to fall asleep. As the slave overseers knew little about the movements of either Palpatine or Darth Vader, or even about the Death Star's layout, Galen opted to ask the construction workers; the slaves themselves. Attacking the Imperials and freeing the slaves, Galen began a revolt. While the Wookiees began fighting, Galen recruited a pair to guide him to the Emperor's location. Led through the confined inner workings of the Death Star, Galen was directed towards one of the superlaser tubes. Following the tube, engaged by the Imperial forces attempting to stop him, Galen reached a convergence chamber. The massive room held the entrance to the Emperor's observation dome, and Galen ascended the catwalks and ledges towards the elaborate portal. Reaching the door platform, he was suddenly confronted by a Shadow Guardsman, reinforced by four Imperial Guardsmen. Galen made short work of the Red Guards, and squared off against the Shadow guardsman. Grappling with the Darksider, Galen ended the fight by breaking his opponent's neck. He then telekinetically activated the locking mechanism to gain access through the massive door that led into the Emperor's observation dome. As he charged along the corridor towards the observation dome, he was spied by the security systems. Darth Vader emerged through the entrance to the dome, lightsaber ignited. Vader acknowledged that he had trained his student well, but declared that Galen still had much to learn, and Galen replied with "you have nothing left to teach me". Vader, utterly confident that he would best Galen easily, opened the battle with a simple double strike. Galen was caught off-guard by the power of the blow, which jarred his wrists and shoulders and nearly disarmed him. Vader used Galen's momentary lack of composure to attack him telekinetically, though Galen managed to sweep aside the missiles. Ducking under two savage slashes, he stabbed at the Dark Lord's abdomen before flicking his blade up, trying to spear Vader through the throat. Vader only barely managed to block, and both combatants momentarily broke off. Galen realized that until this duel, he and Vader had never truly fought as equals; during his training, either Galen would capitulate or Vader would hold back. They fought back and forth, with Galen taking a defensive stance against Vader's overwhelming offense. As he fended off Vader's series of attacks, he danced around the Dark Lord's defenses, testing their limits, all the while taunting Vader. He mocked his former master with the knowledge that, while Galen had broken free from Vader's control, Vader himself lacked the strength to free himself from Sidious. Realizing that there were better ways to kill than to call on his anger, Galen came to pity Vader, seeing the Dark Lord as a result of the same manipulations and abuse as himself, and thus desired to kill him as a way of "freeing" his former Master from the pain of being enslaved to the Sith. Galen's taunts, especially his professions of pity, enraged Vader, who ramped up the intensity of his attack. Galen continued to use his self-taught Soresu to great effect, wasting little energy and turning Vader's would-be death blows into superficial burns. As Vader continued to relentlessly attack, Galen suddenly counter-attacked with a blast of Force lightning, which broke Vader's momentum and forced him onto the defensive for the first time. Galen began to steadily gain ground while Vader fell back. Eventually, Galen saw an opening in Vader's defenses and took advantage of it, slashing Vader across the throat. Surprised but elated, Galen scored two more hits on the Dark Lord in short order before telekinetically pummeling Vader with any and all objects he could find. The last such missile was an energy field generator, which detonated on impact with Vader. The blast severely damaged the Sith Lord's armor and respirator, and destroyed most of his mask and helmet. As Galen approached his former master, intending to finish him, he saw Vader's face uncovered for the first time. Vader, much to the shock and surprise of Galen, was a terribly scarred old man, in whose eyes Galen saw only pain and exhaustion. As he froze, Palpatine approached, praising Galen for his victory. Seeing a perfect opportunity to replace his hobbled apprentice, Palpatine gleefully encouraged Galen to execute Darth Vader and take his rightful place at the Emperor's side. Galen became conflicted and the changes brought on by his recent experiences with the Rebels warring against his desire to continue using the dark side and become a true Sith Lord. In addition, though Vader's horribly scarred visage elicited pity from Galen, a significant part of him still wanted revenge. Rahm Kota, sensing Galen's indecision, intervened and telekinetically snatched Palpatine's lightsaber, using it to kill his guards before rushing the Emperor himself. Palpatine easily fended off Kota with a blast of Force lightning, prompting Bail Organa to call on Galen to help the Jedi General. The sudden violence snapped Galen back to reality, and he realized that he didn't want to go back to what he once was, not after seeing what it did to people. He came to understand that executing Vader would accomplish nothing, whereas saving the Rebels could change the course of history. With his final decision made, he resisted the urge to kill Vader and instead attacked Palpatine. The Emperor managed to pull out his other lightsaber before Galen attacked, and a furious duel began. The two powerful Force-wielders battled back and forth, trading telekinetic, lightsaber, and lightning attacks. Over the course of their contest, Palpatine would occasionally break off and allow intervening Imperial Senate and Royal guardsmen to engage Galen, though the Force-adept made quick work of them. As they fought, Palpatine revealed that Galen had never been Vader's "secret" apprentice, and that he was abducted from Kashyyyk on the Emperor's orders. Darth Vader had been little more than a proxy and it was Darth Sidious who had been Galen Marek's true master all along. Enraged by the sudden revelation, Galen seized the offensive by further pressing his attack against the Emperor. Dodging Palpatine's Force lightning strikes, or channelling them into his lightsaber, Galen closed the distance. Throwing Palpatine off of his feet with a telekinetic shockwave, Galen then blasted the Dark Lord of the Sith against the ceiling of the dome with a Force push before slamming him against the ground. Tossing his comlink to the Rebels so they could call Juno for evac, Galen advanced on the prone Emperor. Darth Sidious rose to his knees and declared that it was Galen's destiny to destroy him, by giving in to his hatred. Galen initially struggled with the urge to do so, but repented in the end, extinguishing his lightsaber. As the Rogue Shadow landed nearby, Starkiller told Kota to get the Rebels aboard, but then Palpatine sprung into action. Snarling at Kota that neither the Rebels nor the Jedi could ever have Galen, Palpatine roared to his feet and fired a blast of lightning into the Jedi Master's back. Without hesitation, Galen immediately stepped into the stream, taking the full brunt of it himself. Overcoming the pain just enough to absorb and gather the energy, Galen advanced on Palpatine as the two remained locked in the chain of lightning. At the same time, he noticed that a squadron of stormtroopers had entered the chamber, with Darth Vader limping behind them, in pursuit of the fleeing Rebel leaders. With no other option left, Galen grabbed the Emperor's shoulders and redirected the lightning into the Dark Lord, causing Sidious to share in the agonizing pain of his own power. Driven by concern for his friends, Galen embraced the Force completely and released all of the pent up energy, resulting in a massive shock wave that killed the stormtroopers and destroyed much of the dome. In the last moments of his life, Galen felt himself leaving his body as death took hold of him. With his final thought centered on Juno Eclipse, Galen Marek whispered his birth name for the last time and died. Although he ultimately perished as a result of the explosion of Force energy, he transcended physical existence and became one with the Force. Six months after the death of Galen Marek, Darth Vader brought his body to Kamino and stored it within the cloning facility of Timira City. The body would serve as the genetic template that Vader needed, hoping to clone a more powerful and obedient version of his deceased apprentice. However, due to side effects caused by the accelerated cloning process and memory flashes used in their training, the clones retained the original Marek's memories and emotions and were constantly haunted by visions of his life, many going insane within months. After numerous failures, Vader finally created a clone that appeared stable enough to be the first success. Unfortunately, however, the clone began to suffer from the same visions that his predecessors did.

Inspired by the death of Galen Marek, the Corellian Treaty is signed, giving birth to the Rebel Alliance. The Treaty was an accord that created the Alliance to Restore the Republic. Signed by the leaders of anti-Imperial resistance groups on Alderaan, Corellia, and Chandrila, the treaty formally declared war on the Empire. Though the meeting to create the treaty at first appeared to have been arranged by Galen Marek, this proved to be a deception by his former master, Darth Vader, who raided the meeting with the Stormtrooper Corps and captured the three senators. Had Galen not survived his confrontation with his former master, the Empire would have effectively ended the Rebellion before it even began. The treaty itself provided a command structure for the Alliance intended to allow each force to govern itself while providing a strong centralized component to coordinate all efforts. It organized the civil aspects such as diplomacy, transport and supply into one tree, bundled all military operations into another, and placed the Commander-in-Chief and Advisory Council at the top. Organa told Bel Iblis and Mothma that he could fund a rebellion, while Bel Iblis would provide ships for its fleet, and Mothma would help provide soldiers.

The Galactic Civil War begins. This was a major galactic conflict fought primarily between the Galactic Empire and the Alliance to Restore the Republic. The Alliance was a rebel faction dedicated to the restoration of the Galactic Republic, the government that the Empire had supplanted at the culmination of the Clone Wars in 19 BBY. Initially, the Empire, especially Palpatine, did not consider the Alliance a threat, but rather as a political tool to further consolidate power that would eventually lead to the Dissolution of the Imperial Senate and a massive, unprecedented military build-up. It would not be until the fateful Battle of Yavin, when rebel Luke Skywalker destroyed the first Death Star, that the threat posed by the Alliance became real to the Empire and more serious measures were drafted to restore Imperial control over the galaxy.

Emperor Palpatine creates the position of Grand Admiral.

Large phrikite deposits are located on Gromas 16.

The religious Cult of Varn is developed on Kamar by the Badlanders.

Han Solo wins the Millennium Falcon from Lando Calrissian during a sabacc tournament on Cloud City.

Hart-and-Parn Gorra-Fiolla, Han Solo, Chewbacca and Odumin disrupted the Bonadan slave trade.

Greedo befriends Anky Fremp on Nar Shaddaa.

Demetrius Zaarin becomes Grand Admiral at New Year Fete Week. A native of the Imperial capital world of Coruscant, Demetrius Zaarin served in the Imperial Navy during the reign of Emperor Palpatine. During New Year's Fete Week, Zaarin was one of twelve officers promoted by the Emperor to the newly created rank of Grand Admiral in an elaborate ceremony. In 0 ABY, eight months after the destruction of the Empire's Death Star battlestation at the Battle of Yavin, Zaarin was joined by Emperor Palpatine on a secret tour of the Outer Rim Territories aboard the Imperial-class Star Destroyer Predominant. During this tour, the Predominant delivered the Emperor to the forest moon of Endor, where construction had begun on a second Death Star and where the Emperor met with Senior Captain Thrawn to discuss the defenses for the shield generator bunker protecting the construction project. By 3 ABY, the Grand Admiral was made the head of research and development for the Empire's starfighter technology. Zaarin used the power that his rank brought sparingly, ensuring that he had all the resources required for his research and development projects but not getting involved in Imperial Court politics. He rarely wore the white uniform of a Grand Admiral, preferring instead to wear the gray uniform of a standard admiral while in Imperial service, and insisting on being referred to only as "Admiral Zaarin." Despite his low profile in the Imperial Court, Zaarin gained the respect of both Emperor Palpatine and Lord Darth Vader, in the process earning the ire of many within the Imperial Navy, including his fellow Grand Admirals.

Corellian Diktat Dupas Thomree is assassinated. Thomree had made a deal with Emperor Palpatine allowing him to govern the Corellian sector as he wished (mostly free of Imperial mandates) as long as he paid taxes, war matériel, and homage to the Emperor.

Han Solo and Chewbacca attempt a clotheslegging scheme in the Cron Drift.

1 BBY

Hundreds of battles & missions are fought between the warring factions as the Galactic Civil War continues.

A group of Moffs led by Trachta, plot to overthrow Emperor Palpatine and Darth Vader. The plot fails and almost all of the conspirators are met with unspeakable deaths. The attempt hinged on a special detachment of cloned stormtroopers, programmed to obey not Palpatine but Trachta. After splitting up Vader and Palpatine, the conspirators would have their stormtroopers, planted within the ranks of the two men's forces, turn on the Sith and kill them. The plot did not go as planned. The members first turned on each other, resulting in the assassination of most of the participants. The surviving members were no more successful, as Vader's and Palpatine's mastery of the Force allowed them to easily defeat the stormtroopers and dispose of the remaining leaders. In the end, all members of the conspiracy but the Imperial assassin Gauer were killed in the attempt.

Darth Vader attempts to create a stable clone of Galen Marek on Kamino. One clone of Marek escapes and becomes a key figure in the early Alliance. Darth Vader is captured by the Alliance during a skirmish on Kamino, but escapes soon after.

THE REBELLION ERA

With the Old Republic gone, an outcry of resistance begins to spread across the galaxy in protest to the new Empire's tyranny. Cells of Rebellion fight back, and the Galactic Civil War begins. This era begins with the Rebel victory that secured the Death Star plans, and ends after the death of Emperor Palpetine high over the forest moon of Endor. The Rebellion starts to reform itself into a body of government, first as the Alliance to Restore the Republic, and later the New Republic. The original trilogy takes place during this era. Specifically, A New Hope takes place in 0 BBY, The Empire Strikes Back in 3 ABY, and Return of the Jedi in 4 ABY.

0 BBY

Fighting continues in the Galactic Civil War for this year

The Imperial Senate is disbanded, giving Palpatine absolute power.

Princess Leia acquires secret plans for the Death Star, but is captured in flight. She gives the plans to C-3PO and R2-D2 who successfully escape to Tatooine where Luke Skywalker comes across them and buys them.

Ben Kenobi hears the message from Princess Leia and gives Luke the lightsaber of Anakin Skywalker.

A squad of stormtroopers kill Owen and Beru Lars, Luke Skywalker's Uncle and Aunt, leaving him without any family that he knows of.

Admiral Natasi Daala is sent to oversee the Maw Installation by Grand Moff Tarkin. The Maw Installation was an Imperial research center for the creation of superweapons. It was built from asteroids in the midst of the Maw Cluster, a virtually unnavigable cluster of black holes.

The Death Star destroys Alderaan and Obi-Wan Kenobi is killed by Darth Vader, but his spirit lives on.

The Battle of Yavin. The Death Star arrived in system escorted by a small support fleet consisting of the Nebulon-B frigate Divad and two CR90 corvettes BB 45 and SB 35. While the Death Star prepared to fire its main weapon, a communications satellite was deployed to coordinate defenses. The Rebels, still planning their attack, knew that any delay to the Death Star's approach could spell the difference between victory and defeat. Therefore they planned a small attack to destroy the communications satellite and disrupt operations. A trio of X-wings, including Keyan Farlander, and a pair of R-22 Spearheads were dispatched to destroy the comsat. While Farlander's wingmen held off Imperial fighters, Farlander ignored the threat and headed straight for the satellite, destroying it with a proton torpedo. The mission was a success, preventing the Empire from calling for reinforcements and disrupting their defenses, although two of the Rebel X-wings were shot down and the pilots had to be rescued later. Other portions of the offensive fleet included two Victory II-class Star Destroyers and two Tartan-class patrol cruisers. A large part of the Alliance Fleet, including MC80 Star Cruisers, Nebulon-B escort frigates, and other Rebel starfighters destroyed those four Imperial starships, however, to allow the Rebel Alliance attack on the Death Star to proceed. Farlander was quickly dispatched again in one of two X-wings charged with clearing some of the defenses around the trench. They succeeded in destroying several laser batteries as well as some small surface hangars, limiting the Death Star's ability to launch fighters. While Red and Gold Squadrons were focused on attacking the exhaust port, Blue and Green Squadrons were ordered to attack the superlaser itself, hoping that they could have some chance of damaging the weapon and if not, they could at least distract some Imperial forces from the exhaust port attack. Meanwhile, down on the ground X2, Shara, and other Rebel soldiers fought off Imperials attacking from space. Various TIE/sa bombers were deployed and doing bombing strafes around the base, and likewise a contingent of Stormtroopers also entered the Yavin 4 Base. X2, Shara, and various Rebel soldiers proceeded to enter the temple as well as avoid the various strafing runs of the TIE bombers. Thanks to the Stormtroopers, the base's anti-aircraft turret was also deactivated, forcing X2 to reactivate the turret's power station. After doing so and then preventing them from taking the Great Temple, Dodonna called X2 and Shara and informed them that Imperials had set up jamming systems that were interfering with the X-wing's engines. X2 and Shara located and destroyed the jamming devices. After fully clearing out the Imperials from the base, X2 then went into space to participate in the battle against the Death Star. Following the preliminary attacks, a fleet of 22 X-wing, 8 Y-wing, and 2 R-22 Spearhead starfighters scrambled to assault the station. The Death Star attempted to use its batteries to defend itself, but the defenses were designed primarily to fight off capital ships, not the small and agile Rebel ships. The fighters destroyed several turrets and a rookie pilot known as Rookie One destroyed a giant ion cannon mounted on the Station, in order to set the stage for the main phase of the assault. Although they managed to infiltrate the Death Star's outer defenses, the Rebel Alliance pilots still needed to destroy the Death Star's ten deflector shield towers that protected the trench. The station commander, Grand Moff Wilhuff Tarkin, dismissed the attack as futile and refused to deploy the station's vast TIE squadrons. But Darth Vader, realizing the material threat, ordered his personal fighter squadron to scramble on his own authority. The TIE fighter squadron attacked the Rebel forces soon after they realized that their laser batteries were failing. An order was passed on, to stop all turbolasers from firing, letting the TIEs do the job, and to avoid the risk of Imperial fighters being shot down by friendly fire. The Rebels engaged in duels with the starfighters, destroying several to clear the way to the trench. As the rest of the Rebel fighters engaged Vader's forces, three Y-wings from Gold Squadron began their attack run on the trench. They were followed by Vader in his TIE/Advanced and two TIE fighter escorts. Vader shot down Tiree (Gold Two) and Jon Vander (Gold Leader) in the trench, then shot down Davish Krail (Gold Five) as he attempted to escape. Following the failure of Gold Squadron, the Rebel tacticians on Yavin 4 directed Red Leader to keep half of the group out of range, and Red Leader instructed Reds Two, Three and Five (Wedge Antilles, Biggs Darklighter, and Luke Skywalker, respectively) to hold back while he led the second trench run, flanked by Reds Ten and

Twelve. Red Squadron made a second bombing run, with Garven Dreis (Red Leader) making the attack itself, while Red Ten and Red Twelve attempted to hold off Vader and his fighters. While both his companions were shot down, Red Leader succeeded in making the run, but his proton torpedoes exploded on the exhaust port's surface, leaving a near miss and also killing some stormtroopers inside from the force of the explosion. The remaining X-Wings attempted to cover Red Leader on his exit from the trench, but Dreis, who had been hit and damaged while exiting the trench, ordered them to maintain their position and prepare for their run, just before being shot down by Vader. During the battle, Vader pursued a shuttle full of Imperial defectors led by TIE pilot Villian Dance, but the ongoing battle forced Vader to turn back. On the Death Star, an officer analyzed the Rebels' attack plan and realized there was actually a good chance they could destroy the reactor and, with it, the entire station. He alerted Tarkin and suggested they consider retreating or evacuation. Tarkin, however, believed the final victory for the Empire was in sight, and would not even consider pulling back. Skywalker was in the lead, while Darklighter and Antilles maintained a greater distance behind him in order to shield him from the Imperial fighters. The three pilots traversed the trench at full throttle in order to keep the TIEs away. Vader and his wingmen gave chase, and opened up on the X-Wings at long range. One of the wingmen's shots scored a minor hit on Wedge's X-Wing, damaging the engine array, and he was forced to abandon the trench run, unable to keep up with his wingmates. Vader instructed his wingmen to let him go and maintain their pursuit of Biggs and Luke. As they closed the distance, Biggs threw his X-Wing into a weave maneuver, erratically moving around both laterally and vertically, to deny his pursuers a clean shot at either his leader or himself. While this was successful against Vader's wingmen, the Dark Lord of the Sith anticipated his opponent's move through the Force and eventually got a clear shot at Biggs, killing Luke's childhood friend from Tatooine and leaving Luke without any assistance in the trench. X2 also arrived at the Death Star at that point to aid Skywalker, and got himself within range of Darth Vader's TIE/Advanced to supply Skywalker with backup. Unfortunately, Vader anticipated X2's arrival and ordered all turbolaser turrets to fire on X2, forcing him to withdraw. Vader and his wingmen then sped down the trench after Luke, as Luke neared the exhaust port. At this critical moment, Luke heard the voice of Obi-Wan Kenobi prompting him to deactivate his targeting computer. The Rebel technicians on Yavin 4 questioned this decision, but Luke reassured them that everything was all right. Vader gained a partial weapon lock on Skywalker's X-Wing, and took a potentially fatal shot. However, the blast only grazed R2, rendering him inoperative for the remainder of the mission but causing no apparent direct damage to Luke's fighter. In the Death Star's control room, master chief gunnery officer Tenn Graneet prepared to fire the Death Star's superlaser. With the Death Star primed to fire, he hesitated, feeling the guilt of the destruction of Alderaan. He called to standby as the others in the control room urged him to shoot. Vader, sensing that the last pilot, Skywalker, was strong in the Force, prepared to kill him (unaware at the time that Skywalker was his own son). However, at the last moment, Han Solo and Chewbacca in the Millennium Falcon surprised Darth Vader and, with a laser blast, destroyed one of his wingmen, Backstabber. In the confusion, the other wingman, Mithel, panicked and collided with Vader's fighter, sending himself crashing into the trench and Vader careening out of control into space. With the Force aiding him, Luke fired his torpedoes, both of which entered the port perfectly. On the Death Star's bridge, Admiral Motti called out that torpedoes were in the main shaft and would hit the reactor. The Death Star exploded just seconds before its main gun would have destroyed Yavin 4. Grand Moff Tarkin and the battle station's entire crew, sans Vader, were killed. Vader himself managed to regain control of his fighter and fled the Yavin system with his life. The Rebel Alliance had won a spectacular victory. Vader managed to make it to the nearby listening post on Vaal. As a result of this battle, the Rebel Alliance gained instant credibility as a legitimate military opponent to the Empire. Between the effects of the battle and the dissolution of the Imperial Senate, thousands of star systems openly joined the Alliance in the months following the Death Star's destruction. As a result, the Empire began occupying worlds it had allowed to remain untouched earlier, both actions resulting in an escalation of the war.

AFTER THE BATTLE OF YAVIN/THE REBELLION ERA

0 ABY

The Super Star Destroyer Executor is launched under the command of Captain Kendal Ozzel. It is dispatched to destroy the Rebel base on Yavin. However, a miscalculation from Admiral Griff allows the Rebels to escape.

1 ABY

Imperial forces seize Bakura, a rich, green and blue planet in the Bakura system of the Shiritoku Spur, located on the isolated edge of the Outer Rim and formally a part of Wild Space.

Han Solo and a small Alliance fleet are hired by an unknown party to assault an Imperial space station to rescue an unidentified imprisoned spacer. They manage to escape aboard the Millennium Falcon to Tansarii Point Station.

Zef Ando, a Rodian squatter; has claimed the abandoned Lars Homestead as his own. Ando later purchased some reconditioned droids off some Jawas, but the droids malfunctioned and attacked him.

2 ABY

An Imperial force led by Darth Vader catches up to some of the Rebels on Ord Mantell. It is here that Emperor Palpatine learns the name of the Rebel who destroyed the Death Star, Luke Skywalker, but withholds this information from Darth Vader until the time is right. While on Ord Mantell, Skorr, a bounty hunter working for Jabba the Hutt, nearly captures Han Solo.

Luke Skywalker and Leia Organa discover the Kaiburr crystal, an ancient Force relic initially located on the planet Circarpous V, on Mimban. The crystal increased a Force-sensitive's power one thousand times over. Among its magnification of abilities were the ability to heal, to further augment a Force-user's connection to the Force, to project Force lightning by those typically unable, and to empower and energize a tired being close in proximity to the crystal. If cut properly, the Kaiburr crystal also worked as a lightsaber crystal.

191

Rogue Squadron is formed by Luke Skywalker. Rogue Squadron, originally dubbed Rogue Flight, and also known as the Rogues, was an elite Rebel Alliance starfighter squadron founded shortly after the Battle of Yavin out of Red Squadron. Rogue Squadron played a key role during several engagements in the Galactic Civil War, serving as the primary defense squadron of the Alliance High Command. The squadron mainly fielded T-65 X-wing starfighters, but flew other craft as well, including T-47 airspeeders, Z-95 Headhunters, RZ-1 A-wing interceptors, B-wing assault starfighters, and BTL-A4 Y-wing starfighters.

A base on Hoth is built by the Rebels. Hoth was the sixth planet of the remote Hoth system. A desolate world covered with ice and snow, located in the Anoat sector, a rarely-travelled portion of the Outer Rim Territories

---

3 ABY

The Battle of Hoth occurs and was a major victory for the Galactic Empire and the single worst battlefield defeat suffered by the Alliance to Restore the Republic. The battle was an Imperial invasion aimed at destroying the Rebel Alliance's Echo Base hidden on the remote ice world Hoth. The base's location was compromised when a viper probe droid deployed by Darth Vader landed on Hoth. When the Death Squadron fleet commanded by Admiral Kendal Ozzel left lightspeed too close to the Hoth system, the Admiral inadvertently alerted the Alliance of the Imperial's presence, giving the Rebels time to prepare for the necessary evacuation and raise the planetary shield. Thus, Vader executed him for that fatal mistake and immediately promoted Captain Firmus Piett to replace him. The Imperial attack force consisted of primarily AT-AT walkers, commanded by Major General Maximilian Veers. His army was tasked with destroying Echo Base's main power generator to allow orbital bombardment of the planet. Spearheading the defense of the generator was the elite Rogue Squadron, manning snowspeeders, commanded by Luke Skywalker.. The snowspeeders did not have the necessary firepower to bring down the walkers, so Skywalker suggested an alternative tactic to trip up the walkers with the tow cables issued to every snowspeeder. Despite the efforts by Rogue Squadron, the power generator was eventually destroyed by Veers. The remaining base personnel proceeded to evacuate, as the 501st Legion, led by Darth Vader, entered the base. It would prove a major victory for the Galactic Empire, and would heavily stymie the Rebels. The Alliance's loss was so great at the time, at least one member of the 501st Legion considered the Battle of Hoth to be the end of the rebel movement.

The Subjugation of Bespin occurs. After the Galactic Empire won the Battle of Hoth and forced the Rebel Alliance offworld. Darth Vader pursued the Rebel leaders, in particular his son, Luke Skywalker. He hired Boba Fett and other bounty hunters to find the Millennium Falcon, the starship carrying the Rebel leaders. Fett spotted the Falcon fleeing the Hoth Imperial blockade and deduced its destination, Cloud City on the gas giant Bespin. Vader arrived before the Millennium Falcon and forged an initial agreement between himself and the Baron Administrator, Lando Calrissian. Calrissian would aid Vader in capturing the Rebels, in exchange for the continued freedom of his colony. The Millennium Falcon entered and landed in Cloud City, piloted by Han Solo and Chewbacca. They also had princess Leia Organa and the protocol droid C-3PO on board. Its crew was greeted as welcomed guests by the Baron Administrator, who gave an especially warm welcome to his old friend, Han Solo. They were given accommodation in which to dwell while their ship was being repaired. After landing, C-3PO wandered off and was shot by a member of Gamma Squad, dismantling him. C-3PO's remains were later sent to the recycling area of Cloud City, although they were intercepted by Chewbacca, who retrieved the parts. After a while, Calrissian invited them to a dinner arrangement, which turned out to be a trap, set by Darth Vader. Solo, upon discovering Vader in the dining room, attempted to shoot the Dark Lord with his blaster, only for Vader to effortlessly absorb the bolts with his right hand, and telekinetically pull the smuggler's blaster away from him with his left. Stormtroopers surrounded the Rebels, ensuring their capture. Later, Lieutenant Sheckil informed Lord Vader of C-3PO's destruction, and Vader visited the wreckage, remembering back when he had created the protocol droid as a young boy, and ordered the droid to be returned to Chewbacca while he prepared to interrogate Solo. He wanted to use Organa, Solo, and Chewbacca's capture as a lure to capture his primary objective, Skywalker. Indeed, Han Solo was tortured but not asked questions in order to trigger a response from Luke through the Force, sending him to rescue his friends. The Imperials disabled the repaired Millennium Falcon's hyperdrive to prevent its escape.

Luke Skywalker discovers Yoda on Dagobah, and trains under him. When he receives disturbing visions of the future he halts his training but promises to return.

Emperor Palpatine contacts Darth Vader aboard the Super Star Destroyer Executor and reveals Luke Skywalker's parentage to Vader. Vader suggests a plan to capture and convert Luke rather than kill him as originally suggested. Seeing the potential a more powerful apprentice would have, Palpatine agrees.

Boba Fett captures Han Solo to take him to Jabba Desilijic Tiure after Solo is frozen in carbonite on Cloud City. Lando Calrissian joins the Rebel Alliance.

Darth Vader cuts off Luke Skywalker's hand and reveals to Luke that he is his father.

Prince Xizor is killed by Darth Vader and Black Sun collapses.

---

4 ABY

The Battle of Endor occurs. The Battle was fought between the Rebel Alliance and the Galactic Empire and was one of the largest and most important engagements of the Galactic Civil War. It signified the decline of the Empire with the deaths of Emperor Palpatine and Darth Vader, as well as many major Imperial leaders, and the destruction of the Death Star II. Plans for the battle began after the Rebels learned that the Empire was building a new Death Star above the forest moon of Endor. In addition, spies had informed Rebel leadership that not only were the Death Star's defense systems incomplete, but also that the Emperor himself would be overseeing the completion of the superweapon's construction. Seeing an opportunity to strike a crippling blow to the Empire, the Alliance planned an attack on the incomplete space station. Part of the Rebels would fight on the moon's surface in an attempt to destroy the shield generator protecting the Death Star, while another group would fight in space, assaulting the battle station in Endor's orbit once the protective shield was deactivated. Unbeknownst to the Rebels, Palpatine had deliberately leaked false information to them, the Death Star was in actuality operational and ready for combat. The Emperor also had a fleet of Star Destroyers waiting to ambush and destroy the Rebel Fleet upon their arrival. On the ground, a group of Rebels led by General Han Solo fought the Imperial stormtroopers stationed on the forest moon in an attempt to destroy the shield generator protecting the Death Star. Meanwhile in space, the Alliance Fleet, led by Admiral Gial Ackbar and aided by Lando Calrissian in the Millennium Falcon, battled the Empire's naval forces and attacked the battle station. However, the Empire held a significant advantage in the space battle due to the massive fleet of Star Destroyers defending the battle station. In addition to the numerical advantage of the Imperials, Palpatine's battle meditation further helped the Imperials by scattering the attacking Rebel forces. Shortly, the Rebels realized that they had been tricked for the Death Star's weapon systems were already operational. Despite this quick realization, the Rebel fleet still suffered severe losses through the Death Star's superlaser, secretly controlled by IG-88, who also planned to overthrow the Empire. With the strike team on the ground still struggling to take down the shield, the Rebels were able to turn the tide of the battle with the help of the native Ewoks and gain access to the generator command bunker and rig it with explosives. After Solo's team was able to take down the shield generator, several squadrons of Rebel snubfighters led by Calrissian and Wedge Antilles began their attack on the Death Star's reactor core. At the same time, Darth Vader brought Luke Skywalker to the Emperor in order to turn his son to the dark side of the Force. Skywalker dueled his father in the Emperor's throne room, and used his anger to emerge as the victor. However, after Skywalker refused to give in to Palpatine's demands and kill Vader, the Sith Lord attempted to torture the young Jedi using his Force lightning. Unable to see his son die, Vader saved his son and killed his master by grabbing him and throwing him down the Death Star's reactor shaft. He had redeemed himself, becoming Anakin Skywalker once again and fulfilling his role as the Chosen One, though due to the damage inflicted by the Emperor's Force lightning, he died in the act. Soon after, Calrissian and Antilles were able to destroy the Death Star's reactor core, setting off a chain reaction that obliterated the entire battle station, along with IG-88 and the other Imperials inside it. The Rebel fleet was able to escape its destruction, as did Skywalker. The Imperials, having seen the destruction of the Death Star and no longer having Palpatine's battle meditation on their side, were forced to retreat. On Endor, Skywalker and the others celebrated their freedom, as did the inhabitants of many other worlds. With its two main leaders dead, the Empire began its long decline, with multiple warlords fighting for power. Many Rebel heroes of the battle, such as Wedge Antilles, were hailed as liberators, and they helped form the New Republic shortly thereafter. While the actions of the battle did not signify the end of the war, they marked the beginning of the end for the Empire and also succeeded in restoring balance to the Force.

Han Solo is rescued from Jabba the Hutt and Jabba is killed by Leia Organa. Boba Fett manages to escape the sarlacc, killing it.

Yoda dies at 900 years of age.

A celebration across the galaxy begins at the fall of the Empire and the death of Palpatine. Still on Endor, Luke catches a glimpse of the ghosts of Obi-Wan Kenobi, Yoda, and his father, Anakin Skywalker off away from the Ewok party.

A small Rebel task force responds to a distress call at Bakura. Converting into the Alliance of Free Planets, the Imperial and Alliance forces sign the Truce at Bakura. Crafted and signed by Imperial Governor Wilek Nereus and Leia Organa, the truce allowed the Alliance aid fleet and the Bakuran defense force to collaborate against the Ssi-ruuk invasion. However, the truce was broken by Nereus, who ordered the Dominant to turn its guns on the Alliance flagship Flurry.

THE NEW REPUBLIC

Having defeated the Empire at the Battle of Endor, the Rebel Alliance must now transform itself from a militant resistance force into a functioning galactic government. As Imperial territory is reclaimed, the New Republic suffers growing pains, having to fend off insurrections, Imperial loyalists, crime lords and wayward warlords. Also, Luke Skywalker, the last of the Jedi, begins to rebuild the Jedi Order and train new apprentices.

---

4 ABY

The New Republic is established.

---

5 ABY

Luke Skywalker attains the rank of General. Six months later, after Imperial forces under the command of Lord Shadowspawn fought to the last man against his army, he retires from the military.

Ysanne Isard engages in a series of political maneuvers to damage the New Republic and seize control of the Empire.

Trioculus takes control of the remnants of the Empire in opposition to Ysanne Isard. He is killed that same year and his position taken over by the imposter posing as Kadann who is killed later.

---

6 ABY

Rogue Squadron reforms under Wedge Antilles

New Republic forces switch from the guerrilla tactics of the Alliance to a campaign of claiming important Core worlds as the Empire's grip crumbles.

---

7 ABY

The New Republic captures Coruscant from the Empire as it continues to deteriorate.

Ysanne Isard leaves an artificial virus called the Krytos virus that infects all non-Humans, behind on Coruscant to drain the New Republic's already strained resources and create an enmity between Humans and non-Humans. Together these are designed to tear the New Republic apart.

Corran Horn learns about his Jedi heritage. Born to Nyche and Valin "Hal" Horn on Corellia, Horn lived his early life unaware that his grandfather was Nejaa Halcyon, a Jedi Master. He followed his father and adoptive grandfather into the Corellian Security Force, where he excelled. However, he came into conflict with his Imperial Intelligence liaison officer, Kirtan Loor, and eventually fled Corellia after the Battle of Endor in order to evade execution. Horn spent a year lying low on Garqi before saving several locals from the Empire and making the decision to join the New Republic. A highly skilled pilot, Horn joined Rogue Squadron in 6 ABY and became a flight leader. He participated in the captures of Borleias and Coruscant, taking the shields of the latter down and being captured by the Empire in the process. He was incarcerated in the infamous Lusankya prison, where he resisted Ysanne Isard's brainwashing and became the first individual ever to directly escape the prison. On his return, he was hailed as a hero, but on learning that the New Republic would not allow the targeting of Isard for political reasons, he led Rogue Squadron in resigning and waging a guerrilla war against Isard's regime on Thyferra. During the course of that campaign, the Bacta War, Horn was married to Mirax Terrik, the love of his life and the daughter of his father's old rival, Booster Terrik. Horn rejoined the New Republic and continued his career in Rogue Squadron, helping defeat Zsinj and Thrawn and free the Lusankya prisoners.

Wedge Antilles and the rest of Rogue Squadron leave the New Republic military and begin the Bacta War against Ysanne Isard. Ysanne Isard had backed a coup that saw a pro-Imperial faction taking over Thyferra. The faction later elected her head of state, allowing her to remain in lawful power, eliminate the Zaltin, control the bacta industry, and start a small but important conflict known as the Bacta War. During the Battle of Thyferra, Rogue Squadron and its allies, operating at the time independent from the New Republic, which for political reasons could not directly interfere, liberated Thyferra from the Empire and imperial loyalists using guerilla tactics, pluck, and native allies. The New Republic later receives the needed bacta from Wedge Antilles and the former Rogue Squadron in the Bacta War to eliminate the plague whilst Isard fakes her death and disappears.

---

8 ABY

Leia Organa marries Han Solo.

Prince Isolder allies the Hapes Consortium with the New Republic. Isolder was the former heir, or Chume'da, of the Hapes Consortium. As the second son of Queen Mother Ta'a Chume, Isolder was not expected to rule. However, after his older brother Kalen was murdered, Isolder went on an undercover quest to hunt down the person responsible. Impressed by his finding of the culprit, his mother granted him the rank of Chume'da. In 8 ABY, Isolder fell in love with Leia Organa when she came to Hapes to discuss a possible alliance between the New Republic and the Hapes Consortium. However, she was kidnapped by Han Solo, former smuggler and New Republic General. With Jedi Knight Luke Skywalker, he followed Han and Leia to the planet Dathomir, where they were captured by the Dathomiri Witch Teneniel Djo. Though she was in love with Skywalker at first, she later fell in love with Isolder, and married him after they defeated Zsinj, an Imperial Warlord.

Imperial warlord Zsinj dies. Zsinj was a Human male from Fondor. Though he bore no first name per the traditions of his father, a Fondorian shipyard mechanic, Zsinj preferred to follow in the footsteps of his more famous mother, Mme. Maarisa Zsinj, a Chandrilan Admiral in the Republic Outland Regions Security Force popularly known as the "Ace of the Spacelanes."

---

9 ABY

Jacen and Jaina Solo are born to Leia Organa and Han Solo.

Grand Admiral Thrawn's attempt to destroy the New Republic and restore the Galactic Empire fails. Mitth'raw'nuruodo, better known by his core name Thrawn, and misinterpreted as Mitthrawdo by Vicelord Siv Kav, was a male Chiss who served in the naval forces of the Galactic Empire and became the only non-Human Grand Admiral. Regarded by many as the best military strategist in the navy, he rose to a position of power despite the Empire's strict speciesist policies.

Obi-Wan Kenobi's spirit moves on.

The Noghri defect to the New Republic when they discover that the Empire has been manipulating them and polluting their world. Noghri (pronounced /ˈno.gɹi/) were a primitive humanoid species. They had steely gray or blue skin, and were extremely skilled assassins due to their abilities in stealth and hand-to-hand combat. Despite their small size, they were efficient killing machines, with claws, fangs, and a sense of smell so acute, they could smell one's bloodline (as exemplified by Khabarakh's identification of Leia Organa Solo as Darth Vader's daughter, which made her the Mal'ary'ush). They were much like the Wookiee species culturally, in that they respected honor above all else. Noghri society was clan-based, revolving around the dukha, or community building, at the center of each village.

Ysanne Isard returns, and helps Rogue Squadron defeat her clone, who is using a warlord to do her dirty work. Isard is killed by Iella Wessiri on the Lusankya, while Wedge Antilles kills the clone and warlord.

---

10 ABY

The Galactic Empire recaptures Coruscant, but splinters into factions, and fights with each other. The New Republic is forced to hide at Pinnacle Base and the Chief of State, Mon Mothma, is forced to consider a last-minute plan for the defense of the galactic capital. However, she never got a chance, since the combined Imperial armada began bombarding Coruscant's energy shield from orbit, causing heavy damage to the heavily populated ecumenopolis below. The Imperials' first target were Coruscant's communication centers, knocking out the ability of the capital to communicate to its forces throughout the galaxy and requiring a number of commandeered courier ships, including the Messenger, to break through the blockade and send word.

Operation Shadow Hand occurs, also known as the "Shadow Hand Strategy", and was the Imperial name for the section of the Galactic Civil War following in the wake of the Thrawn campaign. It was applied to the collective military campaigns that the reborn Emperor Palpatine launched in an attempt to retake control of the galaxy for the Galactic Empire. These were essentially "wave assaults" from Byss and the rest of the Deep Core.

The Empire is brought back under Sith rule when Emperor Palpatine is reborn in a clone body and makes Luke Skywalker his second in command. However Luke turns against him and kills Palpatine with Leia and destroys his flagship Eclipse, a powerful technological tool and a potent psychological weapon, the Eclipse boasted a planet's worth of weaponry and had been almost unstoppable.

The New Republic wins the Battle of Calamari.

Aakin Solo is born to Leia Organa and Han Solo.

---

11 ABY

Palpatine returns again, but Jedi Knight Empatajayos Brand destroys his life-force. Brand dies and Palpatine is ultimately dead, freeing the Empire from Sith rule once again.

R2-D2 destroys Eclipse II and the Galaxy Gun, causing the destruction of the Imperial Fleet, and the planet Byss, where cloning machines of Palpatine are located.[154][155]

The New Republic reoccupies Coruscant.

Luke Skywalker establishes the Jedi Praxeum on Yavin 4 and Leia becomes the Chief of State of the New Republic. The ancient Jedi scholar Karena coined the term praxeum to describe a Jedi academy as a place for the "distillation of learning combined with action." In the days of the Galactic Republic, well-known praxeums included those on Teya IV, Arkania, Ossus and Dantooine. Inspired by the parting words of Obi-Wan Kenobi and the several Force-sensitive individuals he had encountered, Skywalker began planning for a unique institution where new and old Jedi could learn together and in doing so created the Jedi Praxeum.

Battle of Ord Cantrell, a conflict between ex-Imperial Baron Ragez D'Asta and self-proclaimed Galactic Emperor Xandel Carivus, precipitated when Carivus ordered the arrest of D'Asta's daughter Feena for treason. It resulted in Galactic Emperor, Xandel Carivus's, execution by Kir Kanos.

Admiral Natasi Daala and her fleet of Star Destroyers emerge from the Maw after 11 years in isolation.

Kyp Durron, under the influence of Exar Kun, uses the Sun Crusher to destroy Carida. The Sun Crusher was a nearly indestructible craft, no larger than a starfighter, but was capable of unleashing destruction on a magnitude that dwarfed even the Death Star's capabilities. Unlike the Death Star, which destroyed individual planets, the Sun Crusher could destroy an entire star system by causing its target star to turn into a supernova. The key to its near invincibility was layered Quantum-crystalline armor, a material so strong that it could perfectly repel even turbolaser shots. Han Solo once was able to ram the Sun Crusher straight through the bridge of the Imperial-class Star Destroyer Hydra without taking any damage, and during the skirmish in the Maw, it even survived a glancing blow from the Death Star Prototype's Superlaser, which likely would have destroyed any other ship it touched. The Sun Crusher took some engine damage from the blast, as this was its only weakness, but was able to continue to fight. The Sun Crusher was also equipped with a hyperdrive and was designed to slip unnoticed into a system, fire its weaponry, and then escape before its presence was detected. The Sun Crusher's primary weapon was a payload of 11 energy resonance torpedoes. Each torpedo resembled an oval-shaped plasma discharge and was activated when it passed through the Sun Crusher's resonance torpedo launcher. The resonance torpedo then traveled to the system's sun at near-lightspeed velocity.

Corran Horn,a Force-sensitive Human male Corellian pilot who served as a Corellian Security Force investigator, a Rogue Squadron ace and New Republic hero, trains at the Jedi Praxeum on Yavin 4. He later rescues his wife from Leonia Tavira, and destroys the Invids from the inside-out.

Exar Kun's spirit is destroyed after thousands of years in isolation, he attempts to influence Skywalker's apprentices at Yavin 4 to do his bidding, successfully turning the young Padawan Kyp Durron to the dark side and severely wounding Skywalker. However, the rest of Skywalker's apprentices banded together and, with the help of the long-dead shade of Vodo-Siosk Baas, banished Kun's spirit and finally put an end to his schemes.

---

12 ABY

The term "Imperial Remnant" is used for the first time referring to the shattered remains of the Empire, now unified under Gilad Pellaeon. After her defeat in the Assault on Yavin 4, Admiral Daala turns control of the United Warlord Fleets over to Pellaeon, who forms the Remnant.

Darksaber is constructed. The Darksaber battlestation was a superweapon built by the crime lord Durga the Hutt. A member of the Besadii kajidic, Durga wanted to use the superweapon to hold ransom entire planets and spread his influence throughout the galaxy. Based on the set of plans for the original Death Star battlestation stolen by Durga from the former Imperial Information Center on the galactic capital of Coruscant, the Darksaber was designed by the engineer Bevel Lemelisk, the creator of the Death Star and a number of other superweapons. Lemelisk adjusted the plans to the Hutt's wishes, removing all the Imperial padding and leaving only the central superlaser weapon, encased in a cylindrical durasteel shell. The resulting shape closely resembled that of the lightsaber, the traditional weapon of the Jedi Knights, so Lemelisk christened his creation accordingly: the Darksaber.

13 ABY

Tahiri Veila is born to Cassa and Tryst Veila. Tahiri Veila would become a Jedi Knight in the New Jedi Order and later the Sith apprentice of Darth Caedus. The descendant of a Jedi of the Old Order, Veila was born on the planet Tatooine to a pair of moisture farmers, Tryst and Cassa Veila. After the deaths of her parents, an orphaned Veila was adopted by the leader of a Tusken Raider tribe, and thus she was raised as one of the Sand People. Around 22 ABY, Jedi Master Tionne Solusar discovered Veila's Force-sensitivity and brought her to the Jedi Praxeum on Yavin 4. She then formed a friendship with a fellow Jedi Initiate named Anakin Solo, a grandson of the Jedi Chosen One Anakin Skywalker, also remembered as the Sith Lord Darth Vader.

Adumar, a temperate planet located near the Coreward edge of Wild Space first settled by Humans in the Ductavis Era, joins the New Republic as a planetary government. Adumari scoutships had ventured far enough from their homeworld to learn of the events of the larger galaxy; namely, the struggle between the New Republic and Galactic Empire. As Adumar had considerable industrial resources devoted to manufacturing munitions, both sides were eager to gain an alliance with the world. Therefore, both the New Republic and the Empire sent delegations to Adumar, each composed of elite starfighter pilots. The delegations were sent to Adumar's largest nation, Cartann, and during their stay, the perator, or leader, of Cartann decided to take control of the entire planet. While he had aid from the Empire, the New Republic pilots escaped Cartann and rallied the other Adumari nations into the Adumari Union and defeated Cartann and its allies. The Adumari also later routed an Imperial task force sent to aid Cartann and ultimately joined the New Republic. They would remain members of the New Republic and its successor state, the Galactic Alliance, for years, participating in the Yuuzhan Vong War and the Second Galactic Civil War, during which the world broke with the Galactic Alliance to join the Confederation.

14 ABY

Lord Hethrir captures Han and Leia's children, but is defeated. Hethrir had been a male Firrerreo who was at one time, along with his lover Rillao, an apprentice of Darth Vader. Under Emperor Palpatine, Hethrir held the office of Procurator of Justice and with the defeat of the Empire in 4 ABY, became the leader of the Empire Reborn insurgency.

Rise and fall of the Disciples of Ragnos. The Disciples of Ragnos, also known as the Cult of Ragnos, was a Sith cult that worshipped the ancient Sith Lord Marka Ragnos, who died shortly before the Great Hyperspace War some five thousand years before the Battle of Yavin. Their ultimate goal was to resurrect him and use his power to take over the galaxy. The cult's efforts were eventually thwarted by the Jedi but not before they had wrought havoc across the galaxy. The remaining survivors of the Disciples fled to the Maw and found Sinkhole Station, telling the Mind Walkers of their views of the Force. They were brought in and taught the methods of Mind Walking, thus ensuring that the Disciples way of the Force never died out.

Following the collapse of the Empire Reborn movement, and destruction of Disciples of Ragnos cult, major armed conflict between the New Republic and the Imperial Remnant drops off, turning into almost a cold war.

15 ABY

Tahiri Veila is orphaned.

Luke Skywalker confronts Brakiss for his dark side leanings. Brakiss flees Yavin 4. Brakiss was a Human male from the planet Msst who was recruited by the Galactic Empire as a baby after being discovered to be Force-sensitive. He was trained and brainwashed by the Inquisitorius as a tool for their purposes. In 11 ABY, the remnants of the Inquisitorius discovered that Jedi Master Luke Skywalker was planning to recreate the Jedi Order from a Jedi Praxeum on Yavin 4. In an effort to sabotage Skywalker's efforts and steal his training methods, Brakiss' handlers installed him as a spy within the original class of the academy. Skywalker immediately surmised Brakiss' purpose, but sensing his potential in the Force, he decided to keep the young man as a student, working to turn him to the light side of the Force. Brakiss worked alongside Skywalker's original students, helping them defeat the spirit of the deceased Dark Lord of the Sith Exar Kun.

Ailyn Vel concludes that her father, Boba Fett, is dead.

Sliven is injured badly during a battle between his tribe of Tusken Raiders and a group of smugglers.

16 ABY

The Black Fleet Crisis. When the Galactic Empire expanded into the Koornacht Cluster following the end of the Clone Wars, they discovered the Yevetha species and also noted the Yevetha's rapid ability to learn new skills. The Imperials subjugated the Yevethan homeworld of N'zoth and its nearby star systems, built the Black Fifteen shipyards and put the Yevetha to work as skilled slave labor building, repairing and modifying vessels of the Imperial Navy. About eight months after the Battle of Endor, the Imperial garrison at N'zoth was ordered to retreat and destroy the repair yard. Before they could initiate their withdrawal, an assault led by chief commando Nil Spaar took advantage of the Empire's view of the Yevetha as mindless labor and seized control of the vessels undergoing repairs, the operational warships and the yards. All Imperials were killed. Over the next decade and a half, the Yevetha developed their technical capabilities, developed advanced technologies in the form of starship shielding, gravity bombs, Aramadia-class thrustships and D-type trifoil fighters. They established the Duskhan League, which grew to encompass thirteen worlds. In 16 ABY, the Dushkan League came out of its isolation to engage the New Republic, which was enjoying a period of peace marked by increased member applications, economic prosperity and military innovation, as well as the development of a bloated and divided bureaucracy. A delegation led by now-Viceroy Nil Spaar arrived at Coruscant, supposedly to seek a peaceful coexistence.

Given their xenophobia and view of all non Yevethan species as 'Vermin' however, it is more likely that they were there on a mission to sow confusion and disruption prior to their planned war of extermination. Using the New Republic's lack of intelligence on the Dushkan League and Senatorial political infighting to his advantage, Nil Spaar extended his negotiations with Chief of State Leia Organa Solo over a period of weeks. Pressured by military and intelligence advisors who sought answers, and potentially an ally against the Core Imperial strongholds, Organa Solo entered the discussions, only to find herself on the receiving end of a political plot to throw the New Republic into confusion. During this period he played into her empathy towards a species subjugated by the Empire, allowing him to cultivate assets on Coruscant. Unfortunately (or fortunately perhaps for the Yevetha), the Commander of the Fifth Fleet, General A'baht had sent astrographic survey ships to the areas around that of the Dushkan League. The New Republic had lacked accurate Star Charts of the deep core areas formerly belonging to the Empire, a fact which had made the General uncomfortable in the Fifth Fleet's search for the missing Black Fleet. The fleet itself, and the Prowler, were searching outside the space claimed by the League, but that did not stop a Yevethan warship from destroying the unarmed surveying ship, claiming it had violated their space. Spaar used this as his opportunity to set off a series of political machinations that sowed confusion amongst the New Republic. First, he accused Organa Solo of "warmongering" and begged for the Yevetha to be left in peace. Weary of going to war, many New Republic citizens expressed outrage towards the Chief of State and several member worlds even went as far as submitting articles of withdrawal. With the diplomatic outcome a complete catastrophe, Leia ordered the Fifth Fleet to return from the Falax sector to Coruscant, leaving the Black Fleet now completely unhindered to carry out Spaar's plans.

17 ABY

The Almanian Uprising. Almania itself was a little known Wild Space world located not too far from the Corporate Sector. A backwater known to few, the planet was orbited by the moons of wealthy Pydyr, Auyemesh and Drewwa. The planet was relatively ignored by the Empire and Rebel Alliance-sympathetic, Auyemesh and Pydyr the only real intergalactic ports of call in the system. This easily allowed the rise of the Je'har, who became the tyrannical upper caste of the planet, and unfortunately the planet was also keenly raided by slavers. Dolph was a very young Almanian man when he was discovered to have an affinity to the Force. One of the first of Luke Skywalker's Yavin 4 Jedi Academy students, Dolph was enlisted for less then a year when he was informed that his parents had been killed by the Je'har. Enraged, and with few friends despite Brakiss, Dolph took off for his homeworld to identify the corpses. He never returned to Yavin 4. He arrived on Almania to see his parents both impaled in front of the Je'har palace. Overwhelmed with disgust and hatred he fell into the whirlpool of the dark side, vowing to bring down the Je'har regime. Despite his lack of training in the dark arts, he knew enough to focus his anger and became a dangerous savage. He organized his homeworld into a resistance movement and hid himself behind a new identity: Kueller, the name of a long dead Almanian general. As part of his mystique, he always wore a Hendanyn death mask, which made him rather reminiscent of Darth Vader. His forces fell in easily behind him, and his army destroyed the Je'har completely, torching all sympathizers of the Je'har. Seeing himself as a visionary, and misguided by the dark side, similar to Anakin Skywalker's fall into the abyss, he turned his sights on the New Republic, thinking he could prevent mass murder on the scale of the Je'har.

18 ABY

The Corellian Insurrection. Corellia and her four sister worlds had once been a vibrant display of multicultural Core World ideals. Corellia itself maintained a major role in the foundations of the Rebel Alliance thanks to the actions of those such as Garm Bel Iblis, Han Solo, and Wedge Antilles, and was famous throughout the galaxy for the system's shipyards and the Corellian Engineering Corporation. However, after the Battle of Endor, the Corellian system began to quake under the pressure of change. Six months following the death of Emperor Palpatine, Imperial Grand Admiral's Danetta Pitta and Josef Grunger both had their eyes on Corellia. Pitta had bribed the Diktat, a 'traditional' Corellian leader instituted by the Emperor, to his side, and thus the two greedy warlords met in a massive clash above Tralus, which ironically annihilated both of them, including Pitta's Torpedo Sphere and Grunger's Star Dreadnought Aggressor. Their conflict put Corellia on the slow plunge of change, and after two Diktats, Corellia fell into the hands of the New Republic. Corellia became isolated from the rest of the galaxy, its two lucrative trade routes drew in far less income and businesses located elsewhere. The populace lost its fire, and the Sacorrian Triad took advantage of the situation, funding resistance groups throughout the Five Brothers such as the Human League on Corellia, led by Thrackan Sal-Solo, cousin of Han Solo. During this time, the Triad had also managed to draw together a sizable fleet. Corellia was represented by the New Republic Senate by only one member, to the protests of some of the native Drall and Selonians. By 18 ABY, the Corellian Sector was governed by Frozian Governor-General Micamberlecto, but was seen by the natives as little more than an ineffectual figurehead. While the dust of the defeated Empire settled, Chief of State Leia Organa Solo announced a major trade conference on Corellia, the President of the Senate determined to bring Corellia back to its previous state. However, sinister forces were at work, and Organa Solo and her family were headed just where the Triad wanted her. New Republic Intelligence Service remained wary of Corellia, maintaining that the situation at Corellia was unstable. Lieutenant Belindi Kalenda attempted to explicitly warn Han Solo and Chewbacca not to travel to Corellia, or at least not take his children. Untrusting, Solo refused to take her advice, seeing the trip as a family holiday. A few days later, the Millennium Falcon departed, carrying the Chief of State, Solo, Chewbacca, and the children, Jacen, Jaina and the youngest, Anakin Solo. Agent Kalenda arrived at Corellia prior to the Solo's, and was abruptly shot down by Public Safety Service ships. Kalenda barely survived the crash, and was determined to reach Coronet before Organa Solo arrived. Pharnis Gleasry, Human League agent, watched the Falcon take off, Organa Solo hanging a new lightsaber to her belt, as a gift from her brother, Luke Skywalker.

Admiral Gilad Pellaeon resurfaces to launch a major offensive against the New Republic, the last gasp of the once-powerful Empire. NR forces under Admiral Ackbar defeat Pellaeon in the Battle of Anx Minor. The Imperial Remnant is reduced to a mere eight backwater sectors in the Outer Rim Territories, now posing no threat whatsoever to the New Republic and/or the Galaxy at large.

19 ABY

The New Republic and the last fragment of the Empire sign the Pellaeon–Gavrisom Treaty, ending the 21-year-long Galactic Civil War. The Pellaeon–Gavrisom Treaty, also known as the Bastion Accords, was the treaty of peace signed by the Imperial Remnant's Supreme Commander, Fleet Admiral Gilad Pellaeon, and the New Republic's Acting Chief of State, Ponc Gavrisom.

20 ABY

Luke Skywalker marries Mara Jade. Mara Jade Skywalker was, during different times in her life, an Emperor's Hand, a smuggler, and later a Jedi Master who sat upon the Jedi High Council. She was raised as a servant to Emperor Palpatine and became a high-level Force-using operative. As an Emperor's Hand, Jade carried out the Emperor's bidding, killing Rebels and corrupt Imperials alike with cold professionalism, even as a young woman. As Palpatine's assassin, she received top-notch training from experts in a variety of fields as well as training in the Force, which was continued by Luke Skywalker years later. After Palpatine's death, she received his last command, which was to kill Luke Skywalker; however, the death of her Master caused her to go rogue. Eventually she joined smuggler chief Talon Karrde, becoming one of his best smugglers and his second-in-command. During the predations of Grand Admiral Thrawn, she was forced to work with Skywalker, and developed a grudging respect for him. During the Galactic Civil War, Mara Jade proved herself skilled in a variety of fields; she was a good pilot and mechanic and trained in the use of both a blaster and hand-to-hand combat even without relying on the Force. Over the years, she continued to work for Karrde and interact with Skywalker intermittently, training at his Jedi Praxeum on Yavin 4 for a short period of time. She was groomed by Karrde to take over the Smugglers' Alliance and had a brief relationship with Lando Calrissian as part of that role, although she later admitted it was a charade. She also continued to grow closer to Skywalker and worked alongside him on numerous occasions, including the Almanian Uprising and the Corellian Crisis. The two finally realized in 19 ABY while on a mission to Nirauan that they were in love, and wanted to spend the rest of their lives together. After marrying Skywalker, Mara Jade took the surname Skywalker and devoted her life to the New Jedi Order, becoming a Master in her own right

21 ABY

GemDiver Station completes construction. This was a space station that orbited the planet Yavin. It was constructed by Lando Calrissian as a Corusca mining operation. Though there were previous space stations like it, GemDiver Station was the only operation of its kind at the time it was constructed, because financing such an operation was initially extremely expensive. Yavin was also the only planet where Corusca gems could be found.

22 ABY

Jacen and Jaina Solo join the Luke Skywalker's Jedi Praxeum on Yavin 4.

Their younger brother Anakin Solo joins the Junior Jedi Class of the Academy months later and befriends a young Human girl named Tahiri Veila. The two young trainees have several adventures including discovering the Golden Globe and the ancient Jedi Master Ikrit, accompanying their Melodie friend Lyric to her homeworld of Yavin 8 to undergo an important ceremony, visits to Dagobah to discover Anakin's future and the discovery of Kenobi's lightsaber and an ancient Jedi holocron at Bast Castle on Vjun. Anakin later returns to Coruscant where he attended school, developed his piloting skills, and studied under the careful tutelage of C-3PO.

Luke and Mara Jade Skywalker travel to the Unknown Regions where they join a Chiss/Empire of the Hand mission to locate the remains of the ill-fated Old Republic/Jedi expedition Outbound Flight. They discover it in an inaccessible region known as the Redoubt and also learn that the survivors of the Outbound Flight have founded a colony within the wreckage. This combined team also defeats a Vagaari attack.

23 ABY

Jacen and Jaina Solo fight against the Second Imperium which attempts to disrupt the peace between the New Republic and Imperial Remnant, as it has become known, and restart the Galactic Civil War.

Following the defeat of the Shadow Academy, the Jedi Academy is rebuilt. Anakin Solo also came to aid in the reconstruction efforts.

Leia Organa Solo resigns her post as Chief of State and the Bothan Borsk Fey'lya replaces her.

24 ABY

The Diversity Alliance, an extremist anti-Human organization, is defeated by the Solo twins and their Jedi companions.

An attempt by Czethros, a Bounty Hunter who himself had hunted Han Solo years before, to return Black Sun to its former glory is thwarted by the Solo twins and their Jedi companions.

Mon Mothma dies.

THE NEW JEDI ORDER

With the Jedi Knights now over one hundred strong the New Republic has signed a peace treaty with the remains of the Empire. The galaxy is finally enjoying a peaceful respite from decades of war. It's in this era that a horrible alien menace invades the Republic from beyond known space. The Yuuzhan Vong lay waste to entire worlds in their scourge. The Dark Nest trilogy falls at the end of this era. The mysterious Killik encroach upon Chiss-controlled space, inciting a three-way war between the Chiss, the Killik Hive, and the Galactic Alliance, with Jedi falling in on all sides. The sequel trilogy is set to begin in this era, though it is unknown if it will also end in this era.

---

25 – 29 ABY

The Yuuzhan Vong War, also known as the Great War by the Yuuzhan Vong, was a pan-galactic conflict which arose when the Yuuzhan Vong, a warlike species which had long ago fled the destruction of its own galaxy, invaded the Outer Rim. Chief of State Borsk Fey'lya's ill-prepared and inefficient government was unable to prevent the extra-galactic species from driving inexorably toward the Core. Coruscant, the galactic capital, was conquered and remade by the invaders two years after the invasion had commenced, by which time countless species had been rendered extinct and entire planets were now uninhabitable. Utilizing advanced biotechnology in every field of life, the Yuuzhan Vong were masters of adaptation and subterfuge, as well as brute force and terror tactics. The beliefs that the invasion was divinely ordained and that the galaxy was theirs by right were reinforced by Supreme Overlord Shimrra Jamaane and the priest caste, the conduits to the gods all Yuuzhan Vong worshiped. Thus the species attacked with ferocity, their invasion stalling only once the fleet, under command of Warmaster Tsavong Lah, had overextended itself. A vendetta against Luke Skywalker's New Jedi Order, a heretical movement brewing among the lower castes, and rumors that their long-destroyed homeworld haunted the Unknown Regions were only a few of the factors which caused the stagnation of the Yuuzhan Vong empire. After their swift advance, technological parity soon emerged between the New Republic and the Yuuzhan Vong. Once the New Republic had recovered from the loss of its capital, the Yuuzhan Vong were dealt a disastrous defeat at Ebaq 9. Wracked with internal tensions as it was, the Yuuzhan Vong Empire was still able to neutralize many of the threats facing it, including the Yevetha and the Ssi-ruuk, before going once more on the offensive. The New Republic, which was reformed under Alderaanian Chief of State Cal Omas into the Galactic Federation of Free Alliances, was brought to the brink of defeat, and moved toward the fatal deployment of Alpha Red, a pathogen hostile to the Yuuzhan Vong, in response to a renewed Yuuzhan Vong advance upon its temporary capital at Dac. This dangerous end to the war was averted when Zonama Sekot, a seed of the lost living homeworld of the Yuuzhan Vong, emerged over Coruscant, its arrival precipitating the final battle of the conflict. Skywalker and other leading Jedi, who had located Zonama

Sekot and urged its return, defeated Shimrra Jamaane and the true master of the Yuuzhan Vong, Onimi, during the battle, while fleets of warships clashed once more in space. The Yuuzhan Vong War ended with the deaths of the Supreme Overlord and the surrender of Warmaster Nas Choka's armada. The resulting Sekot Accords, which stipulated disarmament and amnesty for the Yuuzhan Vong, proved deeply unpopular for many and both the Yuuzhan Vong, and the aftermath of their devastating war, played a major role in events to come.

---

25 ABY

The Yuuzhan Vong invade the galaxy.

Chewbacca dies at Sernpidal. The events at the Battle of Endor were drastically altered as a consequence of the Rebel defeat at Kamino and Starkiller's choosing of vengeance. Although much of the battle was similar to its canonical counterpart, the main difference was in the form of Darth Vader's Dark Apprentice, the Dark Lord's personal Sith assassin and the only perfect clone of the original Starkiller. With orders from Vader to prevent the Rebel forces from destroying the shield generator bunker, the apprentice did not hold back from rampaging his way through the forest, slaughtering Rebel troops and Ewoks alike. Upon reaching the entrance of the bunker, the Dark Apprentice's path was blocked by the Rebel Han Solo and the Wookiee Chewbacca. While standing above the bunker with a rocket launcher, Solo warned his friend that the clone was approaching and that they had to do everything that they could to buy the Jedi Princess Leia Organa more time to complete the mission. To aid in their effort, Chewbacca utilized a commandeered Imperial AT-ST Walker. Although a combination of the Walker's heavy firepower and quick shots from Han Solo was able to stall the apprentice, neither Solo or Chewbacca were able to kill the clone. After suffering damage to the Walker, Chewbacca called upon the aid of the Ewoks. Once more, their tactics proved ineffective against Vader's disciple who managed to kill the native creatures while simultaneously warding off shots from Solo and Chewbacca. After inflicting even more damage to the Walker, the clone wasted little time in maneuvering his way over to the top of the Walker. Once the hatch was open, the clone began pulling its Rebel occupant out of the cockpit. Chewbacca attempted to resist by relying on his own brute strength, but was effectively incapacitated by the apprentice with one swift punch to the face. Unable to resist any further, Chewbacca was rendered helpless as the clone raised and held the Wookiee by the throat with one hand. Solo attempted to save his friend by firing two shots at the clone. But the Dark Apprentice anticipated this action and quickly used the Wookiee as a body shield to absorb the attack, thus causing Solo to inadvertently kill Chewbacca. With Chewbacca dead, Han Solo quickly followed as the clone impaled the former smuggler through the chest with a lightsaber. Their failure to kill or prevent the Dark Apprentice from entering the bunker led to Leia's death and the Empire's decisive victory over the fallen Alliance.

The New Republic Historical Council sets the year of the Battle of Yavin to the year zero, adopting the current date system.

26 ABY

Ben Skywalker is born to Luke Skywalker and Mara Jade.

Destruction of Kalarba and its moon Indobok when the Yuuzhan Vong crash the Hosk Station into it.

The Jedi Order is driven off Yavin 4 by the Yuuzhan Vong.

Sriluur, a planet in the Tharin sector of the Outer Rim and homeworld to the sentient Weequay species, is overrun by the Yuuzhan Vong.

Nyriaan is conquered by the Yuuzhan Vong. Nyriaan was rich in madilon, a rare, naturally occurring alloy that could be used to make hyperdrives smaller. It was a habitable world, with an atmosphere that was made up mainly of nitrogen and oxygen, and a mean temperature of 40 °C. The planet was covered by a thick, cloud layer, that blocked communications and made unaided landing almost impossible. Large storms were common and could last for months at a time. They posed a constant threat to settlements, so they were monitored by the Tempest Observation Bureau.

27 ABY

The Yuuzhan Vong conquer Coruscant, renaming it for their dead home planet, Yuuzhan'tar.

Anakin Solo dies on Myrkr. In 27 ABY, the Yuuzhan Vong had created a new creature called a Voxyn. This creature was proficient in hunting down and killing Jedi. Anakin and his friends, including Tahiri, Raynar Thul, Lowbacca, Jacen, Jaina, and Tenel Ka, later received a report that their friend from the Praxeum, Lusa, had been killed by a Voxyn. During a meeting, Anakin volunteered to lead a strike mission to kill the Voxyn queen. Though his father was at first set against the idea, the mission was approved, and Anakin selected a small band of Jedi. The mission began when Lando Calrissian, posing as a defector, offered Anakin and his team to a Yuuzhan Vong commander. During the faked capture, one of the team's members, Ulaha Kore, was badly wounded by a Yuuzhan Vong wielding a Coufee. En route to the Koros-Strohna Baanu Rass, which orbited Myrkr, Yaght took Ganner Rhysode, who was acting as team leader, to the bridge, while torturing Kore. Jacen Solo, using a mind meld, linked the strike team together through the Force. When it looked like Kore would be unable to handle any more torture, Yaght asked Jaina to pick a new subject, forcing her to choose between Anakin and Jacen. Anakin insisted through the Force that she pick him, and reluctantly, she did. Anakin whispered something in Kore's ear, and she attempted to impale her hand upon a Voxyn's poisonous spines. Soon, rescue came in the form of two of Lando's YVH droids YVH 2-1S and 2-4S. Jacen confronted Anakin about his discussion with Ulaha, believing he had told her to make the suicidal attack on the Voxyn. However, Anakin told Jacen that he had not done so, and instead told the Bith to reveal the name of Eclipse Station to Yaght. The team successfully rescued Ganner from the bridge, where Tesar Sebatyne shot the Yaght in the face, killing him. Though they successfully reached Myrkr, the Yuuzhan Vong attempted to stop them from landing. Ulaha remained behind to distract the Vong while Anakin and the remaining team members dropped to the worldship. They landed on the worldship, but Kore and the droid 2-1S were destroyed in the process. The group soon stumbled upon an Ysalamir-riddled prison, where Lomi Plo and Welk, two Dark Jedi, were discovered. Anakin allowed them to join the team, but would only give them blasters, not lightsabers. Soon after, 2-4S was destroyed, as well. The group continued and stumbled upon an AT-AT, which was inactive. The Yuuzhan Vong had placed a trap inside, and small bugs bit and wounded Lowbacca and Jovan Drark. They stumbled upon a slave city, where Eryl Besa and Drark were killed, and Anakin was wounded with an amphistaff through his side. Soon afterward, Bela Hara was killed, and Tesar Sebatyne took possession of her white-bladed lightsaber. The teams third Barabel member, Bela's hatchmate Krasov Hara, was also killed with voxyn acid in her face. The team soon discovered an escape ship, the Tachyon Flier. Lomi Plo and Welk, sensing that the mission was taking a downward turn and considering Anakin suicidal since he did not have an escape route, stole the ship, which had the wounded Raynar Thul aboard, and wiped most of the team's memory of them. Shortly afterward, Anakin stayed behind in a Grashal to fight off as many Yuuzhan Vong as he could and give the rest of the team time to accomplish the mission. Tahiri, weeping, rejected him a last goodbye kiss, saying he'd have to return for it. Anakin was unable to return, as the Vong overwhelmed him, and he began fighting them in an intense battle, pouring pure white energy from his fingers to disintegrate the warriors. The Force energy that he drew upon overwhelmed a damaged body; having been mortally wounded going to his sister's aid, as Anakin died a beacon of light surrounded the Yuuzhan Vong. The remaining team members were assisted by the alien Vergere, who gave Jacen Anakin's lightsaber, while Jaina, Tahiri, and some others went to recover Anakin's corpse. Jacen, Tesar, and the rest assaulted the voxyn queen's cavern, and Anakin's older brother killed the queen by using the Force to make her tail go into a void created by a dovin basal. Jaina and the others managed to steal Nom Anor's ship, the Ksstarr, but Jacen was captured. Anakin's death forced Jacen into a prominent role, pushed his sister Jaina to the edge of the dark side, and launched Tahiri into the throes of despair. His sister and the other escapees flew his body to Hapes and the survivors from Myrkr (excluding Jacen) gathered. Everyone recognized Anakin as a hero, including small speeches by Tahiri, Han, Kyp Durron and young Tarc. After a memorial ceremony, Anakin was cremated by Luke Skywalker

Chief of State Borsk Fey'lya dies. A political activist from an early age, Fey'lya's prodigious skill at manipulation and strategy enabled him to emerge as a leading figure in the Alliance to Restore the Republic and retain a base of political power throughout the various crises of the fledgling New Republic. Fey'lya's ultimate ascension to power was secured in 23 ABY, and he led the government as its Chief of State during the Yuuzhan Vong's invasion of the galaxy. In the waning days of the New Republic, as the aliens conquered Coruscant around him, Fey'lya committed suicide in his offices, taking over twenty five thousand Yuuzhan Vong warriors with him to his death and securing his place in history as a Bothan Martyr.

Cal Omas is elected Chief of State. He would serve as the last Chief of State of the New Republic, and the first of the Galactic Federation of Free Alliances, of which he was a founder. He began his service in galactic affairs when he joined the Alliance to Restore the Republic following the destruction of his home planet

Tenel Ka Chume Ta' Djo becomes Queen Mother of the Hapes Consortium. Tenel Ka Djo was a female Hapan Jedi Knight and the daughter of Prince Isolder, Chume'da of the Hapes Consortium, and the Dathomiri witch Teneniel Djo. Although she was the heir of the Hapes Consortium, she preferred the traditions and customs of her mother's people over those of her father's, which angered some Hapans, including her grandmother, Ta'a Chume, and preferred not to be addressed by her full name, Tenel Ka Chume Ta' Djo. Tenel Ka joined Luke Skywalker's Jedi academy when she was fourteen, and became close friends with Jacen and Jaina Solo, Lowbacca, Raynar Thul, and Zekk.

The Bothans declare a state of ar'krai for the first time in millennia. Ar'krai (also spelled ar'kai) was a state of genocidal war among the Bothans. The basic tenets of ar'krai state that if it was declared, all fit Bothans—and usually those that weren't—were required to volunteer for military service against an enemy that threatened the Bothans with extinction—and the Bothans were to repay the enemy in kind. The enemy was to be destroyed to the last individual in an act of speciecide, their name be wiped from history, and their homeworld be ground to dust. In recorded Bothan history, ar'krai was declared only three times. The third was during the Yuuzhan Vong War, after the Battle of Coruscant and the sacrifice of the Bothan Borsk Fey'lya, Chief of State of the New Republic. Ar'krai did not have a concept of ceasefire. Even ten years after the end of the war, Bothan fundamentalists were still attempting to locate Zonama Sekot and destroy the Yuuzhan Vong. The planet, however, remained safely hidden. Even into later years, the True Victory Party wished to carry out ar'krai and completely eradicate the Yuuzhan Vong.

First YVH 1 droid, YVH 1-1A, is released. The YVH 1, or Yuuzhan Vong Hunter One combat droid, was a battle droid developed by Tendrando Arms as a means to effectively combat Yuuzhan Vong warriors. Nearly two meters tall, the YVH 1 droid was built on a reinforced humanoid-type skeleton and protected with layered, self-healing black-gray laminanium armor that resembled the vonduun crab armor used by Yuuzhan Vong warriors. The skull-like head, glowing red photoreceptors, and external circuitry furthered the Vong-like appearance of the droid, which earned them the moniker "Yuuzhandroids". This was meant to demoralize and anger the Yuuzhan Vong warriors making them more prone to mistakes. Their war cry, however, was programmed to drive the Vong mad. YVH units were specifically instructed to maximize the enemy loss ratio while minimizing friendly casualties, and used the phrase "maximum efficiency" to praise one another on this skill. The droids included advanced search-and-identify programming that could penetrate ooglith masquers to sort civilians from Yuuzhan Vong. This programming proved essential in rooting out Yuuzhan Vong sleeper agents and hidden provocateurs. Once identified, the YVH 1 could engage enemies with its right arm's variable-output blaster cannon or the weapon attached to its modular left arm, which was often a heavy laser cannon, sonic rifle, or projectile launcher. The droid could also attack with sheer strength with its servos being capable of crushing light armor with ease. Specialized versions of the YVH 1 droids were created, including adaptable camouflage droids, aquatic versions, and miniature versions fitted into the shells of MSE-series droids for espionage. In addition, certain versions were capable of making use of baradium pellets that dealt a high degree of damage to Yorik coral. It was an optional quality for laminanium to be introduced into the droid though it enhanced the endurance of the war droids in combat if used. This armor was capable of surviving a coralskipper's plasma cannon blast and regenerating the damage in less than a day, though the laminanium ingot and the droids power pack would need to be replaced afterwards. After a series of successes, newer YVH-1 droids were modified to include a vocoder package which mimicked Lando Calrissian's voice of war cries, taunts and insults in the Yuuzhan Vong. Lando, founder of Tendrando Arms, was particularly proud of the taunts that proclaimed the YVH 1 superior warriors to the Yuuzhan Vong, a powerful insult considering the Yuuzhan Vong's intense hatred of machines and automatons. The droids' Vong-like appearance, appropriate taunts, unique programming, and incredible combat effectiveness made the YVH 1 a walking blasphemy and strong demoralizer to the Yuuzhan Vong. Since the Yuuzhan Vong had a strong hatred of technology, the creation of these droids proved to be an efficient and creative method of demoralization.

Jacen Solo is imprisoned by the Yuuzhan Vong.

The Battle of Ebaq, also known as the Battle of Ebaq 9, was a major battle between the New Republic and the Yuuzhan Vong, considered the turning point of the war in favor of the New Republic. The battle plan was conceived and coordinated by an ailing Admiral Ackbar, former Supreme Commander of the New Republic Defense Force, and was put into practice by several of the Republic's most able officers, including General Garm Bel Iblis and Admiral Kre'fey. After striking small raids on, and seizing, poorly defended worlds captured by the Yuuzhan Vong, Ackbar lured their Warmaster Tsavong Lah to the trap at the moon Ebaq 9 by giving Lah evidence of a fortress called the Final Redoubt at the moon there. With Supreme Overlord Shimrra's permission, he took a large fleet to the moon to decimate the New Republic forces there. With the Solo twins and other Jedi at the moon as well, Lah was especially motivated to win the battle and decimate the forces there. However he was drawn into a trap by General Keyan Farlander's battle group at the moon, where he was soon ambushed by Admiral Traest Kre'fey. Eventually, a large New Republic task force led by Garm Bel Iblis and Jedi Master Luke Skywalker trapped the Warmaster. With his fleets doomed, Lah led 10,000 troops to eliminate the Jedi on the moon. However, all of his troops were killed when Vergere, a Jedi Knight who initially joined the Yuuzhan Vong, sacrificed herself by crashing her ship on the moon's surface, causing explosive decompression in the mines inside it, to save Jacen. Lah survived, and confronted Jaina, along with her Jedi friends Lowbacca and Tesar Sebatyne. Jaina was able to kill the Warmaster, and all of his troops battling the New Republic fleet were killed as well. The subsequent New Republic victory resulted not only in the death of Warmaster Tsavong Lah, but a large portion of the already weakened Warrior caste along with him. The battle was a major morale victory for the Jedi and failing New Republic, and turned the tide of the war onto their side. It also proved to be the catalyst for the formation of the Galactic Federation of Free Alliances, as well as a disastrous and humiliating defeat for the newly christened Yuuzhan Vong empire.

28 ABY

The YVH-M droids are created. The YVH-Ms were mouse droids made by Lando Calrissian, designed to seek and follow Yuuzhan Vong infiltrators. They had the special ability to sense Vonglife and the ability to track it as well. Several YVH-Ms were responsible for finding all of Nom Anor's spy rings on the planet Mon Calamari in 28 ABY.

The New Republic is reorganized into the Galactic Federation of Free Alliances. Following the New Republic's decisive victory at the Battle of Ebaq 9, Chief of State Cal Omas realized that a new government was needed if the galaxy was to survive the horrors of the Yuuzhan Vong War. During the invasion, political infighting and weak leadership led the New Republic to a great number of defeats. Omas realized that the cumbersome organization of the New Republic could not withstand the pressures of the galactic war. As a result, Omas instituted a massive reorganization and streamlining of the government. Named the Galactic Federation of Free Alliances, or Galactic Alliance for short, it began the long task of bringing the galaxy back together. Another name thought of by Omas for the reorganization of the New Republic was the Federal Galactic Republic.

Nas Choka is escalated to Warmaster. Nas Choka was a distinguished Yuuzhan Vong warrior who rose through the ranks of his caste to become the final warmaster of his species. He was known more as a tactician and strategist than a martial warrior.

Ssi-ruuk foiled attempt of a second invasion of Bakura. The Ssi-ruuk, Ssi-ruu in singular form, were a saurian species that invaded from the Unknown Regions of the galaxy and initiated the Invasion of Bakura in 4 ABY, shortly after the Battle of Endor. This race relied on a technology called entechment that involved extracting the life-energies of sentient beings and using them as power sources for their mechanical technology. They had a sizable war fleet and ruled an empire called the Ssi-ruuvi Imperium in the Ssi-ruuk Star Cluster near the galaxy's rim.

Jacen Solo escapes his imprisonment.

---

29 ABY

Radical, and still partially obscure, changes occur in the Chiss Expansionary Defense Force and Chiss society in general.

Admiral Ackbar dies.

Coruscant is liberated from the Yuuzhan Vong at the Battle of Yuuzhan'tar, also known as the Recapture of Coruscant or the Second Battle of Coruscant, was the final battle of the Yuuzhan Vong War, fought between the Galactic Alliance and its allies against Yuuzhan Vong empire. After the arrival of the living planet Zonama Sekot to the Coruscant system, and the retreat of the fleet under Warmaster Nas Choka from the battle at Mon Calamari, the Galactic Alliance set route to Coruscant, or Yuuzhan'tar as the invaders had renamed it, to take it back and end the war. The battle was long, with the biggest fleets both combatants could gather. The fighting had several fronts in space and on the surface of terraformed Yuuzhan'tar, and at the end, the Galactic Alliance was victorious, helped by Yuuzhan Vong followers of the Jeedai heresy, the Shamed Ones and Workers. It ended with the death of Supreme Overlord Shimrra and his secret puppeteer Onimi, and afterwards, the Yuuzhan Vong went to exile on Zonama Sekot so they could redefine their culture in peace.

Zonama Sekot forges a peace accord between the Galactic Alliance and the Yuuzhan Vong. The war ends after five years of fighting. Zonama Sekot (Ferroan for "World of Body and Mind") was a living, sentient world capable of traveling through space. Zonama was the planet itself, while Sekot was the living intelligence of Zonama. It was also the seed of the original Yuuzhan Vong homeworld, Yuuzhan'tar, which had been destroyed during the Cremlevian War.

Jacen Solo begins his search for the Force in an effort to determine if Vergere is right.

35 – 36 ABY

The Dark Nest Crisis. The Dark Nest or Gorog was a secret nest of Killiks that was hidden from the rest of the Colony. It was also the most violent—it sought to use the rest of the nests against the Chiss after the Killiks absorbed the three Force-sensitives who escaped from Myrkr in 27 ABY during the Yuuzhan Vong War: Lomi Plo, Welk, and Raynar Thul. The first two were absorbed by the Dark Nest, Lomi became the Unseen Queen of the Gorog while Welk became the nest's Night Herald, thus giving Gorog its qualities of secrecy and manipulation; while Raynar was absorbed by Yoggoy, eventually became UnuThul and forming Unu so that the rest of the Colony took on his attributes of respect for life.

35 ABY

Efforts to rebuild galactic civilization after the Yuuzhan Vong war continue, with many war-torn worlds still under reconstruction. The Jedi, struggling to come to terms with a new role in the galaxy and a new philosophy on the Force are called upon to act as police and diplomats by the Galactic Alliance, despite the wishes of Luke Skywalker.

Luke Skywalker sees an image of his mother for the first time through R2-D2.

A mysterious alien race called the Killiks with a leader very strong in the Force, who are ancient enemies of the Chiss return, with some of the younger members of the Jedi interfering, and becoming part of their alien "Hive," physically and mentally joined to each other.

Voren Na'al publishes the New Essential Chronology.

36 ABY

The Swarm War occurs. The Swarm War was the title given to the brief, but devastating, war fought between the Galactic Federation of Free Alliances, the Chiss Ascendancy, and the Colony, which consisted of Killiks and their Joiner allies. A continuation of the Dark Nest Crisis in 35 ABY, although the Galactic Alliance attempted to ally with the Chiss, elements of the Jedi sided with the Killiks, thus the Chiss believed the Alliance was aiding the Colony, and for all intents and purposes it was a three-way war; a completely free-fire zone.

Luke Skywalker witnesses a hologram, kept by R2-D2, of his father leading the slaughter at the Jedi Temple, as well as another one in which Anakin was Force-choking his mother.

The Conclave on Ossus convenes. The Conclave on Ossus was the first full Jedi convocation of the New Jedi Order. During the convocation, Luke Skywalker declared himself the Grand Master of the New Jedi Order, and declared that the Jedi would serve the Galactic Alliance. He also commanded that the Jedi had to put the good of the Order above everything else, or they should resign. Danni Quee resigned, citing that her life was on Zonama Sekot now, as did Tenel Ka, as she was Queen Mother of Hapes, and she needed to continue to be Queen mother for the foreseeable future to prevent a civil war. Corran Horn attempted to resign over his role in the schisms the Order had been experiencing, but Skywalker refused it, saying that Horn should stop shouldering the blame for the disagreements and for the Destruction of Ithor.

Allana is born to Jacen Solo and Tenel Ka Djo.

THE LEGACY ERA

Having reached peace with the Yuuzhan Vong, the newly formed Galactic Federation of Free Alliances (commonly referred to as Galactic Alliance or GA) struggles to keep itself working as a single government. But many threats from inside are joined by a danger that comes from the remains of the Dark Side, that threaten to give rise to a new Sith Lord more powerful than Darth Vader or Emperor Palpatine. The new Jedi Order created by Luke Skywalker faces a new era as the heirs of the Skywalker legacy grow up. Jacen Solo has partnered with a nemesis from Luke Skywalker's past, Lumiya, who has promised him only if he becomes the next Sith Lord will he be able to bring peace to the galaxy. The Legacy of the Force novels are set at this time. Following the culmination of the Legacy of the Force novels, a series titled Fate of the Jedi begins, involving Luke as he tries to correct the blemish left on the Jedi Order by Jacen Solo. Much later in this era, as suggested by the title, is the Legacy comic series. Set one-hundred thirty years after the films, these comics follow the story of Cade Skywalker, a descendant of Luke Skywalker who has to confront a resurrected Galactic Empire under the control of a new Sith Order. Volume 2 follows the adventures of Ania Solo, a descendant of Han Solo as she wanders the galaxy trying to stop the plots of the evil Darth Wredd.

---

40 ABY

Jacen Solo and Ben Skywalker return from a covert mission on Adumar. The Mission to Adumar was to investigate whether or not Adumari missile-manufacturer Dammant Killers were developing concussion missiles for planets close to rebellion, as Alliance regulations chafed against planetary interests. The master and apprentice posed as Jedi inspectors for the Galactic Alliance, with the two exploiting Jedi mystique to intimidate the Adumari. Ben Skywalker acted as an interpreter for Jacen's "telepathy" as their guide, Testan ke Harran, nervously toured them around the facility. The adept Jedi detected uneasiness from their guide and fellow Adumari workers pertaining to a certain part of a wall. Astonishing their guide, Ben Skywalker cut open the hidden door where a further production facility was discovered to be manufacturing missiles which were not reported to the Galactic Alliance. Despite being engaged by up to twenty Adumari guards, Skywalker managed to record evidence of the facility while his Master entered a pitched firefight. The two Jedi managed to escape the facility in a display of Force acrobatics around Cartann – destroying an odd Adumari starfighter and killing her pilot in the process. Skywalker then transmitted the evidence gained by the investigation while two Jedi took off for Coruscant in Jacen Solo's modified Lambda-class shuttle. The crimes of the Dammant Killers were reported to Galactic Alliance authorities.

The Galactic Alliance, in an attempt to silence malcontent among its members, begins a deterrent campaign against Corellia, leaving the galaxy on the edge of a full-scale war.

Tensions begin to grow between members of the Skywalker-Solo clan.

Lumiya reveals herself after a 20 year hiatus

Jacen Solo falls to the dark side and becomes a Sith apprentice to Lumiya.

The first civil war since the Galactic Civil War breaks out between the Galactic Alliance on one side, and the Confederation on the other.

Boba Fett discovers the existence of a clone that fought at Geonosis and lived a further 70 years.

Mara Jade Skywalker is killed by Jacen Solo. Jade Skywalker tracked Jacen to Hapes, where he was visiting with Tenel Ka and Allana. When he left Hapes, Jade Skywalker ambushed him in her StealthX, and after a dogfight in Hapan space, they ended up on the planet Kavan. In the tunnels of Kavan, a fight between the two ensued that degraded into a brawl. Initially, Jade Skywalker trapped Jacen beneath rubble by collapsing the ceiling and attempted to shoot him with a blaster. The ambush backfired when Jacen used a Force Wave so strong it blew the blaster bolt and the cave stones off himself which also knocked her backwards. She kept fighting Jacen with her shoto and vibroblade even after sustaining a scalp injury and being painfully thrown into a brick wall several times, using her assassin's training and physical skills to good effect. As she prepared to finish off her opponent, Jacen stared into her eyes and instantly created the illusion of Ben's face beneath her by using the Force, causing Jade Skywalker to hesitate for a split second. Jacen used the time to stab a poisoned dart into her thigh, causing a slow, paralyzing, and painless death. Her final words expressed her belief that Jacen had become worse, more vile and cruel than Palpatine, and that Skywalker would defeat and strike him down. Jade Skywalker left her body behind instead of allowing it to become one with the Force to leave evidence of the identity of her killer as well as to give her family something to say goodbye to. Her last uses of the Force were to whisper in Ben's mind and to ruffle Skywalker's hair. Other Jedi, including Leia, also felt her passing through the Force

Lumiya is killed by Luke Skywalker. Lumiya was a Force-sensitive Human female born on Imperial Center during the height of Galactic Emperor Palpatine's reign over the majority of the galaxy. Brie's dedication to the tenets of the Imperial New Order doctrine garnered the interest of Palpatine's chief enforcer, the Sith Lord Darth Vader, who sped the young woman's advancement in various Imperial-sponsored programs, including her enrollment into the Intelligence Academy of Carida. After she graduated with top honors and was promoted to the rank of major by Vader himself, Brie was given a highly classified mission to infiltrate the Rebel Alliance and either cause the death or ostracism of Rebel hero and Jedi Luke Skywalker amongst his peers. Brie achieved the latter, but the events that ended in Skywalker's disgrace also left her horribly disfigured and near death. She was recovered by Darth Vader, who rehabilitated her with cybernetic replacements much like his own. Brie then began to train in the dark side of the Force at the feet of Vader under the assumed identity of Lumiya, Dark Lady of the Sith.

Jacen Solo becomes a full Sith Lord, Darth Caedus.

Luke Skywalker forms the Jedi Coalition, a coalition government between both the New Jedi Order and the Alliance-in-exile, as well as the Maw Irregular Fleet and the Mandalorians, formed after the Battle of Kashyyyk, in response to Darth Caedus' rule of the Galactic Alliance. The Coalition's primary objective was to remove Caedus from power in order to peacefully end the Second Galactic Civil War.

Centerpoint Station is destroyed. Centerpoint Station, known to the Killiks as Qolaraloq or the World Puller, was an ancient space station that was capable of moving entire planets with its tractor beams. It was created by the Thuruht hive c. 100,000 BBY. This would make it perhaps one of the oldest artifacts known to the Jedi in the Yuuzhan Vong War era. Seeing that the balance of power would tip greatly in favor of anyone who possessed its enormous destructive force, Grand Master Luke Skywalker and the New Jedi Order carried out a raid upon the station in order to finally destroy it. Jedi Master Kyp Durron led the raid, with Toval Seyah, a Galactic Alliance scientist and former spy who had worked on the station in the past. Seyah was able to modify Centerpoint's galactic data reserves in such a way that all coordinates in the galaxy were altered to become those of the station. During the pitched battle between Confederation and Galactic Alliance forces, a technician named Rikel, who had lost his wife on the galactic capital of Coruscant to the Galactic Alliance Guard, was left in charge of the station's fire-control chamber. He tried to set the coordinates to target Coruscant itself, and therefore set the targeting coordinates to [0, 0, 0]. But Centerpoint's aim coordinates were relative to itself, and when he fired Centerpoint, the massive construction targeted itself. The resulting gravitic pulse detonated the station, wiping all traces of the enigmatic structure from the system, killing all on board, and destroying countless vessels in its blast radius. As a result of Centerpoint's destruction, Sinkhole Station in the Maw began to malfunction. This caused the shell of black holes that composed the Maw to begin to slide apart, creating a "crack" in the otherwise complete shell of black holes. This then allowed Abeloth to reach out from the Maw, which seemed to have blocked her influence when it was intact (as Abeloth was previously only able to influence those within the Maw, such as the Jedi younglings at Shelter). According to Thuruht, the destruction of Centerpoint was a direct result of Jacen Solo's attempt to change what he saw in his vision at the Pool of Knowledge. By trying to change the future, Jacen apparently altered the Current of the Force and unleashed Abeloth, the Celestial embodiment of Chaos.

41 ABY

Admiral Daala returns to fight in the war. Natasi Daala was a Human female who became the first woman to reach the rank of admiral in the Imperial Navy, and later was named Chief of State of the Galactic Federation of Free Alliances. Daala enlisted in the Imperial Navy on Carida, but was discriminated against due to her gender. However, she achieved success thanks to Moff Wilhuff Tarkin, who discovered her after she defeated many skilled Imperial opponents in simulated battles, using an alias to hide her true identity. Tarkin took her under his wing, and as he rose in the ranks, so did she. She became his lover and was eventually promoted to admiral by him. Shortly after, she was sent to oversee the top-secret Imperial research facility known as the Maw Installation. There, some of the best scientists in the galaxy worked on new concepts, designing superweapons for the Empire. She resided there with four Imperial I-class Star Destroyers for eleven years, unaware of what was happening in the galaxy.

Gallactic Alliance Naval Officer Gilad Pellaeon is killed by Tahiri Veila. Tahiri Veila was a female Human Jedi Knight in the New Jedi Order and later the Sith apprentice of Darth Caedus. The descendant of a Jedi of the Old Order, Veila was born on the planet Tatooine to a pair of moisture farmers, Tryst and Cassa Veila. After the deaths of her parents, an orphaned Veila was adopted by the leader of a Tusken Raider tribe, and thus she was raised as one of the Sand People

Darth Caedus makes Tahiri Veila his Sith apprentice.

Isolder is killed by Darth Caedus. Isolder was the former heir, or Chume'da, of the Hapes Consortium. As the second son of Queen Mother Ta'a Chume, Isolder was not expected to rule. However, after his older brother Kalen was murdered, Isolder went on an undercover quest to hunt down the person responsible. Impressed by his finding of the culprit, his mother granted him the rank of Chume'da.

Darth Caedus is killed by Jaina Solo at The Battle of Uroro Station. This was the final battle in the Second Galactic Civil War. During the battle, Jaina Solo dueled and killed her brother, Darth Caedus, and Luke Skywalker convinced the Imperial Remnant to join the Jedi Coalition under the leadership of Jagged Fel. The Confederation was forced to surrender, and the war was ended.

At the end of the war, Natasi Daala is named the new Chief of State of the Galactic Alliance.

43 ABY

Han Solo and Leia Organa Solo embark on a journey to investigate into the history of the Millennium Falcon.

Jedi Grand Master Luke Skywalker is charged with dereliction of duty by Chief of State Natasi Daala. Luke is exiled from the New Jedi Order and the Galactic Alliance afterwards and Kenth Hamner becomes acting Jedi Grand Master.

The Unification Summit is held on Coruscant in an effort to reunite the galaxy in the aftermath of the Second Galactic Civil War. During the first public meeting of the three major powers, it was noticed by Luke Skywalker and other attendees that all three Heads of State—Jagged Fel of the Imperial Remnant, Natasi Daala of the Galactic Alliance, and Turr Phennir of the Confederation—all had strong ties to the former Galactic Empire. Daala and Phennir served as an Admiral and General, respectively, while Fel was the son of leading Imperial fighter ace, Soontir Fel. A committee was set up by the Galactic Alliance Senate to prepare for the Unification Summit. It was headed by Bothan Senator Tiurrg Drey'lye.

44 ABY

Widespread slave uprisings spread throughout the galaxy, inspired by the Freedom Flight organization. Freedom Flight had been secretly created by Moff Drikl Lecersen in 38 ABY with the false objective of the elimination of slavery throughout the galaxy. Lecersen's true objective was to aid in the Imperial-Alliance conspiracy's rise to power in the galaxy by creating more uprisings throughout the galaxy than Galactic Alliance Chief of State Natasi Daala would be able to handle, leading to her downfall. However, due to the Freedom Flight's structure, wherein each operative only knew a few other beings in the organization, the majority of its members worked simply to free individuals from slavery and help them begin new lives. Also, if a member of Freedom Flight was captured, the being could only betray a few other members. When communicating, the organization referred to things using aviation terms such as flight path, pilot, and cargo, so that anyone who overheard them would not be suspicious. The movement was behind the slave revolts on Blaudu Sextus and arranged for reporter Madhi Vaandt to be present so as to show the Mandalorians' brutality in putting down the movement. When the situation reached the ears of the Jedi Council, they concluded that Freedom Flight had to have a spy in Daala's office, as no one knew that she was using Mandalorians to put down the movement. During the suppression of the slave movements, the Mandalorians discovered Lecersen's movement, which eventually was learned by Daala through Boba Fett. Galactic Alliance Chief of State Natasi Daala responds to these revolts with overwhelming and brutal force, leading to Imperial withdrawal from the Unification process.

The Jedi Order leads a coup to overthrow Daala, ending her reign and leading to her imprisonment. Luke Skywalker's exile is ended.

The Dark side entity known as Abeloth manipulates the Galactic Senate to elect Rokari Kem, whom it possesses, as Chief of State. Chief of State Kem is used as a figurehead for Abeloth and the Lost Tribe of Sith to attempt to rule the galaxy.

At the Liberation of Coruscant, the Jedi Order defeats the Lost Tribe of Sith and Abeloth. Wynn Dorvan is elected as Chief of State in the aftermath.

The Jedi Order is commanded by the Galactic Senate to leave Coruscant. The Jedi Temple is abandoned and the Order relocates to the academy on Shedu Maad.

Boba Fett helps Daala escape from prison, as she begins a campaign of revenge and conquest, intending to conquer the galaxy. The Imperial Remnant, led by Jagged Fel, declares war on Daala's forces.

104 ABY

R2-D2 tells the Keeper of the Whills about the Skywalker family's history through the Clone Wars and the Galactic Civil War.

127 ABY

The Sith-Imperial War. The Sith-Imperial War was a conflict occurring from 127–130 ABY, which saw the return of the Empire as the dominant galactic power. Darth Krayt, Dark Lord of the One Sith, set out to destroy the New Jedi Order, sending all his minions to commit the murderous sprees in his name. Following the war, the Galactic Federation of Free Alliances surrendered, though surviving portions of its military reformed into the Galactic Alliance Remnant, intent on keeping up the opposition against the Empire and the One Sith. However, the Sith revealed their deception and took control of the former, causing Fel and his followers to form the True Empire.

The Galactic Alliance, Jedi Order and Yuuzhan Vong complete a successful terraforming of the war devastated planet Ossus. As a result, Yuuzhan Vong terraforming technology is implemented on a hundred other planets. The One Sith sabotages the program, causing renewed hostility to the Yuuzhan Vong and distrust of the Jedi.

The resurgent Galactic Empire (formerly the Imperial Remnant) starts a secession movement against the Alliance, in part due to the failure of the Ossus Project.

The Empire declares war on the Alliance, claiming violations of the Treaty of Anaxes. The Treaty had been invoked by the Moff Council to initiate the Sith–Imperial War. Initially, the treaty was to have the Galactic Alliance and the Fel Empire defend each other in case of attacks such as by the Yuuzhan Vong. It was used in supporting the repair of planets' ecosystems through Yuuzhan Vong bio-technology.

The Sith form an alliance with the Galactic Empire through the Director of Imperial Intelligence Nyna Calixte.

130 ABY

The Galactic Alliance is defeated at Coruscant and its remaining territories are absorbed by the Empire which becomes the new galactic government. The Jedi Order is nearly destroyed during a massacre at Ossus, with Kol Skywalker as one of the casualties.

The Galactic Alliance Remnant, a military resistance movement founded from units of the Galactic Alliance Defense Force following the surrender of the Galactic Alliance government in the Sith-Imperial War, under Gar Stazi begins it's campaign against the Empire.

The One Sith turns against Emperor Roan Fel and his Imperial Knights. Darth Krayt usurps the Imperial throne, though some parts of the Empire remain loyal to Fel. Darth Krayt founded the One Sith, or the New Sith Order, on Korriban, the ancient Sith burial world. In this new Sith cult, most of the followers were trained from birth, sported a red-and-black tattooed appearance and carried lightsabers with a yorik coral-styled hilt design. This Sith Order was considered heretical by the holocrons of Darth

Andeddu and Darth Bane. By the year 130 ABY, the One Sith had risen to take the place of Lumiya's Sith faction, itself the remnant of Darth Bane's Order

---

137 ABY

Cade Skywalker, bounty hunter and descendant of Luke Skywalker, lives in self-imposed exile from the Jedi. He begins to rediscover his destiny as a Jedi Knight and as a member of the Skywalker family, and rises to fight the new Sith. He embarks on a series of adventures aboard his starship Mynock.

Darth Krayt is killed by Darth Wyyrlok III, a Chagrian Lord, after the Battle on Had Abbadon. He is then resurrected on Korriban.

Galactic Alliance Remnant and Fel Empire-in-Exile forces unite against Darth Krayt's Galactic Empire.

---

138 ABY

Darth Krayt kills Darth Wyyrlok (III) and regains control of the Empire. Sith Trooper project unveiled.

The Hidden Jedi Temple falls, though many of it's defenders are able to evacuate.

Jedi, Galactic Alliance Remnant, and Empire-in-Exile forces launch an assault on Coruscant, defeating the Krayt Empire. Darth Krayt is killed for a final time by Cade Skywalker. Emperor Roan Fel falls to the dark side and is killed by the Imperial Knights.

Marasiah Fel becomes Empress. Marasiah Fel, affectionately known as Sia, was a female Human princess and Imperial Knight who is the daughter of Emperor Roan Fel and Empress Elliah Fel until she became the first Empress of the Fel Empire during the end of the Second Imperial Civil War against the Dark Lord of the Sith Darth Krayt and the One Sith. Through her father, Princess Fel was a great-granddaughter of Jagged Fel, the first Emperor of the Fel dynasty. She was also a distant cousin of Ania Solo. Like her father, Fel possessed a strong connection to the Force, thus enabling her to join the Knights of the Empire. The lover of fellow Imperial Knight Antares Draco, she was captured by the One Sith and taken to Korriban, where Draco nearly died in an attempt to rescue the woman he loved.

The Galactic Federation Triumvirate is formed. Following eight years of galactic rule by the One Sith, the combined military might of the Galactic Alliance Remnant, the Empire-in-exile, and the New Jedi Order defeated the Dark Lord of the Sith Darth Krayt and his Galactic Empire. The Galactic Triumvirate was set up after the war to merge the various factions into one, cohesive government. The new government immediately set about restoring stability to the galaxy. Reconstruction efforts began on the planet Coruscant which had suffered damage during the battle to seize it from the Sith. The Imperial Mission, abused by Darth Krayt, was disbanded. However, efforts to improve the galaxy's infrastructure were continued beginning with a communications array that would link the Outer Rim Territories with the Core Worlds. Though not an especially costly project, it did cause political tensions.

The One Sith decide on the new strategy of taking over governments planet by planet.

Darth Wredd's insurgency begins. The genesis of Darth Wredd's insurgency can be traced to one event in the last years of the Second Imperial Civil War. The One Sith Vul Isen tested a bioweapon on a backwater world called Mala. This test succeeded in wiping out all life on Mala and even knocking the planet out of its orbit, turning Mala into a rogue planet which wandered through the galaxy. The sole survivor of this genocide was the man who became Darth Wredd, whose Force-sensitivity was recognized by an unidentified Sith master. This Sith Master sense Darth Wredd's Force potential and took on him as a Sith apprentice. While Darth Wredd ultimately embraced the dark side and became a Sith, he harbored a desire for revenge against the people that had destroyed his family and homeworld. Darth Wredd's opportunity for revenge came during the aftermath of Darth Krayt's death during the Battle of Coruscant. Following the defeat of the Sith, the One Sith was once again driven underground and embarked on a strategy of infiltrating governments across the galaxy in order to restore their "golden age." A new galactic government called the Galactic Federation Triumvirate was formed which consisted of an alliance of the Fel Empire, the Jedi Order, and the Galactic Alliance. Under the leadership of Empress Marasiah Fel, the Triumvirate embarked on a program to create a galactic-wide communications network to link the Outer Rim Territories with the wide galaxy. Under this program, the Imperial Knight Yalta Val was dispatched to supervise the final stages of the construction of a communications station in the remote Carreras system.

Darth Luft's operation to build a hidden Sith fleet in the Mon Calamari Shipyards discovered and destroyed. The Liberation of the Mon Calamari Shipyards was a battle that occurred between Darth Luft's pirates and a Galactic Federation Triumvirate taskforce at a set of shipyards above the world of Dac. While on a quest to hunt the rogue Sith Darth Wredd, junk dealer Ania Solo and Imperial Knight Jao Assam discovered that another rogue Sith Darth Luft and his pirate associates had started a slaving ring operating in the Mon Calamari Shipyards above the planet Dac, which had been rendered lifeless during the Second Imperial Civil War. Jao Assam informed his superior Yalta Val, who convinced the Galactic Federation Triumvirate Admiral Gar Stazi to liberate the Mon Calamari and Quarren slaves. A joint Galactic Alliance Navy and Imperial Knight force was dispatched to assault the Mon Calamari shipyards. During the fighting, the Galactic Alliance Navy used the tanker Trand Cappa to flood the shipyards, neutralizing the pirates. Imperial Knights and seatroopers then liberated the shipyards and apprehended the pirates. Ania Solo and her companions also succeeded in closing space doors to the shipyards, saving many Mon Calamari and Quarren slaves. Jao Assam also dueled and killed Darth Luft. Following the battle, the liberated Mon Calamari and Quarren slaves settled in the flooded shipyards. However, Jao and Ania quickly discovered that they had merely played into Darth Wredd's hands by eliminating Darth Luft. This brought Darth Wredd closer to his goal of destroying the One Sith and reinstating the Rule of Two.

139 ABY

Battle of the Floating World. This was to be the conflict of Darth Wredd's insurgency which occurred on the floating world known as Mala in 139 ABY. During the battle, the rogue Sith Darth Wredd lured both the Fel Empire and One Sith onto Mala with the intent of using the former to destroy the latter. In addition, Darth Wredd wanted to kill Galactic Empress Marasiah Fel, who was also the leader of the Imperial Knights. However, he was thwarted and killed in combat by the Imperial Knight Jao Assam and the junk dealer Ania Solo.

INDEX

Q

R

S

14826560R00131

Printed in Great Britain
by Amazon.co.uk, Ltd.,
Marston Gate.